The Constitution
and American Racism

The Constitution and American Racism

Setting a Course for Lasting Injustice

DAVID P. MADDEN

McFarland & Company, Inc., Publishers
Jefferson, North Carolina

LIBRARY OF CONGRESS CATALOGUING-IN-PUBLICATION DATA

Names: Madden, David P. (David Phillip) author.
Title: The Constitution and American racism : setting a course for lasting injustice / David P Madden.
Description: Jefferson, North Carolina : McFarland & Company, Inc., Publishers, 2021 | Includes bibliographical references and index.
Identifiers: LCCN 2020045151 | ISBN 9781476683942 (paperback : acid free paper) ∞
ISBN 9781476641751 (ebook)
Subjects: LCSH: Race discrimination—Law and legislation—United States. | Discrimination in justice administration—United States. | Constitutional law—United States. | Civil rights—United States. | Race discrimination—Law and legislation—United States—States. | Civil rights—United States—States. | Equality before the law—United States. | Slavery—Law and legislation—Untied States.
Classification: LCC KF4755 .M34 2021 | DDC 342.7308/73—dc23
LC record available at https://lccn.loc.gov/2020045151

BRITISH LIBRARY CATALOGUING DATA ARE AVAILABLE

ISBN (print) 978-1-4766-8394-2
ISBN (ebook) 978-1-4766-4175-1

© 2021 David P. Madden. All rights reserved

No part of this book may be reproduced or transmitted in any form or by any means, electronic or mechanical, including photocopying or recording, or by any information storage and retrieval system, without permission in writing from the publisher.

Front cover image © 2021 Sascha Burkard/Shutterstock

Printed in the United States of America

McFarland & Company, Inc., Publishers
Box 611, Jefferson, North Carolina 28640
www.mcfarlandpub.com

Acknowledgments

So many people have helped me with this book. My wife Brandy has been my rock, editor and inspiration. My son-in-law Jim has fixed computer problems for me. My daughter Amanda and her husband have proofed; historian Paul Finkelman read the draft of my first chapter and offered many helpful suggestions; Jill Swenson has guided the boat; Colonel Ken Clevenger, retired Army judge, has read and debated my ideas with me; and many others have just listened. I dedicate this book to them and my beloved children, Amanda, Joshua, and Brandy Lynn and my grandchildren Lizzie, Noah, Logan, Sam, Gannon and Harley, who bring me joy at its simplest level. There are no self-made persons, only those who have had opportunity and someone to reach back and pull them forward.

I did not do enough.

"Nonetheless, while I do not completely agree with Oscar Wilde's assertion that our only duty to history is to rewrite it, I think we who live in the present have a responsibility, not only to re-examine the past, but also to make moral judgments about that past.... Without moral judgments about traditional resolutions of legal problems we are apt to rely unquestioningly upon those past resolutions, even though their underlying values and norms are wrong and oppressive."

—Barbara Holden-Smith, Professor of Law, Cornell Law School (quoted from "Lynching, Federalism, and the Intersection of Race and Gender in the Progressive Era")

Table of Contents

Acknowledgments   v
Preface   1
Introduction   3

1. "The security the southern states want..."   5
2. "The Peculiar Institution"   30
3. The Law of Slavery   49
4. States' Rights as Revisionist History   70
5. "The Constitution is colorblind"   97
6. Tyranny of the Republic   123
7. The Power Vested in the President   136
8. Civil Rights   149
9. Democracy Is Government "by and for the people"   160

Chapter Notes   177
Bibliography   191
Index   201

Preface

This book is about constitutional failure. It reviews the history of the Constitutional Convention and the men who were delegates, and the operation of the Constitution since ratification. It examines the idea that the Constitution was a pro-slavery document written by men who profited handsomely from the blood, sweat and tears of African American slaves. The Constitution was written in a way to give slave states a dominant say in the government. Southerners were clear at the Constitutional Convention: no protection for slavery, no union. Slavery was possible because of racism. The notion that slavery was OK because slavery is in the Bible or other societies relied on it just doesn't square with the idea of American democratic values or the writings of the founding fathers, particularly Jefferson. Veneration of the Constitution is perilous and gives far too much liberty away. Historians like Paul Finkelman and David Wiecek and political scientists like Sotirios Barber and Sanford V. Levinson have been critical of the idea of constitutional veneration and emphasized the undemocratic aspects of the document. They have good company among fellow historians and political scientists.

The Constitution and its government have nearly always worked to the disadvantage of African Americans and now represent an absolute political failure for all fair-minded Americans expecting to live in a democracy. The excuse that it created a republic and not a democracy is pabulum that grows thinner at every election. What the Constitution did because of its protection of slavery was give us 750,000 deaths in the Civil War, Jim Crow, segregation and public terror in the form of lynchings, bombings and water cannons. In the twenty-first century, the Constitution's government has no checks or balances and has given us the greatest disparity of wealth in our history. It has resulted in minority governments, senators and congressman winning election because of gerrymandering and other questionable measures aimed at voter suppression

Preface

and voter nullification. Slavery justified by racism was the law in America before the Civil War, and racism was institutionalized in law after the end of Congressional Reconstruction. It is in some respects fitting and ironic that the president who withdrew federal troops from the South didn't win the popular vote but did win the electoral vote because of the contested votes of three southern states. In the 2016 presidential election the Electoral College, a pro-slavery mechanism in the Constitution, again delivered the presidency to the candidate with the smaller share of the popular vote.

Introduction

The Constitution is a failure. There are no consistently effective checks and balances. As rightly pointed out by George Mason at the Constitutional Convention in 1787, before its ratification, Madison's checks and balances work only if the same faction does not control the presidency and the Senate. The Constitution is a failure because it provided no way to end slavery without secession and the deaths of 750,000 Americans. It is a failure because once Reconstruction ended, veneration for the Constitution did not prevent lynching, voter intimidation and segregation. There never were any separate but equal facilities for Black Americans. Even after a Civil Rights revolution led by figures such as Dr. Martin Luther King, Jr., there is no equal protection under the law.

This book is meant to inform and persuade Americans that Madison's Constitution is dead, and veneration will not improve its workings in the face of politicians who do not care about the rule of law. The rule of law requires equality of law. Madison said in *Federalist* 39: "we may define a republic to be, or at least may bestow that name on, a government which derives all its powers directly or indirectly from the great body of the people.... It is essential to such government that it is derived from the great body of society, not from an inconsiderable proportion or favored class of it; otherwise a handful of tyrannical nobles, exercising their oppressions by a delegation of power, might aspire to the rank of republicans and claim for their government the honorable title of republic."

Let's be clear, race and money have always dogged this Constitution. From the founding, racism and money were the justifications for slavery. When it came time to write a national constitution, slavery was a delegate in Philadelphia from the very first day, and southern delegates molded and shaped the document to protect their property. It is argued that the delegates to the Constitutional Convention had to compromise to get a national government. Compromise means mutual concessions, but most

Introduction

of the concessions at the Constitutional Convention came from the delegates of the northern states. Southerners got increased representation by way of the three-fifths clause and federal protections for slavery, while northerners got a republic that would be unable to find any compromise on slavery without being drenched in blood. In federalist America right up to the Civil War, slavery was the rule of law. As Andrew Delbanco has said, the last Fugitive Slave Act was the fuse that lit the explosion that was the Civil War.

Racism has permeated the operation of the Constitution from ratification. Slavery was the dominant engine of southern economics, and the South sought to control the federal government to defeat abolitionism. When the South lost the Civil War, it embarked on a racial war marked by lynching, violation of basic human rights, voter suppression and segregation. It did not look for racial accommodation. In fact, it thrived on the benign neglect of the federal government in the face of murder and political tyranny. Today, with voter purges, gerrymandering, the Electoral College and money, the forces of a minority party use racism as a tool to cultivate fear and demagoguery. The following chapters describe racism in the writing of the Constitution and its operation as a political device for nearly 240 years. Madison's Republic is dead. It was bought and sold on the backs of Black Americans and today is the foil of a government by minority faction. Even as I finish this book a deadly epidemic is enveloping America, and its leader, the president who lost the popular vote by the widest margin in American history, is ineffective, capricious and failing to provide for the "general welfare."

1

"The security the southern states want…"

> "The security the southern states want is that their Negroes may not be taken from them, which some gentlemen within or without doors have a very good mind to do."
> —Pierce Butler, delegate, South Carolina, Friday, July 13, 1787, Philadelphia Constitutional Convention

James Madison managed the creation of a republic that legalized and protected slavery and limited popular government. The Constitution was negotiated and written to protect American slavery by men who profited from human bondage. American slavery was based on white racism, the economics of forced labor, and the blood of millions of Africans kidnapped, brought to America, bred for sale and worked into the ground. It was an evil, pernicious system inconsistent with any of the expressed democratic libertarian sentiments of the American Revolution, especially the unqualified declaration that "all men are created equal" by nature's law.[1]

There were men who led the Revolution who knew slavery was wrong and said so before, during, and after the war with Britain for American independence.[2] James Otis, Nathaniel Appleman, the Rev. Samuel Webster, John Allen, Tom Paine, Benjamin Rush, Samuel Hopkins, Anthony Benezet, Colonel John Laurens, Robert "Councillor" Carter, John Randolph and others raised their voices against slavery and freed their slaves.[3] Thomas Jefferson, a slaveholder, tried to shift moral guilt for slavery from the colonists to Great Britain in a draft of the Declaration of Independence, but southern delegates to the Continental Congress successfully argued references to slavery should be deleted from the document.[4]

The Constitution and American Racism

The Constitution was written by men who were part of a small aristocracy that included southern supporters of slavery who mistrusted popular government.[5] The Constitution was an obstacle to the abolition of slavery. It established a national government that legalized and protected slavery and rejected popular government. The Constitution was made nearly impossible to change by requiring super majorities for amendments in Congress and ratification by three-fourths of the states.

The popular narrative of American history is a tale of the struggle to establish republican democracy through the efforts of those who claimed to believe that "all men are created equal." The truth is many founders believed white, male, educated, privileged property owners like themselves were entitled to personal liberty and the control of government, to the exclusion of other citizens. The traditional history of democracy in America is told by ignoring or minimizing the impact of slavery and racism on the development of political and cultural institutions in the colonies and the United States.

Developed by white English colonists in the West Indies on sugar plantations and southern North American colonies on tobacco, rice and indigo plantations, American slavery was based on race.[6] "Between 1735 and 1775, six out of seven slaves imported into South Carolina came from Africa, one from the islands, and only a statistically insignificant number from other mainland colonies."[7] Historian Betty Wood wrote in her book *The Origins of American Slavery*, "Albeit with the benefit of hindsight, it would seem that from the outset American slavery was characterized by an awareness of ethnic difference that over the course of a century hardened into an overt racism, a racial contempt and hatred that was deliberately cultivated by those who stood to gain financially from the employment of enslaved Africans."[8]

Black slaves were forced to labor their entire lives in bondage and lived in a system based on coercion and punishment. There were no white slaves in America forced to labor for life on a plantation chopping cotton or in an always-wet rice field. Those who embraced slavery believed Africans were their cultural, religious, physical and mental inferiors. White masters, white politics, and white religion dehumanized slaves by claiming they were cursed by their color, lazy, stupid, and unable to govern themselves. Masters claimed Blacks were unable to provide for their own well-being, and slavery was not a curse but a civilizing blessing.[9]

The Constitution authorized Congress to pass fugitive slave acts, created the Electoral College to protect the southern vote for president and

1. "The security the southern states want..."

created an unrepresentative Senate that could stop any actions taken by a popularly elected House of Representatives. The authors of the Constitution gave the southern states disproportionate membership in the House of Representatives and Electoral College by making a slave three-fifths of a person.[10]

The Constitution, ratified by white men, protected slavery, and according to Chief Justice Roger Taney of the U.S. Supreme Court in *Dred Scott*, free Blacks could not be citizens of the United States, and those who were owned and labored on plantations were but property, and had no rights. Because the founders intended to protect slavery, the government of the United States could not abolish or restrict the spread of slavery.[11]

The constitutional protection of slavery doomed the country to a civil war that killed over 750,000 Americans.[12] The South could block an amendment to end slavery, and abolition was possible only after the secession of the southern states. That slavery could be abolished only after a bloodbath of this proportion should give pause to anyone considering the success of the Constitution as a governing document: "there is no other way to understand the Civil War than as a failure of the constitution...."[13]

After the South lost the Civil War, Southerners refused to accept defeat and sought to re-establish white racist governments throughout the South. Through violent intimidation, including beatings, burnings, lynchings and murder by organizations like the Ku Klux Klan, "White Regulators," and ordinary citizens, white Southerners built a political and cultural power structure to oppress Blacks. By attacking the most basic democratic right of a citizen, the right to vote, they muted the voices of black men and women throughout the South and made segregation based on the white lie of "separate but equal" the rule of law. In the Jim Crow South and elsewhere in the United States everything was separate but nothing was equal. The racism that justified slavery and helped shape the Constitution not only made possible an anti-democratic blueprint for government, but survived the abolition of slavery.

Without exception, from 1877 until 1965 the federal government failed to enforce the Thirteenth, Fourteenth, and Fifteenth Amendments to the Constitution and the Civil Rights Acts passed during Reconstruction, whether legislatively, judicially, or through any concerted action by the national government. The national government created by the Constitution failed to require representative governments in states that embraced segregation and thus ignored the Constitution's guarantee of a Republican form of government. The anti-democratic provisions of the

Constitution and indifference in the federal government, in combination with racism as a political tool, were utilized in post–Civil War America to keep whites in power by segregating Blacks and discriminating against them educationally, economically, and socially.

A Debtor Nation

The debt left over from the Revolution was staggering. The French, the Spanish and the Dutch had all loaned money to the Confederation and the individual colonies to keep the Continental Army and state militias in the field and fund the war against Britain. Without French supplies, and their army and navy, victory at Yorktown would not have been possible and the British might have outlasted the colonists. The Continental Army was never well armed or clothed, and pay was a promise more often not kept. At the start of the Yorktown campaign in 1781 the Continental Army had received no pay for over a year. Soldiers who stayed the course were promised land by the national government and states because that is what the states had in abundance, although the states could not even agree on who owned the western lands.

The Revolution ended with the Peace of Paris in 1783, which was ratified by the Americans in January 1784. The treaty contained mutual obligations by all signatories, and as time passed these mutual obligations became more problematic for Americans.

While the states argued over land titles, the British continued to occupy forts in the Northwest Territories because they could, and there was no army to force them out of the western lands. The treaty ending the war had promised to compensate some loyalists for property that had been destroyed and confiscated by the patriots, but most of the states had no money to fulfill this obligation and believed that this article of the peace treaty was unjust. The United States was a debtor nation with almost no credit anywhere. Paper money had no value and hard currency consisted of Spanish pieces of eight and British coins.

Farmers in Massachusetts, burdened by taxes collected by their state to pay war debts, rebelled when they began to lose their farms because they could not pay the taxes. The militia was called out to put down Shay's Rebellion in Massachusetts and some states issued money without security and wrote stay laws to help their farmers and prevent foreclosures. The separate states also claimed the right to tax interstate commerce and levy tariffs as they saw fit. There was no money to run the national government because there was no tax revenue or contributions by the states. Men like Madison and Washington saw the situation as apocalyptic, calling for action to bring order to the former colonies by amending or replacing the Articles of Confederation to address the problems of an ineffective national government.

George Washington had earned the admiration of his countryman during the Revolution and still commanded great respect throughout the states. He believed changes were needed and soon or the fruits of the Revolution would be lost to the states. Washington's forte was not politics, but he would lend his name and support to those who sought a stronger union of the states. No man had struggled harder to work for the success of the Revolution, and he understood firsthand the failures of the Continental Congress under the Articles of Confederation. During the Revolution Congress had failed to feed, clothe and pay the Continental Army. For Washington, the idea of a strong national government was not a philosophical question. It was a matter of survival.

The Delegates

The states named seventy-four delegates to the Constitutional Convention. Only Rhode Island, referred to by contemporaries as "Rogue Island," did not participate in the convention.[14] These white male delegates were chosen by the state legislatures. Of the seventy-four only fifty-five actually participated in the debates and on a given day only thirty to forty of the delegates were on the floor of the Convention considering provisions for the new constitution.[15] Delegates came and went at their whim; some actively participated and some attended occasionally.[16]

The delegates did not resemble the typical American in 1787. At the time of the Convention in 1787, most Americans were small farmers, owning and working farms of 90 to 160 acres. By this measure only two of the fifty-five delegates could claim to be farmers.[17] Many southern delegates owned large plantations and lived off the labor of slaves. They were all white males, almost all Protestant, lawyers, owners of large estates, land speculators, or had held public office. Six had signed the Declaration of Independence, and twenty-six were soldiers who had served in the Revolution.[18] All of these men had local and national reputations; Jefferson described them as "demigods."[19] Neither Jefferson, who was in

France as ambassador, nor John Adams, who was in London as ambassador to Great Britain, attended the Convention. Jefferson had reservations about a strong national government, but Adams was firmly behind the idea. Other patriots like Virginia's Patrick Henry believed that a national government could be used to abolish slavery and did not attend because he "smelled a rat."[20]

Of the fifty-five delegates who were regularly involved in the business of the Constitutional Convention, twenty-five owned slaves.[21] Among those were Charles Carroll and Luther Martin of Maryland, and John Dickinson of Delaware. Benjamin Franklin had owned slaves but by the time of the Convention he'd become an advocate of gradual emancipation. George Mason, James Madison and Edmund Randolph of Virginia owned hundreds of slaves. Madison acknowledged slavery's evils and warned of its debilitating influence in a democratic republic, and Jefferson talked about the damage slavery did to the masters, but neither founder emancipated his slaves or recognized the damage that slavery did to its victims. In 1787, both Madison and Jefferson had no occupation but politics and public service and so lived off the labor of their slaves. Charles Cotesworth Pinckney and Edward Rutledge of South Carolina, Robert Morris of Pennsylvania, and George Washington of Virginia owned slaves. Of these founders, Washington alone had urged an end to the slave trade in Virginia before the Revolution.

The Rake

The men who made the Revolution and drafted the Constitution had distinct characters shaped by their times and their environment.[22] Born on an estate in what is now the Bronx in New York City, Gouverneur Morris was a rake, a roué, and a man who viewed himself as an aristocrat. An interesting man who brooked no fools, he was far too fond of other men's wives. He was in many ways representative of the anti-democratic delegates to the Constitutional Convention. He made money in his own right and was considered a successful businessman. A brilliant man critical of those he did not believe his equal, he responded to concerns about the dangers of an American aristocracy at the Constitutional Convention, telling the delegates that "there never was, nor ever will be, a civilized society without an aristocracy."[23] Morris once described a crowd of American Revolutionaries as "poor reptiles!" He had been an active patriot during

1. "The security the southern states want..."

the Revolution and despite his aristocratic tendencies was an adamant foe of slavery, urging its abolition in New York. He called it a "nefarious institution" which was "a curse of heaven on the states where it prevailed."[24]

As the man who "wrote" the Constitution, actually penned it, Morris authored the phrase "We the people...." As a delegate to the Constitutional Convention in 1787, he made more speeches than any other member of the Convention.[25]

Madison's plan for the government called for three branches, each providing a check on the other. There would be a legislature, chief executive, and a judiciary; not only did the nature of the representational basis of the legislative branch cause debate but the office of president drew vigorous discussion. According to Madison's notes of the Constitutional Convention, Morris argued "One great object of the executive is to control the legislature. The legislature will continually seek to aggrandize and perpetuate themselves," and "the executive magistrate should be the guardian of the people...."[26]

Morris had a political career that spanned the years from the Revolution to the early Republic. He considered himself a Federalist, a believer in a strong central government, but when the War of 1812 began, he gave comfort to New England secessionists and called Madison a "sexless drunkard." He believed the Constitution was a failure and it was time to get rid of it.[27]

The Architect

James Madison was born into wealth and the life of a colonial patrician at Montpelier, the Madison manse in Orange County, Virginia. His father's estate was comprised of thousands of acres and many slaves. Madison was never burdened by work but his youth was remarkable for not being spent riding across the countryside raising hell like so many of his young wealthy contemporaries, but reading the books in his father's library. A graduate of Princeton, he completed the three-year course of study in two. He had embraced the Enlightenment ideas of natural rights and individual liberties at Princeton, and was active in politics in Virginia and the Continental Congress during the Revolution. Although he was critical of slavery, his beliefs regarding the natural rights of men did not extend to his slaves, and he lived off their labors all his life. He was shy. When he finally married at age forty-one, it was to a widow seventeen years his junior.[28]

The Constitution and American Racism

Madison was a member of the Virginia House of Delegates, where he met Thomas Jefferson in the fall of 1776, and later actively supported him on the issue of religious tolerance. He wrote "all men are equally entitled to the free exercise of religion."[29] He had no military experience, but because of family connections he served briefly as a colonel in the Virginia militia during the Revolution. He saw no active service but in 1779 went to the Continental Congress until at war's end he returned to Virginia and served in the House of Delegates.[30]

Because of his service in the Continental Congress, Madison was well aware of the shortcomings of the national government during and after the Revolution. Before the Constitutional Convention he wrote a memorandum, "Vices of the Political System of the United States," in an attempt to identify the problems with the Articles of Confederation and the various state governments.[31] The Articles of Confederation had proved ineffectual as a framework for unified government because there was no power in the legislative branch, and the states could always override their delegates' votes. The Congress had no power to tax, and states resisted efforts to force them to pay contributions for the expenses of the Confederation. All the states acted like small republics. Madison was critical of the states and argued that they could not operate collectively based on recommendations but only if compelled by laws. There was no common defense or foreign policy. All of the states had interests but none seemed to coincide or bring them together to act as allies in addressing common problems. Madison was also critical of the form of government some states had adopted. He believed it too democratic and subject to the whims of the people.[32]

In 1787 there were over 600,000 slaves in the former colonies, mostly in the South. By the time of the Constitutional Convention, slavery had been recognized by Americans for over one hundred and sixty years.[33] Most slaves lived in the South on large plantations, growing tobacco, rice, indigo, and wheat. In the upper South, in Virginia, Maryland, and North Carolina, tobacco was the cash crop of choice, but in the lower South, in South Carolina, rice and indigo were the main cash crops. It was only after ratification of the Constitution and the invention of the cotton gin that cotton became the "king" of cash crops.[34]

In pre-revolutionary America, huge numbers of slaves had been kidnapped from Africa by slavers. When brought to the colonies, they spoke no English. If they survived the horrible ordeal of transport to the American colonies known as the "Middle Passage," many died while being

1. "The security the southern states want…"

"seasoned" on the plantations.[35] In the years before the Revolution, many slaves were born on the plantations and the planters in the upper South began to sell their surplus slaves to white planters further south.

Resistance to slavery at the time of the Convention can be seen in the passage of the Northwest Ordinance of 1787, which was passed by the Continental Congress in July, after the Constitutional Convention began meeting. It provided, "There shall be neither slavery nor involuntary servitude in said territory…." The Northwest Territories consisted of the present states of Ohio, Indiana, Illinois, Michigan, Wisconsin and Minnesota, all north of the Ohio River. There was no enforcement provision in the ordinance, but as historian Paul Finkelman has said, "the ordinance can be seen as an example of the tension between liberty and property inherent in Revolutionary America."[36]

Philadelphia in the Summer of 1787

Philadelphia had been the home of the Continental Congress during most of the Revolution. It is located on the Delaware River and has hot and muggy summers, and for years after its founding, the city was plagued with malaria and yellow fever epidemics. Five thousand residents died in a 1793 outbreak of yellow fever. The delegates to the Constitutional Convention chose to meet in the Philadelphia State House where the Declaration of Independence had been debated and ratified. It was a two-story brick structure with ample room for the delegates.

The delegates agreed on the need for secrecy so their work would not be influenced by public debates, so the first-floor windows were nailed shut for confidentiality and to keep flies out during what proved to be a hot and humid summer.[37] George Washington was chosen as president of the Convention, although in practice someone else managed the proceedings. Much of the real work of the Convention was done by committees, but the Convention adopted a rule that even after the delegates had approved a proposal, it could be considered again by the Convention as a Committee of the Whole.[38]

James Madison took the most detailed and extensive notes, and these are considered by many historians the best evidence of the proceedings.[39] Madison's notes were not published until after his death, well after the Constitution was ratified. From the beginning, some states took positions on issues that promised to complicate discussions on the idea of a union of the states and the nature of the government that would bind the former colonies. Delaware instructed its delegation not to agree to any proposal that adopted proportional representation, and the southern states made it clear slavery would be protected.[40]

The first meeting of a quorum of the delegates was on Friday, May 25, 1787, and the Convention adjourned on September 17, 1787. The organization and structure of government to replace the ineffective Articles of Confederation was the soul and substance of the debates at the Convention. The Convention had been called to amend the Articles and some thought was given to amending them, but not for long, and the delegates moved quickly to the idea of establishing a new system of government.

Madison arrived at the Convention ready with what became known as the "Virginia Plan" based on what he described as a republican form of government. He was enthused with the idea of a representative government, not a government ruled by the popular will.[41] Madison and his fellow delegates were not trying to devise a democratic government, they were trying to devise a system that centralized certain authority in a national government and left other authority in the hands of the states. Since the delegates at the Convention represented a thin slice of what aristocracy existed at the birth of the nation and definitely were not representative of all the people,[42] they wanted limits on any government surviving the debates at the Convention. Many saw government as a threat and sought to create a government that reflected their values and protected their political and economic status.

Early in the Convention, Governor John Randolph of Virginia proposed Madison's "Virginia Plan." The plan called for a legislative branch consisting of two houses, an executive and a judicial branch.[43] The legislature would be a national congress, the House of Representatives, with proportional representation from the states, and a smaller upper house serving for a longer term and elected by the House, not the people. The smaller states were opposed to proportional representation because they believed larger states would dominate them and run roughshod over their interests.

William Patterson, a delegate from New Jersey, argued he would rather submit to a "monarch, a despot," than a government that did not protect the smaller states. At the other end of the argument, delegate James Wilson of Pennsylvania was adamant that "as all authority is derived from the people, equal numbers of people ought to have equal numbers of representatives, and different numbers of people different numbers of

1. "The security the southern states want…"

representatives."[44] Presciently, Wilson also argued that a senate that gave equal representation to each state would result in the minority ruling the majority. If each state had an equal vote, small states could combine and dictate policy to those large states not joining them.[45]

Madison believed the real difference between the states represented at the Convention was not size, but slavery.[46]

Eventually, the delegates argued over how the population of each state would be determined for calculating a state's representation in the House. In 1783, while serving in the Confederation Congress, Madison suggested that the states should contribute to the operating costs of the Confederation based on their population and the Southern states should include three-fifths of the number of slaves in determining their population. For purposes of raising revenue, Southerners thought Madison's proposal overvalued slaves and Northerners thought it undervalued them.[47]

The use of the ratio became the basis of counting each slave as three-fifths of a person for purposes of determining representation in the House of Representatives. On this point Gouverneur Morris, who opposed slavery, objected on the grounds it gave Southern states great benefits and such a formula would encourage the slave trade.[48] Despite objections, on July 16, 1787, the Southerners prevailed on the point and the Convention adopted the three-fifths clause and so enhanced their representation in the House of Representatives and Electoral College.[49] The smaller states got a Senate with equal representation, all the states having the same vote.

Debate over the chief executive centered on what sorts of powers the president would have. Alexander Hamilton, who appeared only occasionally at the Convention, in June admitted he was no friend of republics and urged the delegates to adopt a monarchical form of government.[50] Hamilton's proposal died a just death. An Electoral College was devised to elect the president rather than have it done by popular vote. The South would benefit from the three-fifths rule by increasing the slave states' representation in the Electoral College.[51] As a result, four of the first five presidents were from Virginia, and nine of the first sixteen presidents would be from the South. Most of these men were slave owners.

Gouverneur Morris observed that the chief executive was the protector of all the people and would need to "be the guardian of the people, even the lower classes, against legislative tyranny," because "wealth tends to corrupt the mind, and to nourish its love of power and so stimulating it to oppression."[52] Benjamin Franklin counseled, "the first man put at the helm will be a good one. Nobody knows what sort may come afterwards.

The Constitution and American Racism

The executive will be always increasing here, as elsewhere, till it ends in monarchy." George Mason pointed out to the Convention that given the powers of the President and the Senate, if the two branches were controlled by the same party, they would be able to subvert the Constitution.[53] There would be no separation of powers.

So it went. The Convention adopted some of Madison's suggestions, changed some, rejected some, and adopted some proposals of other delegates. In the end, Gouverneur Morris was asked to reduce the Constitution to writing with help from the Committee of Style. The document had 4,453 words. It was divided into seven Articles, each having sections and clauses. When ratified it had no Bill of Rights.

The first three Articles lay out the general architecture of the government: establishing a bicameral legislature, a chief executive and a supreme court. Article IV gives Full Faith and Credit to the public acts, records and judicial proceedings of every state. It gives citizens moving from one state to another the same legal rights and treatment. The article also gives legal authority for the passage of fugitive slave acts.

Article V provides the process for amending the Constitution, prohibits the national government from outlawing the slave trade before 1808, and directs that the Senate shall be bound by equal state representation.

Article VI provides for the enforceability of debts incurred before the adoption of the Constitution; has a supremacy clause providing that the laws of the United Sates shall be the supreme law of the land; and the final clause prohibits a religious test as a qualification for holding office. The last Article, VII, required ratification of the Constitution by nine states.

Without ever using the word "slavery" in the original text of the Constitution as written and ratified, the supporters of slavery made sure that the Constitution recognized and protected rights in humans as property. The representatives at the Convention decided union was more important than conflict over slavery. Madison insisted that the Constitution not mention slavery.[54] Slavery, the most undemocratic of the legacies of the "founding fathers," would be abolished only after the deaths of hundreds of thousands of Americans in the Civil War. The Constitution as ratified protected slavery and made Black men and women property by its acknowledgment of the institution and its protection of a dehumanizing system of labor based on total and complete obedience. Racism, the root of slavery, has survived extirpation and still yet dominates state and national

1. "The security the southern states want..."

politics, such as the Republican Party's strategy over the past fifty years of attracting racists through the guise of favoring "states' rights" or "limited government."[55]

All Other Persons, the "Three-Fifths Clause"

> **1. Article I, Section 2, Clause 3, Representatives and direct Taxes shall be apportioned among the several States which may be included within this Union, according to their respective Numbers, which shall be determined by adding of the whole Number of free Persons, including those bound to Servitude for a Term of Years, and excluding Indians not taxed, three fifths of all other Persons.**

This is the infamous "three-fifths clause." The Southerners couldn't even use the word slave; instead "all other Persons" described a hellish institution made legal by the Constitution. Madison had first proposed a three-fifths formula to be used as the basis for taxation during debates on finances in the Confederation Congress in 1783.[56] The proposal in the Constitutional Convention counted slaves to determine proportional representation in the House of Representatives. This calculation inflated the South's representation in the House of Representatives and the Electoral College. It insured Southerners a disproportionate impact on all decisions in Congress. This clause defined the South's power inside the new government. This inflation of the South's political power insured fugitive slave acts, gag rules, and multiple southern presidents despite the North having a larger voting population. It made possible the Missouri Compromise, the Compromise of 1850, the Kansas-Nebraska Act, and ultimately meant the Constitution's government would fail to provide a peaceful solution to slavery.[57]

According to Madison's notes on the Constitutional Convention, Pierce Butler, delegate from South Carolina, framed the issue succinctly for Southerners: "The security the southern states want is that their negroes may not be taken from them."[58] While not a firm believer in representative government, Elbridge Gerry, delegate to the Convention from Massachusetts, opposed the three-fifths clause: "The idea of property ought not to be the rule of representation. Blacks are property, and are used to the southward as horses and cattle to the northward...."⁵⁹ In September, Gerry voted against acceptance of the Constitution.

The three-fifths clause also provided that if a direct tax were levied by the national government, for example a poll tax or head tax, a slave would only be counted as three-fifths of a person. The South by this Article boosted its representation in Congress and diminished its financial contribution to the federal government.

The Slave Trade

2. Article I, Section 9, Clause 1, The Migration or Importation of such Persons as any of the States now existing shall think proper to admit, shall not be prohibited by the Congress prior to the Year one thousand eight hundred and eight, but a Tax or duty may be imposed on such Importation, not exceeding ten dollars for each Person.

George Mason, delegate from Virginia, blamed Britain for the slave trade in the constitutional debates and admitted, "Every master of slaves is born a petty tyrant."[60] But Mason, who owned 200 slaves, never freed one during his life or at his death.[61] The founders were too embarrassed to use the words "slave" or "slavery" in the Constitution, and here we see the euphemisms "migration" and "importation" used to describe slave trafficking. To be sure, this clause did not require Congress to end the slave trade in 1808, but it prohibited it from doing so sooner. By the time of the Constitutional Convention, ten of the thirteen states had already banned the import of slaves from outside the United States.[62]

This provision allowed some Southern states that had ended the trans–Atlantic slave trade to reopen it, although it did not affect the domestic slave trade. Some Southerners had an interest in ending the international slave trade because states like Virginia had developed a surplus in their slave populations and were interested in "selling their slaves South." The Atlantic slave trade officially ended in 1808 after Congress passed a bill ending it in 1807, but because the prohibition was not actively enforced by the United States, some Atlantic slave trade continued until the Civil War. As late as 1860, fifty-two years after Congress ended the trade, some Southerners were still attempting to bring Africans into the country,

1. "The security the southern states want..."

and in July of that year, the ship *Clotilda*, a slaver, ran aground in Mobile Bay, Alabama.[63] When Great Britain ended the slave trade, it sent naval forces to Africa to enforce its ban on the trade, confiscating ships and freeing cargoes of human beings intended for slavery. In contrast, the United States did not consistently or forcefully police the Atlantic slave trade.

Taxes

> **3. Article I, Section 9, Clause 4, No Capitation, or other direct, Tax shall be laid, unless in Proportion to the Census or Enumeration herein before directed to be taken.**

Although Southerners wanted slaves treated as property instead of people, they opposed taxation of their slaves. This clause is redundant because it provides that if a capitation tax or head tax was ever imposed by the national government, a slave would have to be treated as three-fifths of a person.[64] This clause shows the length to which the Southerners went to keep their property from being taxed and the length to which Madison was willing to go to accommodate his fellow Southerners and slave holders. According to historian John Rakove, a "tax imposed on products cultivated by slave labor might ultimately operate as a tax on slavery itself."[65]

Fugitive Slaves

> **4. Article IV, Section 2, Clause 3, No Person held to Service or Labour in one State, under the Laws thereof, escaping into another, shall, in Consequence of any Law or Regulation therein, be discharged from such Service or Labour, but shall be delivered up on Claim of the Party to whom such Service or Labour may be due.**

Historian Andrew Delbanco describes the Fugitive Slave Act of 1850 as the fuse that led to the Civil War.[66] Article IV made possible the passage of federal fugitive slave acts providing for the capture and return of runaway slaves in the United States. There was no serious opposition in the Convention to this Clause. In February 1793, Congress passed the first national Fugitive Slave Act. (A second act was passed in 1850.) Many northern states enacted "personal liberty" laws to protect runaways and prevent Black freedmen who were kidnapped from being sent south into slavery. Federal courts, in enforcing fugitive slave acts, often ignored the "personal liberty" laws. The issue of resistance to enforcement would be a cause for Southern resentment, and enforcement by Southerners shaped northern attitudes about slavery. Public attitudes in the North about slavery changed enough that an "Underground Railroad" organized by private citizens to help fugitive slaves effectively aided many escaped slaves to reach freedom. As more slaves escaped and Southerners demanded more active help of state and federal officials in returning their property, more fugitive slaves found it necessary to flee across the border to Canada, beyond the reach of the Constitution.

Amending the Constitution

> **5. Article V. The Congress, whenever two thirds of both Houses shall deem it necessary, shall propose Amendments to this Constitution, or, on the Application of the Legislatures of two-thirds of the several States, shall call a Convention for proposing Amendments, which, in either Case, shall be valid to all Intents and Purposes, as Part of this Constitution, when ratified by the Legislatures of three fourths of the several States, or by Conventions in three fourths thereof, as the one or the other Mode of Ratification may be proposed by the Congress; Provided that no Amendment which may be made prior to the Year One thousand eight hundred and eight shall in any Manner affect the first and fourth Clauses in the Ninth Section of the first Article; and that no State, without its Consent, shall be deprived of its equal Suffrage in the Senate.**

This Article makes it virtually impossible to amend the Constitution. Any attempt to abolish the slave trade prior to 1808 was prohibited. South

1. *"The security the southern states want..."*

Carolina, in fact, reopened the trans–Atlantic slave trade and wanted to make sure that the trade could not be ended by the national government before 1808.

Article V made a political, constitutional, non-violent end to slavery nearly impossible by requiring two-thirds of both houses of Congress and three-fourths of the states to approve any amendment. Ultimately, fifteen states made slavery legal. Today, those fifteen states could block an attempt by the remaining thirty-five states to abolish slavery. Only thirteen of the fifteen states would be necessary to block the Thirteenth Amendment abolishing slavery. "Requiring amendments to be approved by supermajorities in both houses of Congress and the states creates a virtually insuperable barrier to serious constitutional revision."[67]

The last sentence of Article V ordains "that no State, without its Consent, shall be deprived of its equal Suffrage in the Senate," and insures the anti-democratic nature of the government because it does not reflect the principle of one person–one vote. It gives states with smaller populations the same weight as states with large populations in the course and conduct of the government. States with small populations can block measures beneficial to the whole, such as the abolition of slavery, making lynching a federal crime, the Equal Rights Amendment and the elimination of the Electoral College.

Suppressing Slave Rebellions

6. Article I, Section 8, Clause 15, To provide for calling forth the Militia to execute the Laws of Union, suppress Insurrections and repel Invasions.

This Article permitted the militia to be used to suppress insurrections. It was used to suppress Nat Turner's rebellion and John Brown's raid on Harper's Ferry. Because there were often more slaves than slave owners in the South, there was always a fear among the whites of a slave insurrection. On the eve of the Civil War the total population of the South was 9 million; 40 percent were slaves.[68] Thirty-one percent of the families in the seceding states owned 3,521,110 slaves.[69]

In 1788 during the ratification debates, Hugh Hughes, one of the anti-federalists from New York, who styled himself as "a countryman from Duchess County," penned opposition pieces to the ratification of the Constitution: "Should the new constitution be sufficiently corrected by a substantial bill of rights, an equitable representation ... and relinquishing every idea of drenching the bowels of Africa in gore, for the sake of enslaving its freeborn innocent inhabitants, I imagine we might become a happy respectable people.... I have no idea of marching 500 or 1000 miles to quell an insurrection of such immigrants as are proposed by the new constitution, to be introduced for one and twenty years."[70]

No Export Taxes on the Products of Slavery

> 7. **Article I, Section 9, Clause 5, No Tax or Duty shall be laid on Articles exported from any state.**

This clause benefits slavery. The slaves who worked on large plantations produced mainly wheat, tobacco, rice, indigo, sugar, and eventually cotton as cash crops. This clause prohibited the national government from levying export taxes on the fruits of slave labor.

More Tax Support for Slavery

> 8. **Article I, Section 10, Clause 2, No State shall, without the Consent of the Congress, lay any Imposts or Duties on Imports or Exports, except what may be absolutely necessary for executing its inspection Laws: and the net Produce of all Duties and Imposts, laid by any State on Imports or Exports, shall be for the Use of the Treasury of the United States; and all such Laws shall be subject to the Revision and Control of the Congress.**

The South feared individual states would levy tariffs on imports and exports. This provision served the slave states because the products of slavery were almost always exports, and the plantations were able to import European consumer goods without state taxes levied on them.

1. *"The security the southern states want..."*

Electoral College

> 9. Article II, Section 1, Clause 2, Each State shall appoint, in such Manner as the Legislature thereof may direct, a Number of Electors, equal to the whole Number of Senators and Representatives to which the State may be entitled in the Congress: but no Senator or Representative, or Person holding an Office of Trust or Profit under the United States, shall be appointed an Elector.

Federalists James Madison, James Wilson and Alexander Hamilton, among others, had proposed direct election of the president. The method of election of the president was a divisive issue in Philadelphia during the Convention.

Slavery drove this controversy. Review of Madison's notes shows the Southerners expressed concerns about direct election because if only Southern whites voted they could not furnish a large enough base for their candidate to win. Madison himself expressed a preference for direct election, but he knew such a system would be unacceptable to the South.[71] The southern solution was to use the three-fifths formula to count slaves in determining the number of electors in the Electoral College.

The Electoral College protected slavery. The Constitution increased the influence of the southern states through the three-fifths rule, which meant increased numbers for the South in the House of Representatives. Remember, electors were equal in number to a state's House and Senate delegations. Until the 12th Amendment, the top two candidates receiving votes after the Electoral College voted were President and Vice President respectively, unless there was a tie. Thomas Jefferson and Aaron Burr tied, but Alexander Hamilton famously hated Burr more than Jefferson and used his influence in the House of Representatives to help swing the election to Jefferson. Jefferson had a history of opposing Federalist ideas regarding the direction of the country and the divisions between the two factions were deep. He still professed to believe in the superiority of an agrarian country with a limited national government. Hamilton sought a big government solution to debt and other problems. Burr was a bit of a self-serving scoundrel who cared more for himself than the country and hated both Hamilton and Jefferson.

The Constitution and American Racism

The problem with a system that counts slaves at three-fifths of a person is shown by the 1800 census where Pennsylvania had 10 percent more free persons in its population than Virginia but received 20 percent fewer votes in Congress than Virginia because of slaves being counted. In debates over the Twelfth Amendment in the House of Representatives, Massachusetts Congressman Samuel Thatcher documented the disparity: "The representation of slaves adds thirteen members to this House in the present Congress, and eighteen Electors of President and Vice President at the next election."[72] The Electoral College was designed to protect southern interests. Its history makes it unnecessary, and its effect undemocratic today. The country deserves direct election of the President by a simple majority of Americans. Even Madison was in favor of direct election of the President. Governors and representatives and senators are elected this way. Political party, Congressional, and state legislative opposition to eliminating the Electoral College indicates a fear of democracy and direct participation of the people in their government.[73]

The vote of the Electoral College has failed on four occasions to reflect the popular vote for President, twice in the last twenty years.

New States

> **10. Article IV, Section 3, Clause 1, New States may be admitted by the Congress into this Union; but no new States shall be formed or erected within the Jurisdiction of any other State; nor any State be formed by the Junction of two or more States, or Parts of States, without the Consent of the Legislatures of the States concerned as well as of the Congress.**

The drafters of the Constitution recognized that new states would enter the Union. In 1784 Jefferson proposed a clause in an ordinance that would have barred slavery after 1800 from any states admitted from the Western territories, North or South.[74] The proposition failed by one vote.[75] The Northwest Ordinance of 1787, drafted and ratified under the Articles of Confederation by the Confederation Congress while the Constitutional Convention met, prohibited slavery in states carved out of the Northwest Territories, including the states of Ohio, Indiana, Illinois,

1. "The security the southern states want..."

Wisconsin, Michigan and Minnesota. There were efforts after the ratification of the Constitution to repeal this ban. Southerners wanted to maintain a balance between slave states and free states. This clause in the Constitution allowed for the admission of new slave states to the south and west.

After the Constitution's ratification and during Jefferson's presidency when the Louisiana Purchase was made, a treaty provision of the purchase protected the right of Spanish and French residents to keep their slaves. Jefferson, concerned about the legality of the Louisiana Purchase, drafted a constitutional amendment, never acted on by Congress, that legitimized the purchase and reserved it for Native Americans.

Westward expansion meant expansion of slavery. New territories that would become new states led to arguments over whether these new states would be slave or free. These arguments led to the Missouri Compromise, the Compromise of 1850, and the Kansas-Nebraska Act. All of which were intended to preserve the southern states' interest in blocking any efforts to limit or abolish slavery by prohibiting slavery in the territories or entry of slave states into the Union. The Missouri Compromise in 1820 signaled the beginning of a serious moral, intellectual, and political divide in the United States on the issue of slavery. John Adams opposed Missouri's entry into the Union as a slave state. He wrote his daughter that she would think him mad if she knew "the calamities that slavery was likely to produce in the country."[76]

Missouri applied for admission as a slave state in 1819. At the time there were 22 states in the Union—11 free and 11 where slavery was legal. While slavery had been legal in the area that was the Louisiana Purchase, slaves had travelled to Missouri with Southerners from the "old" South. New York Congressman James Tallmadge introduced an amendment that would prohibit the further importation of slaves to Missouri and require the eventual emancipation of the children of Missouri slaves. "I know the will of my constituents, and regardless of consequences, I will avow it; as their representative, I will proclaim their hatred to slavery in every shape." The bill passed in the House and failed in the Senate. Then the northern part of Massachusetts, now Maine, sought admission as a state. The compromise hammered out permitted the admission of both Maine and Missouri, thereby preserving the balance of free and slave states. It also prohibited slavery north of a line 36 degrees 30 minutes in the Louisiana Purchase, but strengthened fugitive slave laws by requiring the return of any runaway slave who made it north of this line.

A Republican Form of Government

> **11. Article IV, Section 4. The United States shall guarantee to every State in this Union a Republican Form of Government, and shall protect each of them against Invasion; and an Application of the Legislature, or of the Executive (when the Legislature cannot be convened) against domestic Violence.**

This is known as the "guarantee clause" because it guarantees a "Republican Form of Government." A republican form of government was never defined by the Constitution or the Supreme Court, and this clause has never been enforced or used by the Supreme Court despite the many abuses in southern states after the Civil War.

Madison defined a Republican form of government in *Federalist* No. 39: "It is essential to such a government, that it be derived from the great body of the society, not from an inconsiderable proportion, or a favored class of it; otherwise a handful of tyrannical nobles, exercising their oppressions by a delegation of their powers, might aspire to the rank of republicans...."[77]

Forced segregation, suppression of Black voters, and the terrorism sanctioned by the southern states is the definition of tyranny rather than a republican form of government.[78]

The guarantee clause also gave the national government authority to assist in putting down slave rebellions. The national government promised it would protect states from domestic violence. Because of the disparity in white and slave populations in all the southern states, whites expected a slave rebellion and they wanted military force available to put it down. It is not surprising that people—torn from their homeland, brutalized by those who did not recognize them as persons—would seek to free themselves.

The laws passed by the national government demanding both cooperation and punishment for those who might lend succor to fugitive slaves recognized, protected and enabled slavery to flourish in the United States. Resistance by slaves resulted in brutal private and public "correction" sanctioned by the law. Slaves rebelled by personal resistance and insurrections, including the Stono Rebellion in 1739 in South Carolina, and the New York City Conspiracy in 1741.[79] During the Revolution thousands of slaves

1. "The security the southern states want…"

fled plantations and took up arms against the colonists when provided protection and freedom by British forces. Thousands of these slaves were evacuated with loyalists and British forces after the peace treaty. When British General Carleton evacuated New York in 1783 he took some four thousand former slaves with him.[80]

The Legacy of a Pro Slavery Anti-Democratic Constitution

The Constitution blocked democratic reform of the new government through a cumbersome amendment process. It counted a slave as three-fifths of a person to placate Southerners worried about federal restrictions against slavery and increased southern influence in the government. It made the United States a slave country despite the moral irony acknowledged by Jefferson and Madison. The government became a protector of slavery by requiring personal, state and federal aid in the return of runaway slaves and suppression of insurrections. The Constitution created a legislative branch strongly influenced by slave interests and there were repeated constitutional crises resulting in compromise with Southerners to protect slavery. The Constitution created a Supreme Court that made Black slavery the rule of law.

The delegates to the Constitutional Convention made amending the Constitution so hard it has only been done twenty-seven times in over 225 years. The abolition of slavery by the Thirteenth Amendment, passage of the Fourteenth Amendment making native born persons citizens, and the Fifteenth Amendment guaranteeing freedmen the right to vote were possible only because the southern states seceded and were therefore unable to prevent its passage. The direct election of Senators and a woman's right to vote only came 125 years after ratification. The Constitution, because it was a pact with the devil, resulted in a civil war that killed hundreds of thousands of Americans, and the racism that permeated slavery is still the source of injustice throughout America.

The Constitution guaranteed disproportional representation in the federal government and continues that tradition today. Because each state has the same number of votes in the Senate, regardless of population, the Senate can be controlled by one party whose members do not represent the majority of Americans. The Senate confirms cabinet appointments and the nomination of federal judges and can block bills by

The Constitution and American Racism

vote, filibuster, and skewed operating rules favoring the party in power. The Senate is not the greatest deliberative body in the world; it is the greatest obstacle to representative government in the United States. When both the executive and legislative branches are controlled by the same party there are no checks and balances. One party with control of the presidency and the Senate can control the government.

Racism was inherently embedded in the U.S. Constitution with its legal protection of slavery and the way it sanctioned a system of laws to enforce property rights in humans. The federal government ceased, after the election of 1876, to intervene in the southern states to stop lynching, black voter suppression, and the institutionalization of discrimination and segregation with Jim Crow laws. Today the national government functions as a servant of monied interests whose agenda does not align with the majority of Americans. Voter suppression continues and the Electoral College ignores the vote of the majority of Americans.

The Constitution did not create a government that embodied Jefferson's words that "all men are created equal." The founding fathers did not encourage or protect a government "by the people and for the people." The federal government created by the Constitution has failed repeatedly throughout American history to protect Black Americans and to intervene to ensure that all Americans are the beneficiaries of a republican form of government. Madison's Republic has failed all Americans, and racism still provides a way for political parties to gain control of the government, and it is legal.

The Constitution fails as the framework for a democratic government answerable to all of the people. Gerrymandering sanctioned by the Supreme Court and an Electoral College designed by delegates to the Constitutional Convention to protect the influence of southern states and the Senate, which in Republican hands represents a minority of Americans, continue to limit the influence of the popular vote. Presidents are elected without a majority of the popular vote and legislation that benefits all Americans is thwarted by a non-representative Senate that rewards its constituencies with legislation reflecting lobbying and money more than democratic ideals.

For Congress the Constitution does not provide for term limits and this has made possible the establishment of a class of professional politicians maintained by huge sums of cash from lobbyists whose influence extends to almost all areas of the commonweal. The federal government, ruled by a minority faction, is not accountable to the public and does not

1. "The security the southern states want..."

promote the general welfare or serve the interests of "We the People." It has on occasion served the common good. In the 1960s a confluence of public outrage over the violence that enforced segregation, the work of Martin Luther King, Jr., and other Civil Rights icons, a progressive Supreme Court, and the improbable intervention of Lyndon Johnson caused a Civil Rights revolution. The gains made by the Civil Rights Revolution have been eroded by the Republicans in Congress and on the Supreme Court. Racism has been an ally of Republican politics masquerading as states' rights and originalism.

2

"The Peculiar Institution"

Native Slaves

The Europeans did not discover the Americas, they invaded them. The Spanish, the Portuguese, and the Dutch were trying to get somewhere else when they blundered into two huge continents by accident and chance. Luck, and modest technological improvements in navigation, ships, and sailing made possible landfall in places that were already populated by millions of people. Islands in the Caribbean and the vast land masses of the North and South American continents had civilizations and cultures that had existed without European intervention for thousands of years. The Europeans considered the inhabitants of these islands and continents primitive infidels, part of the wildlife to be killed, enslaved, or converted from their native beliefs to a religion that considered them damned without Christian salvation.

The first Europeans came for gold, silver, fur, and timber and colonized land for cultivation of cash crops like sugar and tobacco. They exploited and killed the native peoples they encountered, destroyed their cultures, and took their land on the way to establishing European footholds in the Americas that became revenue producing colonies and part of their empires. By 1494, one Spaniard claimed 50,000 Taino Indians had already died after contact with Europeans. The Taino withered from a population estimated at 300,000 in 1492 to 500 by 1548.[1]

At first the Spanish and Portuguese and later the English colonial systems sought to enslave Native Americans as a readily available labor force. On his second voyage, Columbus kidnapped 550 Taino Indians from the islands he had claimed for his Spanish employers Ferdinand and Isabella, and sent them back to Spain to be sold as slaves to pay for his expedition.[2] In their colonies the Spanish put natives to work in mines, and later haciendas, and the Portuguese and British tried to use

2. "The Peculiar Institution"

them as forced labor, slaves on their sugar plantations in Brazil and the Caribbean.

At almost first contact Native American Indians died from European diseases for which they had no natural immunity, not having been exposed to contagions brought by the explorers and colonists from Europe. Diseases like smallpox, measles, chickenpox, typhus, whooping cough and pneumonia killed millions of natives.[3] Population estimates for American Indians in North and South America at the time of Columbus range from 10 to 20 million.[4] It is estimated that some five million American Indians lived north of the mouth of the Rio Grande in civilizations that thrived from organized agriculture and hunting.[5] An estimated 95 percent of pre–Columbian Native American populations died as the result of these first encounters with white Europeans.[6]

European diseases, murder, and the toil of slavery quickly reduced native populations wherever the white man encountered them. Deaths from disease were increased by concentrating Indians as slaves made to work in mines and on haciendas and plantations where epidemics raged.[7] Native Americans not enslaved or killed deliberately for their land, by labor or by disease moved away from the conquistadors and colonists and sought refuge in the "wilderness."[8]

The English and Native American Slavery

The English were enemies of Spain, and declared that their colonial efforts would not be heavy handed like the Spanish when it came to natives. Because of their almost continual state of warfare with the Spanish over religious and then imperial conflicts in the Americas, there were Englishmen who saw the colonial effort as an opportunity to free natives enslaved by the Spanish.[9]

Except for war and debts, the English had no tradition of enslaving people. In one of history's great ironies, the man who helped save the Puritan Colony in New England from starvation in 1620, the Pequot Squanto, was among two dozen Indians who had been kidnapped by an English sea captain in 1614, taken to Spain and sold into slavery.[10] Somehow Squanto managed to escape slavery in Spain and make it back to Plymouth in time to save the Pilgrims.

There was no English common law recognizing or regulating slavery. There was no act of Parliament that recognized or regulated slavery.[11]

The Constitution and American Racism

English law recognized the European tradition of enslaving captives from "Just Wars," particularly if they were non–Christians, but this slavery was not race-based. In 1625, Philosopher Hugo Grotius articulated a doctrine that recognized slavery as repugnant but declared that captives from "Just Wars" could be enslaved. Grotius also endorsed the Roman concept that the children of a slave mother were themselves slaves, a doctrine that was taken up by the British colonists in the South.[12]

Native Americans in both the northern and southern British colonies in North America soon resisted English efforts to displace them from their land and resources. In 1622, the Powhatan Confederation attacked the Puritans in New England and killed many of the colonists, but hundreds of Pequot were captured, and many were put to death. Among the Indian captives after the war were seventeen Powhatan men and boys transported in 1637 to a small Puritan colony in the Caribbean and declared "cannibal negroes" and made slaves for life. The use of the word Negro in their classification was a recognition that Black slavery was becoming the primary method of obtaining forced labor for Britain's American colonies, and so the word Negro was used to denote slaves. Many more Pequot were held captive in New England and made "servants."[13]

When Indian confederations again tried to halt English expansion in New England during King Philip's War in the 1670s, large numbers of Indian captives were enslaved by the colonists after their surrender. These Native American captives were sold out of the colony to other colonies and plantations in the West Indies, some even ending up in Spanish galleys. They were sold because it was profitable, it freed up land for the colonists that the Indians formerly occupied, and it made sure they could not escape into the interior of the colony to once again resist the growing and expanding white colonial population.[14]

An already acute labor shortage resulted in Virginians turning to Indian slavery. In 1682, the House of Burgesses declared any Indians sold by tribes or any other entity as slaves would be considered slaves. Increasingly in Virginia, Indians were lumped into the same category as Black slaves. They were considered heathens, as were Africans, and fair game for enslavement and regulated by the same laws used to structure the Black slave society. Eventually, racism meant white Virginians, rich or poor, considered themselves the master class and racially better than any of the slaves of color.

The same attitudes and labor shortage spread. The southern colonies, and South Carolina particularly, began Indian slave trading in

2. "The Peculiar Institution"

earnest, enslaving some 30,000 to 50,000 Native Americans.[15] Indian slavery continued into the eighteenth century; North and South Carolina sent over 50,000 Native Americans as slaves to British sugar plantations in the Caribbean.[16]

By the 1770s thousands of American Indians were slaves, laboring on plantations in the South and homes in New England. Oddly, in either place there was no presumption from their color that Indians were intended to be slaves. Indians who were slaves did bring freedom suits in the colonies. Many of these actions sought to prove the plaintiff had a white mother and therefore had not been born a slave. Indian slaves, while included by law and custom in some parts of the colonies with Black slaves, existed side by side with free Indians. Free Indians and their tribes were their own racial class separate and apart from Blacks and enslaved Indians.

In the eighteenth century, George Mason was one of Virginia's largest slave holders. He was the author of the Virginia Declaration of Rights and became an opponent of slavery by word, not deed. A delegate to the Constitutional Convention, he refused to sign or support the Constitution because it permitted the Atlantic slave trade, the "infernal traffic" to continue. His opposition was not because of moral objections to slavery, but because he thought the trade weakened the United States by making it vulnerable to foreign attack.[17] In 1772, he represented twelve Indian slaves in a freedom suit against their master. Mason argued in *Robin v. Hardaway* that they were free because Virginia had repealed a statute that provided for Indian enslavement.[18] Mason not only relied on "positive" law to argue that Indian slavery had been abolished, but also argued that the law of Virginia recognizing Indian slavery was contrary to natural law. Mason argued the settlement of Virginia by the English was an invasion, and the resistance by the Indians was a "just war," and so if captured during these wars they could not be made slaves. Mason's clients won but it took many more freedom suits for the full liberating impact of *Robin* to become settled law in the southern colonies.[19]

"American slavery was peculiar because all the slaves were defined by race."[20]

Black slavery began to replace Native American slavery in the North American southern British colonies in the early seventeenth century. By 1518 the colonizers of Hispaniola imported slaves from West Africa to work in their cane fields and mines. Thus began the great transport of slaves from Africa to the Americas. Prior to 1840 over two-thirds of emigrants from the old world to the Americas were slaves.[21]

The Constitution and American Racism

The Portuguese were the first to actively conduct an Atlantic African slave trade. Beginning in the sixteenth century, the Portuguese and Spanish forcibly brought Africans to their colonies for labor on their haciendas, forts, and missions in North America and sugar cane plantations in the Caribbean and South America.[22] The English followed to provide their colonies with a predictable, stable labor force that was not paid and had no rights. Slavery began and grew in all of the European colonies because of economics; selling slaves was profitable, owning slaves was profitable, and the labor of slaves was profitable. The British Empire and its colonists needed more men and women to labor in their Caribbean and North American colonies on large plantations producing cash crops. The Africans initially had nowhere to escape and proved physically hardy because of their prior exposure to malaria, which was rampant in the Caribbean and the lowlands of the North American southern colonies.[23]

The old quarrels of Europe came to North and South America with Portuguese, Spanish, British and French exploration and colonization. The British missed out on the gold and silver discoveries made by the Spanish, and so they made fortunes intercepting Spanish gold and silver ships on the way to Spain. Despite these ill-gotten gains, they wanted a mercantile system that exploited their colonies and produced revenue for the mother country. The British developed huge sugar cane plantations in the Caribbean to feed Europe's new sweet tooth and these plantations needed a reliable labor source. Native labor was quickly used up, dying from disease and overwork, and because of the terrible conditions on these sugar plantations. The British turned to African slaves and became customers and competitors of the Portuguese and the Spanish in the slave trade.[24]

Thinking their claims in North America must also have gold and silver, Britain's first colonies were fool's errands, gentlemen looking for gold in places like Virginia and the Carolinas.[25] These first colonies failed, and some disappeared with their colonists. Ultimately, in Jamestown, English colonial policy was saved by a weed that could be smoked—tobacco. Tobacco, like sugar, took Europe by storm and made the English huge sums of money. As British colonial expansion moved into the Carolinas, rice, indigo, sugar and eventually cotton enabled the southern colonies to prosper.[26]

In the colonies, as the demands of the monoculture of cash crops like tobacco, sugar and rice grew, the demand for labor became insatiable. Tobacco could be cultivated on small plantations by indentured servants and the plantation owners working together in the fields.[27] Larger

2. "The Peculiar Institution"

plantations—sugar, rice and eventually cotton—required large labor forces. Initially, the British transported unwanted orphans and criminals to the colonies to work.[28] As time went by an Englishman could get to Virginia or any of the other colonies by agreeing to be an indentured servant. An indentured servant was bound to work for his or her master for some specified time. One reason slavery was preferred as a labor source was that if white indentured servants survived their contracts, they became competition to established planters. They could begin their own lives and settle land and rise in social status. In the last half of the seventeenth century wages improved in England, the population decreased as the result of several factors, and being an indentured servant in the colonies became less attractive to a native Englishman.[29]

Monoculture was the financial engine for English plantation owners in the southern colonies and the West Indies. Great sums of money were made from these pursuits, and as tobacco markets declined, sugar, rice, wheat and indigo became profitable. A triangular trade became the engine for English fortunes. Slave ships traveled to Africa to purchase slaves in the first leg of this traffic. In the second leg, they took their cargo of slaves to the colonies and sold humans like cattle. After emptying their ships of slaves, they picked up cargoes of sugar or rum or tobacco, indigo, and rice and traveled back to England where they sold these items, which were in great demand, and then started all over again. Eventually, in the late eighteenth century cotton became the cash crop and "King" of the South.[30]

After Jamestown was established in 1607, Black slavery came to North America. In 1619, a Dutch ship brought Africans to the Jamestown colony. Eventually a slave in the British North American colonies was Black, Native Americans or of mixed racial heritage. Adopting the old Roman rule of slavery, and breaking with established English law, the race of the mother was used to determine the status of the child. A white southern defender of slavery said, "the black color of the race raises the presumption of slavery."[31] James Madison, architect of the Constitution, said racial prejudice derived "principally from the difference of color."[32]

The racism that justified and made Black slavery possible in the South, and dominated local society, culture and law, survived the Thirteenth Amendment to the Constitution abolishing slavery. It persists in our politics, economy and society. Racism has endured because it was embraced by white colonial Southerners culturally, socially and politically as a justification for slavery. It became law in the slave codes. It was woven by politics at the Constitutional Convention into the fabric of the

The Constitution and American Racism

Constitution. The Supreme Court and local southern courts developed a jurisprudence of slavery making it the rule of law. The national government constantly compromised with slave interests to preserve the Union. These compromises ranged from Fugitive Slave Acts and the rendition of runaway slaves to the expansion of slavery throughout the new territories.

The Constitution was designed to protect slavery based on the economic interests of its authors. The government created by the Constitution thwarted the eradication of the evil of racism by its original anti-abolition and anti-democratic bias. Culturally and politically racism has endured because it became the culture of the South and was part of being white. It was reinforced by political and economic incentives, intergenerational transmission of family beliefs as to race and reinforced by government that enforced segregation and fought equality.[33]

African slave traders captured, kidnapped and purchased men, women and children in war and raids for the purpose of selling them to white traders. These captive souls were brought to America in hellish conditions aboard slave ships in what became known as the "Middle Passage." The brokers, the factors, the sellers, assembled the captives at forts on the coast of Africa and at "factories" where they were sold to buyers to be carried to the Americas by ship and sold again. The Royal Africa Company is estimated to have brought 900,000 Africans to the English colonies to work on sugar plantations in the Caribbean.[34]

By the 1700s England was the leader in the slave trade. Probably 1.4 million Africans were taken from Africa on British slave ships and probably 200,000 of them died on the way during the "Middle Passage." Ships would arrive at the factories on the coast of Africa and load hundreds of slaves on board. They were confined below decks, in spaces where they could not stand or sit and where they lay in their own waste for much of the voyage. They were fed inadequate rations and had little to drink. The crews often tossed babies into the water when their mothers were loaded on the ships because they were troublesome.[35]

Some slaves mutinied on board the ships before they could get away from the coast, and many slaves were killed by pike, sword, musket and bayonet. Living slaves thrown overboard with their chains attached met gruesome ends, drowning within sight of the ship.

> With our ships, the great object is, to be full. When the ship is there, it is thought desirable, she should take as many as possible. The cargo of a vessel of a hundred tons, or little more, is calculated to purchase from two hundred and twenty to two hundred and fifty slaves. Their lodging-rooms below the deck, which are three (for

2. "The Peculiar Institution"

the men, the boys, and the women) besides a place for the sick, are sometimes more than five feet high, and sometimes less; and this height is divided towards the middle, for the slaves lie in two rows, one above the other, on each side of the ship, close to each other, like books upon a shelf. I have known them so close, that the shelf would not, easily, contain one more.[36]

In 1781 Englishman Luke Collingwood took command of a captured Dutch slave ship, the *Zong*. Collingwood, a doctor who had worked on slave ships, sailed the *Zong* already loaded with 244 slaves, a full cargo for a 110-ton ship, back to Africa and bought 200 more slaves. With 444 slaves crowded below decks in August 1781, he was supposed to have headed for Jamaica. He made landfall after a long voyage of eleven weeks but, for some reason, despite being low on food and water, he turned back out to sea.

Since the voyage began, the *Zong* already had over 60 slave deaths.[37] At some point Collingwood threw 132 living slaves, chained together, into the sea, and then made his way back to Jamaica. By this time in the slave trade, slavers could insure the ships and their human cargo. Making a horrendous story even more despicable, the *Zong*'s owners sued the insurers because necessity required them to "jettison the slaves," intentionally killing live human beings, destroying the cargo.[38] While there was no English legal precedent for African slavery, because the slave trade was so lucrative, the English courts and insurance companies transformed human beings into property, carving out a special niche in English contract law. This made the slave cargoes insurable. The slavers claimed the intentional murder of these men, women and children was justified and that they could be insured because it was necessary to save the rest of the cargo.

After "slavers" brought people from their African homeland to North America, they were sold in scrambles or auctions. The age and physical condition of the slaves were keys to establishing the price for their sale to plantation owners and others. The captives were degraded at these auctions by being displayed as so much cattle, in part to break them in spirit. Once purchased, they were then transported by ship or foot to the plantations where they were destined to work until another sale, or death. Planters "seasoned" or broke men, women and their children to the yoke and squeezed them till they died from disease, overwork and punishment, poor in property and spirit.[39] Slave traders and plantation owners destroyed families, brutally punished and murdered rebellious and reluctant slaves and justified it all in the name of profit and based upon their perceived moral and the intellectual superiority of the white man and his institutions.

> Planters required both men and women to engage in hard physical labor, and they worked in marshy rice fields, hot and humid tobacco fields, dusty wheat fields, and dangerous backbreaking lumber camps. Workers on rice plantations spent days standing in the water of the rice field, prey to insects and disease, with a minimal diet to sustain them. Children were expected to work as soon as they were deemed old enough to be useful. Pregnant women worked, and after childbirth women returned to the fields quickly, with little time lost. All worked under the compulsion of the overseer's or slave driver's lash, and they were liable to be lashed for working too slowly.... [W]omen working in the owner's house were especially vulnerable to sexual exploitation.[40]

So profitable was the traffic in human bondage that in 1640 Britain's King Charles II participated in the formation of the Royal Africa Company to supply slaves to English colonies in the Caribbean and North America. The English political philosopher John Locke was a member of the Board of Trade for the colonies and in 1669 wrote the Fundamental Constitution for South Carolina that provided "Every Freeman of Carolina, shall have absolute power and authority over Negro Slaves, of whatever upbringing or Religion soever."[41]

Investors profited handsomely from bankrolling ships to go to Africa to purchase slaves, and then take them for sale to the sugar plantations in the Caribbean or the plantations and haciendas of North and South America, from where they returned with valuable cargoes of sugar, tobacco, rice and eventually cotton. The Lloyds Insurance syndicates would insure these ships and their cargos so that if the ship or its cargo were lost, investors would not suffer an economic loss.[42]

Since there was no precedent in the English common law for regulating African slavery, custom, and then local law, improvised while the system expanded, became the law on the plantations and in the colonies.[43] And it was done with the active participation of the law-making bodies in the colonies. Virginia and other southern colonies created a legal system for southern slavery with slave codes that deprived the victims of their most basic rights. When a man or woman entered American Black slavery, he or she lost their personhood and, because of the master's law, became property on the bottom rung of a slave society where racism was the central governing principle.[44]

"By law, every negro is presumed to be a slave...."[45] Coercion and brutality marked the work in the fields and compassion was believed a sign of

2. "The Peculiar Institution"

weakness. In 1705 the Virginia Slave Code stated that "All negroe, mulatto, and Indian slaves shall be held, taken, and abridged to be real estate." The slave codes also protected whites from being held accountable for violence they inflicted on Blacks. A white master could administer physical punishment to a Black without fear of punishment. The incidental death of a slave during such punishment was not a crime.

The slave codes made the rape of a white woman by a Black man a crime punishable by castration or death, but did not make the rape of a Black woman by a white man a crime. The slave codes permitted the use of slave patrols to stop, search, and coerce slaves at any time and to pursue them if they were suspected of being runaways. The militia was used to assist slave patrols and put down slave uprisings. Slaves could not testify against whites; they could not possess guns; and they were denied an education. Blacks could not marry. They could not gather in groups without a white person present.[46]

After the Revolution and the adoption of the Constitution, state laws in the South made it more difficult for an owner to free his or her slaves. Some states even forbade freed Blacks from living within their borders for fear they would be a poor example to their slave brothers and sisters.[47]

Any percentage of color was enough to make a person Black and therefore a slave. Among many other provisions, according to the original Virginia Slave Code:

> *And also be enacted, by the authority aforesaid, and it is hereby enacted,* That all servants imported and brought into this country, by sea or land, who were not Christians in their native country ... shall be accounted and be slaves, and such be here bought and sold notwithstanding a conversion to Christianity afterward. And for encouragement of all persons to take up runaways, *Be it enacted, by the authority aforesaid, and it is hereby enacted,* That for the taking up of every servant, or slave, if ten miles, or above, from the house or quarter where such servant, or slave was kept, there shall be allowed by the public, as a reward to the taker-up, two hundred pounds of tobacco; and if above five miles, and under ten, one hundred pounds of tobacco.[48]

Every southern colony and state enacted similar codes to protect masters' interests in Black slaves.

The whole system was built on the racial belief that Africans were inferior in every way and in the notion that slavery was a civilizing institution. Society in the South was based on the idea of hierarchy and domination. Black was synonymous with slave.[49]

The Constitution and American Racism

The racism that justified slavery, maintained it and shaped the post–Civil War South persists in our culture and politics. While slavery is as old as the history of man, it was different in colonial America because it was based on race.[50] In the ancient world captives from piracy, raids and war became slaves regardless of race. In ancient Greece, city states like Sparta made captives and then slaves of their competitors and neighbors as war and interest suited them. In the Roman Empire, Greeks were slaves of Romans, as were many other people, including Germans, Saxons, and residents of competing city states in the Mediterranean who looked very much like Romans. Race was not the basis for enslavement or a marker of who was a slave.[51] In the Roman Empire race was not the thing that set slaves apart. Roman slaves could be freed by their master during the master's life or when he or she died. Slaves worked as bureaucrats, soldiers, teachers and philosophers. Former Roman slaves could even become citizens of the Empire.[52] "Nowhere in the pre–Columbian world was color or race a mark of slavery nor was enslavement tied to race."[53] American Indians might have treated captives as slaves but they also could be adopted by the tribe, losing their status as slaves.

The arguments for colonial slavery ranged from economic necessity to paternalism, but were based on racism. White slave owners claimed Blacks were inferior in every way and needed white guidance and protection, and slavery would civilize its victims.[54] Aristotle's ideas of human hierarchy and ethnocentricity gave comfort to those Englishmen and colonists who saw racism and slavery as consistent with ancient ideas of racial superiority. Aristotle's ethnocentricity believed all other societies were inferior to Greeks. His theory that extremely hot and cold climates bred inferior humans who were unsuited for independence influenced those who traded in African slaves and in their minds justified their barbarism.[55]

Sixteenth-century Englishmen embraced many ideas of race to justify enslaving Africans, including the biblical story of Ham from Genesis. Blacks were considered the descendants of Ham and were Black because of Noah's curse. "Curse theory" persisted throughout the period of slavery in the United States. Others believed that since Adam was white, Blacks or other people of color could not be descended from the Adam in the Bible. Some even believed Black Africans were descended directly from apes.[56]

One Englishman, Robert Gainish, traveled to Africa to buy slaves in 1554 and called Africans a "people of beastly living, without a God, law, religions, or commonwealth." Another English writer called slavery a curse for sins and a result of "civil condition," or barbarism. The British scientists

2. "The Peculiar Institution"

Robert Boyle and Isaac Newton both adopted racist ideas based on color. Boyle described black as an ugly deformity and white as the purest color in all of nature. John Locke, a doctor and the English rights philosopher, claimed that Blacks were descended from apes and had no rights.[57]

But even those who owned slaves recognized slavery as an evil. Jefferson wrote in his draft of the Declaration of Independence that the slave trade was an "execrable commerce ... this assemblage of horrors," and a "cruel war against human nature itself, violating its most sacred rights of life and liberties." Despite this view Jefferson wrote later in his *Notes on the State of Virginia* that "the real distinction [between whites and Blacks] which nature has made went beyond color and other physical attributes."[58]

Colonists in the Northern colonies owned slaves and profited from the slave trade. Quaker Moses Brown, brother of John Brown and a resident of Providence, Rhode Island, profited from and defended the trade.[59] Northerners carried slave cargoes in their ships and made fortunes in the slave trade. But it was New Englanders who first denounced slavery in the colonies in the clearest terms. A Puritan judge, Samuel Sewall in Massachusetts, as early as the 1600s wrote about slavery: "all men, as they are sons of Adam ... have equal right unto liberty." Of the slave trade Sewall wrote, "How horrible is the uncleanliness, immorality, if not murder, that the ships are guilty of that bring crowds of these miserable men and women."[60] The powerful orator and Boston lawyer James Otis called for the "immediate liberation of the slaves" in 1765. "The colonists of Massachusetts are by the law of nature free born, as indeed all men are white and black.... Does it follow that it is the right to enslave a man because he is black?" Boston rebel Samuel Adams—the street-tough agitator for American independence—and his wife received the gift of a slave girl in 1765, and immediately emancipated her. His cousin, John Adams, future revolutionary and President, would come to call slavery a "foul contagion in the human character."

English common law posed a dilemma for colonial slave owners because it did not recognize slavery. In 1569 the English courts found that English law did not recognize slavery when an Englishman tried to bring a slave back from Russia. In 1701, an English court ruled that a slave was free as soon as he or she set foot in England. The famous Englishman Blackstone, in his Commentaries on the British law, wrote as late as 1765, when England was the dominant mover in the slave trade, that "The spirit of liberty is so deeply implanted in our Constitution [English], and rooted even in our very soil, that a slave or a Negro, the moment he lands in England, falls under the protection of the laws and so far becomes a freeman though the master's right to his service may possibly still continue."[61]

James Somerset was a Black slave purchased in Boston by Charles Stewart, a British customs agent. Stewart returned to England in 1769, taking Somerset with him. Somerset escaped from Stewart's custody in London in 1771 and was befriended by English men and women who sponsored his baptism into the Christian faith. In November 1771, Somerset was recaptured, and Stewart sent him to be held on a ship bound for Jamaica where he was to be sold as a slave to a sugar plantation owner. Upon learning of Somerset's plight, the sponsors of his baptism made application to the King's Bench for a writ of *habeas corpus*. Granville Sharp, a leading English abolitionist, helped Somerset procure legal assistance and eventually he was represented by five very able lawyers.[62]

Somerset's lawyers argued that while colonial law might make slavery legal, slavery had never been recognized at English Common Law, and Parliament had never passed a law recognizing its legality. Chief Judge of the King's Bench, William Murray, 1st Earl of Mansfield, heard the arguments in the case. Lord Mansfield tried to get the parties to settle on the basis of setting Somerset free. But the case attracted attention and was not settled, and Mansfield had to decide Somerset's fate. Mansfield's opinion set Somerset free. He wrote in part, "a foreigner cannot be imprisoned here [England] on the authority of any law existing in his own country [the colonies]: the power of a master over his servant is different in all countries, more or less limited or extensive; the exercise of it therefore must always be regulated by the laws of the place where exercised." Mansfield found that because Somerset had been brought to England the law of England had to be applied, and since England had no laws recognizing slavery, Somerset must be freed. News of this decision travelled to Britain's North American colonies in the South, where the planters resented and feared the decision.[63]

In 1780, during the American Revolution, the legislature in Massachusetts wrote in Article I of the Massachusetts Declaration of Rights that "All men are born free and equal...." Quock Walker was a slave in Massachusetts owned by Nathaniel Jennison, who beat him. In the trial of the charges against Jennison (*Commonwealth v. Jennison*), the judge presiding in the case charged the jury that from his reading of the Declaration of Rights, "slavery is in my judgment as effectively abolished as it

2. "The Peculiar Institution"

can be by the granting of rights and privileges wholly incompatible and repugnant to its existence." It was the first of many cases; slavery was effectively ended in Massachusetts.[64]

Slavery and the Founders

The *Somerset* case decided in 1772 energized Southerners who now saw independence from Britain as a way to protect slavery.[65] Some southern slaves learned of the *Somerset* decision and tried to find English ships to take them to England. By 1772 the southern system of slavery was the force propelling a successful commercial agricultural system that made the owners wealthy. Because of their ownership of slaves and the value they represented, because the crops they grew were valuable and had ready commercial markets, and because the slaves had cleared huge tracts of land enhancing its value, Southerners were the richest men in the British North American colonies. They were suspicious of the Northerners and their attitudes towards slavery, but in the end, saw joining in revolution with them as a way to protect slavery.[66]

Jefferson and almost all the prominent men of the South who supported the Revolution owned slaves. After the Declaration of Independence was published, men in England thought that the colonists were hypocritical in demanding equality when they owned slaves. The British government eventually offered freedom to slaves who would leave their masters and support the Crown against the Rebels, and thousands did. Despite the prominence of slavery and its legality in the colonies, North and South, free Blacks did join the rebel colonists and fight for the cause of American Independence.

Apologists for Jefferson, Madison, and a host of signatories to the Declaration of Independence and the Constitution argue we must judge men by their times and what was acceptable then among their peers. What is important is that there were men, including Jefferson and Madison, who recognized that slavery was an evil. Despite expressing this belief Jefferson in his writings showed that he was a racist who was unable to see Blacks as equals. Years after writing the Declaration, he did not even free the Black mother of his children.

There were men before Jefferson, and who were his contemporaries, who spoke out against slavery. In the 1600s in New England, Judge Samuel Sewell, of the Massachusetts Bay Colony, attacked it as inconsistent with divine law. Later, fellow New Englanders James Otis, Nathaniel Appleman, the Rev. Samuel Webster, and John Allen condemned slavery. The patriot Tom Paine and Dr. Benjamin Rush joined in condemning slavery. Quakers like Benjamin Lay, John Woolman, and Anthony Benezet agitated against slavery. In 1776, after the Declaration of Independence was written, Samuel Hopkins, in his pamphlet, *A Dialogue Concerning the Slavery of the Africans,* wrote of the link between racism and slavery and called on the Continental Congress to abolish it.[67]

At the time of the Revolution and the Constitutional Convention, many advocates of slavery knew it was wrong and engaged in moral somersaults to justify the system. To these men the climate and curse theories were sufficient justifications, but they also embraced a more basic racist argument regarding ugliness, indolence and ignorance as reasons for their participation in and advocacy for the peculiar institution.

Thomas Jefferson, James Madison's mentor and friend and the author of the Declaration of Independence, owned slaves but emancipated few of them, despite his writings on the rights of colonial Americans. He fathered children by one of his slaves, Sally Hemings. He emancipated only five slaves at his death. His reasons for refusing to emancipate his slaves were primarily economic, even in death. Despite his relationship, romantic or simply sexual, with Sally Hemings, he did not free her or all their children. We do not know his reasons except by his writings on race. Jefferson would come to write, "The whole commerce between master and slave is a perpetual exercise of the most boisterous passions, the most unremitting despotism on the one part, and degrading submissions on the other."[68] He called slavery a moral depravity and a hideous blot. He believed it was the greatest threat to the survival of the Republic. But he owned more than 600 slaves during his lifetime. He hired men to pursue his runaway slaves, and we know from his journals and letters that he ordered slaves as young as ten to be flogged when their labor failed to meet his expectations.[69]

Jefferson's personal writings show his innate racism, and his often-precarious financial affairs help explain his failure to give up his slaves. Thaddeus Kosciuszko was a Polish nobleman who fought for the American colonies in the Revolutionary War. The American he admired most was Thomas Jefferson. At the end of the Revolutionary War, before leaving America Kosciuszko wrote a will specifying that part of his estate upon his death was to be used to free Jefferson's slaves and educate them to enable them to be free and independent:

2. "The Peculiar Institution"

5th day of May 1798
 I Thaddeus Kosciuszko being just in my departure from America do hereby declare and direct that should I make no other testamentory disposition of my property in the United States I hereby authorise my friend Thomas Jefferson to employ the whole thereof in purchasing Negroes from among his own or any others and giving them Liberty in my name, in giving them an education in trades or otherwise and in having them instructed for their new condition in the duties of morality which may make them good neighbours, good fathers or mothers, husbands or wives and in their duties as citizens teaching them to be defenders of their Liberty and Country and of the good order of Society and in whatsoever may make them happy and useful, and I make the said Thomas Jefferson my executor of this.—T. Kosciuszko[70]

When Kosciuszko died in 1817 it was discovered that he had written three subsequent wills, but Jefferson, who was supposed to be executor of the estate, declined the duty due to his age.[71] What is remarkable is that Jefferson's words in praise of political equality had such a profound effect on Kosciusko that he tried to find a way out of the great moral dilemma of the time for his hero. Despites Kosciusko's efforts, Jefferson never resolved his moral dilemma, his attachment to slavery during his long life, in his will or on his deathbed.

The phrase "We hold these truths to be self-evident, that all men are created equal," is as plain and exceptional in its stirring prose as any statement of political beliefs ever made before or since. People all over the world have heard these words and embraced them in their own struggles for liberty and equality. The rubric contains no qualification. "Self-evident" in contemporary eighteenth-century usage meant axiomatic, rather than merely obvious. In describing this axiomatic truth Jefferson had originally written that it was "sacred and undeniable."[72] But, if we judge men not by what they say but by what they do, it is apparent Jefferson did not believe in the equality of man.

From his personal notes we know Jefferson certainly did not believe all men were created equal. He believed that the African was inferior to the white man. It is impossible to square Jefferson the patriot, calling on his countryman to rise and redeem by force their freedom, with Jefferson the slaveholder and racist. Jefferson said that slavery is a "moral and political depravity" but never gave any public support to abolition of the depravity. As a trial lawyer John Adams said during his closing argument on behalf of British soldiers in the Boston Massacre trial, "Facts are stubborn things and whatever may be our wishes, our inclinations, or the dictums of our passions, they cannot alter the state of facts and evidence."[73] In one of history's great ironies, often used by British critics of the American Revolution, white Southerners such as Jefferson proclaimed the cause of liberty just, but owned slaves and profited from their labor.

As Commander-in-Chief of the Continental Army, George Washington never had enough men to fill the ranks of his army. We have this image of the embattled farmer firing from behind every wall and tree, striking down Redcoats at every turn and winning the Revolution—a good tale, but not history or entirely factual. The British retreat from Concord and Lexington and the subsequent siege of Boston by the militia were not the usual conduct of the militia during the Revolution. As much as we are in love with the vision of an enraged patriot at freedom's barricade, the militia was an irregular force led by amateurs, and armed haphazardly. For the most part they were men who did not want to leave home. Nevertheless, they performed well, acting within the scope of their training, equipment, and leadership. The Revolutionary War was won by battles fought by the Continental Army, sometimes supplemented by local militia who went home at day's end. Washington recognized that to beat British regulars the colonials would need full-time soldiers: "I am wearied to death all day with a variety of perplexing circumstances, disturbed at the conduct of the militia, whose behavior and want of discipline has done great injury to the other troops, who never had officers, except in a few instances, worth the bread they eat." Writing about the "Summer Soldier," Tom Paine described most colonists' participation during the Revolutionary War: "These are the times that try men's souls: the summer soldier and sunshine patriot, will in this crisis, shrink from the service of his country.... The soldier who had the freedom to hide behind fences and trees also had the freedom to flee."[74]

In March 1778, Rhode Island sent a Black regiment, the First Rhode Island, to General Washington. Slaves who enlisted in the regiment were promised their freedom. Although Washington had some reservations about Black troops, he remembered their service in the French and Indian War and recalled they were reliable soldiers. The Continental Congress prohibited enlistment of Blacks after the fall of 1775, but despite this bar over 5,000 Blacks served in militia and Continental forces. Many stayed with the colors from Bunker Hill through Yorktown. Five percent of the Continental Army was Black.[75]

Many Blacks enlisted because of bounties, ideology, and promised freedom. They served in integrated units, the last time for 175 years.[76] Before the Revolutionary War, Washington had spoken out against

2. "The Peculiar Institution"

slavery, having introduced a bill in the Virginia House of Burgesses to halt the transportation of slaves to Virginia. He described the slave trade as "wicked, cruel, and unnatural."[77] Prior to the Constitutional Convention in Philadelphia in 1787, Washington wrote the patriot Robert Morris, saying that "there is not a man living who wishes more sincerely than I do, to see a plan adopted for the abolition of it [slavery]." Nine presidents owned slaves; only Washington freed his.

The legacy of slavery and the racism that sustained it has been enduring. Inventing a legal system to manage and regulate slaves meant that the rule of law was based on racism. The promise of the Revolution was meant only for white men. Thomas Jefferson was a racist, and the brilliance of his pen may have resulted in the Declaration of Independence, but his public silence on slavery and his racist musings in his *Notes* make clear he had no plan for emancipation, and was consumed by the basest kind of racism. He could not even bring himself to emancipate Sally Hemings. Examining Jefferson on his own terms and by the actions of his contemporaries leaves him wanting as a man who claimed to believe in equality.[78]

The racism that justified and made possible slavery continues to affect the ways we view and judge Black Americans. Economics and racism have combined to thwart Black economic, educational, and social success in our society. If we can recognize that current racism has its roots in a moral and political ideology that sought to justify the unjustifiable, perhaps we can deal with racism and make changes in our government that reflect Jefferson's lofty words that "all men are created equal."

The current economic condition of Black Americans is a result of slavery and policies adopted by state and federal governments and economic institutions after the Civil War. Those policies discriminated on the basis of race. Failure to provide an adequate education or integrate Black Americans into society, restrictive racial covenants burdening property, and excluding Blacks from job and social opportunities have resulted in an economic and political system weighted heavily against Black Americans.

The judicial system has been no less of a culprit. The Rule of Law has not been applied to Black Americans equally. Cash bail makes release virtually impossible for most Black Americans because of their economic circumstances, and only enriches bail bondsmen. The sentences received by Black Americans in the American penal system are harsher and longer. The Black incarceration rate is 35 percent of all jail inmates while the Black population constitutes 12 to 13 percent of the American population. American Indians are also disproportionately represented in U.S. prisons, as are Hispanics. The United States now has the highest incarceration rate of any country in the world.

Racism justified American slavery. Whites were not enslaved or forced to work for life on plantations without any rights or hope for a better future. American Indians were once considered slaves by the same men who wrote the Black slave codes. But the American Indian only escaped slavery in the South by a different racist calculus. The color of his skin was used to justify a racism directed at the American Indian that legalized the theft of his lands, the murder of his families, and destruction of his culture. But whites chose Blacks to be their slaves and did so because of paternalistic and racial arguments. Many slave owners considered themselves to be doing the right thing in enslaving a whole race. They believed the Black slave society that they created based on force and intimidation was humane. Racist belief that Blacks were inherently inferior to whites both held together and permeated Southern society.

While paternalism and racism may seem separable, they are not. Paternalism was possible because of racism. A study by three political scientists, published in 2016, *The Political Legacy of American Slavery*, ends with this conclusion:

> whites who currently live in counties that had high concentrations of slaves in 1860, are today on average more conservative and express colder feelings toward Blacks, than whites who live elsewhere in the South. That is, the larger the number of slaves per capita in his or her county of residence in 1860, the greater the probability that a white Southerner today will identify as a Republican, oppose affirmative action, and express attitudes indicating some level of racial sentiment.[79]

This racism has not only remained intractable but has been a political tool of the Republican Party since the days of the "Dixiecrats." These attitudes are tools of the right and those who seek a less democratic government.

3

The Law of Slavery

British Colonists established and made slavery legal in the English colonies in the Caribbean and North America. The largest concentration of African slaves in the American colonies first appeared in the West Indies in the 1600s, in places like Barbados and Jamaica, where sugar cane production became profitable by using slave labor. In the 1640s, British colonists in Barbados grew tobacco, cotton, ginger, and indigo. Most of the labor for this agricultural production was white indentured servants, but by 1660, the main cash crop was sugar and the main labor source was slavery. These sugar plantations had extremely high mortality rates and consequently a high demand for slaves from the Atlantic slave trade. The Royal Africa Company delivered over 100,000 slaves to Barbados between 1672 and 1713.[1]

Customs and procedures for the organization and management of slavery were developed on large sugar cane plantations in the West Indies. Customs became unofficial norms and then were made into law. Slaves were treated cruelly on these sugar plantations, including brutal beatings and brandings. One visitor recorded that he had witnessed a slave having his ear cut off and then being forced to eat the roasted ear. Slaves were killed without any punishment for the killer.[2]

The white colonial assemblies on Barbados and Jamaica passed comprehensive slave codes. The Assembly in Barbados passed its first slave code in 1661. The act permitted the use of disfigurement to punish slaves who struck a master. The slave could be whipped, have his nose slit, and face branded. If a slave was killed during punishment no crime was committed. In 1684 Jamaica passed a slave code, later adopted by the South Carolina Assembly in 1696.[3] The slave codes passed by the colonial assemblies were unified in relying on brutality and death as the basis for their operation.[4]

Each North American English colony had some form of legislative

The Constitution and American Racism

body like Virginia's House of Burgesses, and these legislative bodies made laws to control the slaves. These codes defined who was a slave and the limits of their conduct, what they could not do, and how they could be punished. The colonial assemblies made the customs developed on the plantations legal and used the law as a shield to protect slavery and its masters.

Customs on the plantation and slave codes made by the legislatures controlled all aspects of the life of a slave. Both custom and law denied a slave's right to move about, marry, nurture and raise his own family, or choose an occupation, a dwelling, even his clothing. Education and religion were prohibited by the masters and the laws of the states. Learning to read was a crime. There was no income, no economic or social future. The codes of social order robbed children of their freedom at birth to a Black mother. All of the children of a slave mother were considered slave property, born into slavery, meant to be cursed with all of the horrors of a system that bound them to hard labor for life, on a sugar cane or cotton plantation subject to physical and mental abuse at the whim of men who considered them property to be bought and sold.[5]

In the British colonies in the Americas, slavery was possible because of racism. A white person could not be a slave. If you were Black, it was assumed you were a slave and slavery meant subordination in all things.[6] The system required obedience and the price of disobedience was whippings, beatings, and forms of torture intended to make all slaves, men, women and children do what they were ordered to do by a white man. Killing a slave was excusable during "correction" and there were few white men ever prosecuted for the death of a slave.

There had been no slavery in England. There had been serfs or villeins when England was a feudal state. Serfs were laborers who worked the land and their complicated status was defined by their relationship to the land and the lord who had title to the land. They could own their own property and had some autonomy. Serfs retained some measure of legal and personal rights. As explained by historian Betty Woods, they had never been slaves.[7] By the late fifteenth century villeinage and serfdom had largely died out in England.[8] "Slavery was not in any historical sense a continuation of villeinage."[9] Color did not determine who was a serf or villein. Serfs were not slaves without any rights.

Over hundreds of years the English developed a legal system that was based on rights theory, courts and due process. The development of the idea that the king's subjects had rights that even the king could not

3. The Law of Slavery

ignore was a response to the absolutism of monarchs who believed they answered only to God. Absolutism was resisted by the nobility when the king needed money and soldiers. Richard the Lionheart was a warrior and the King of England only incidentally. He was the son of Henry the II, the "Lawgiver" who had increased the number of courts in the realm and tried to rationalize the laws of inheritance. Richard's younger brother John was content to stay home and claim the throne. John in fact paid a foreign king to keep Richard, who had been captured on the way home from the Crusades, in prison. When Richard was killed on one of his military expeditions in France, John became King.

John could never live within his means and was always asking the nobles for money. Eventually, the nobility joined forces in 1215 and forced John at Runnymede to acknowledge their rights. The result, the Magna Carta, was meant to protect the nobility and not the commoner. Much credit is given to the Magna Carta as a liberal democratic document establishing basic political rights, but there were several versions of the great charter, and the provisions mostly dealt with complaints of the nobles. But the Magna Carta enumerated rights such as the supremacy of the law, the right to a trial by your peers, and a check on the king's power to tax. Oliver Cromwell and Parliament took a king's head in the seventeenth century, and ultimately the Glorious Revolution in 1688 ended with Parliament ascendant and choosing the king.

English colonists came to North America during the political struggles in England between the Crown and Parliament and brought their beliefs as to the evolving nature of the relationship between a free man and the state. When the colonists in the West Indies moved to a system of African slavery to work the sugar cane plantations, the basis for the system was anti-democratic and racist. Rights were restricted to white educated Englishman. The accident of birth, whether as a king or an African, still affected English beliefs as to the value of a person in society. Blacks were inferior in the minds of the white colonists because they were not Christians and they looked different. Race alone justified their enslavement. Because they were infidels, Africans were not entitled to any of the benefits of being a Christian. The first slave codes enacted in the West Indies were based on these beliefs and used as a blueprint for similar codes in the southern colonies.[10]

British colonialism, the planters, and colonial assemblies made the slave a commodity without any power to alter his or her status.[11] A slave could be bought and sold, used for collateral, and like other property could be inherited. The American slave had no choice in any matter. The master's will was his or her life and the value of that life was measured in terms of the productivity of the slave. Southern slavery advanced as the result of the colonial adoption of customs developed while the institution matured as a labor system to produce cash crops.[12]

Slavery in Africa was not the same as slavery in the colonies. Africans captured by Africans might be considered slaves in the context of African tribal society but were treated differently than they were in the American colonies. Many African slaves in these tribes could not be distinguished from their masters. Some were leaders, some were workers, some were not for sale. The differences between African slavery and American southern slavery are significant, and comparisons at best difficult. The major difference in America was color was the marker of a slave. At some point in the British colonies, only Black or some shade thereof was the marker of the slave.[13] These slaves would never become part of the tribe; they would have to be freed by their master to lose their status and until then they would live at the whim of their owner.

Slave codes served several purposes.[14] They regulated slaves and gave legal cover to their inhuman treatment. By making custom law, the slave codes made the treatment of slaves legal and made a place for slavery in the rule of law. The codes in the southern colonies made slavery a lifetime condition; made the status inheritable from the mother; made color a mark of slavery; and made slaves property. There had been some question initially about what kind of property slaves constituted, but the law eventually settled on them being chattels, not real estate. A chattel is movable property, such as cattle or lumber or crops after harvest, and unlike real estate, it can be loaded on a ship and bought and sold.[15]

Nine colonies adopted slave codes before the American Revolution. The codes mandated the length of a workday, fourteen to sixteen hours a day with Sunday off unless "necessity" or family requirements required work on that day. Owners were required to provide minimal food and clothing. The South Carolina code identified Negroes, Indians that had been bought or sold, and mulattoes as slaves. The codes placed the burden of proof on the person of color claimed to be a slave to prove they were not. Whipping and beating were defined as legal punishments by owners for slaves. This kind of discipline for refractory slaves was unsupervised and its severity determined by the master or overseer. "Moderate correction" statutes exonerated owners when they killed a slave

3. The Law of Slavery

while punishing him or her for some infraction when the slave resisted punishment.

Slaves could not own boats or canoes. "Trucking" statutes made it illegal for slaves to sell any commodity including produce they had grown. They could not be taught to read or write and couldn't vote or hold office. Slaves had to wear clothes consistent with their status, made from slave cloth. They were required to carry written permission of their owners if they left the plantation. They were forbidden to serve in the militia unless the service was labor to assist the white militia. They could not testify against whites but could testify against other Blacks.

Runaways could be punished by branding, lashes, and death. A runaway could have an ear cut off and his or her Achilles tendon cut above the heel. Slaves were forbidden to congregate or own any kind of weapon. They could not build churches or travel in groups without a white man. They could not travel at night and were subject to curfews, and they were forbidden to ride horses.

Criminal offenses were established by the slave codes and many offenses were left to the owner to prosecute and determine punishment. Petty offenses might include striking a white for the first time and simple theft, but striking a white a third time could result in a death sentence. For major crimes like murder, insurrection, arson and rape, courts composed of multiple judges and owners would hear the evidence and mete out punishment. Many punishments assumed medieval proportions, and in one case of insurrection in Maryland, a slave's right hand was cut off and his body torn into four pieces, with the head and quarters displayed as a warning to other slaves. In New York a slave found guilty of insurrection was burned slowly for ten hours. Slaves were broken on the wheel, hung in chains until they starved to death, and were impaled on stakes.

All whites were required to serve on slave patrols. These were informal formations of white men who patrolled the countryside looking for runaways or slaves who might be involved in resistance to the lash and whip. Enlistments in the patrols might be for as long as a year and there was no pay or drinking while on duty. Whites who helped runaways were punished. The slave codes were applied to free Blacks who lived in the colony or state, although they were encouraged to leave. Manumission or freeing slaves was discouraged and eventually illegal in the southern states. During the Revolution the royal governor of Virginia and British military forces promised freedom to slaves who would desert their masters and join the British. When the British left New York in 1783, they angered George Washington by taking thousands of such men and women with them.

Colonial law and later southern state law before the Civil War departed from the British trend to broaden political rights and make government more representative. It was a white man's government. Colonial law made every effort to protect slavery and the system of economics that made sugar, tobacco, indigo, rice and cotton profitable. The mere existence of slavery in the British Empire made libertarian ideals of representative government articulated by British Enlightenment political philosophers like John Locke hypocritical and hollow, particularly when viewed in the context of the brutality of the system from the shores of Africa to the sea islands of South Carolina.

The slave codes were not static. After the Revolution, with new states recognizing slavery, the codes changed, sometimes in the apparent harshness of the details that made the system so barbaric. But all of the codes worked on two principles: The white man was supreme, and the Black man was property. In the states of the Deep South with huge plantations and hundreds of slaves, the codes were uniformly onerous. Criminal codes applying to Blacks criminalized conduct that went unpunished for whites. The codes were meant to suppress freedom and insurrection. In most situations it was not legal for a Black man, however provoked, threatened or abused, to strike a white man. A white man killing a Black man or woman almost always went free to do it again.

New Republic, New Protections

The delegates to the Constitutional Convention agreed to end the Atlantic slave trade. Some northern delegates thought ending the slave trade would lead to abolition. It did not. The southern delegates agreed to end the Atlantic trade because there were now enough slaves in the states for slave trading to be self-sustaining. Older colonies like Virginia and North Carolina had a surplus of slaves because of declining tobacco production and began to sell them south. Thomas Jefferson remarked to a friend that he could make more money from breeding his slaves for sale than from their labor.[16]

The delegates at the Constitutional Convention gave the Southerners a way to pursue and capture runaway slaves who crossed state lines. In

3. The Law of Slavery

1793 Congress passed the first Fugitive Slave Act. Article IV, Section 2, of the Constitution was the legal justification for the act:

> No Person held to Service or Labour in one State, under the Laws thereof, escaping into another, shall, in Consequence of any Law or Regulation therein, be discharged from such Service or Labour but shall be delivered up on Claim of the Party to whom such service or Labour may be due.

While the Constitution never mentions slavery, a slave was referred to as a "person held to Service," and Madison's notes confirm that this clause was meant to protect slave owners. The Act gave slave owners and their "agents" authority to hunt for runaway slaves within the borders of free states. Once found, the slave could be taken under compulsion before a federal or state judicial official for an order finding he was a slave and permitting removal from the state. The owner or agent could merely swear the Black person had been his slave by affidavit or oral testimony. The Act made children of any Black female born while she was a runaway slaves in perpetuity. It punished by a $500 fine anyone who helped a runaway slave. The Act contained no procedural due process for the slave to object, and once the slave disappeared into a slave state, whether he was a free Black man who had been kidnapped or a runaway, he would never be returned. Many northern states refused to enforce the law because they considered the Act little better than kidnaping, and eventually abolitionists organized safe houses and networks to aid and hide runaway slaves.

Between 1824 and 1840, Pennsylvania, Indiana, Connecticut, New York, and Vermont passed Personal Liberty Laws to protect runaways and free Blacks within their borders. These laws required a jury trial to determine whether the person was a slave, and in some instances, provided counsel to the putative slave. The creation, propagation and protection of slavery in the United States was made possible by a legal system supposedly built on the idea of the equality of all men and the operation of the Rule of Law. The Constitution and the law at federal and state level actively protected slavery. The Rule of Law was slavery.

With the invention of the cotton gin in 1793, the growth and sale of cotton became more and more profitable. England proved an insatiable consumer of raw cotton for its mills. Grow more cotton, process more cotton, sell more cotton. There was a boom in the international slave trade after the Revolution, and 20,000 slaves came to Georgia and South Carolina from Africa in 1803 via the Atlantic slave trade. As Southerners moved south and west, so did cotton and slaves. At least 100,000 slaves moved west every decade after 1810 until the beginning of the Civil War. States that had produced tobacco now produced slaves, selling and trading slaves, destroying families and Black lives.

The new national government began efforts to slow the Atlantic slave trade in 1794, when Congress prohibited the use of any U.S. port or shipyard for building or outfitting ships for use in the international Atlantic slave trade. The Act was meant to prohibit the export of slaves *from* the United States. It required bonds of and imposed fines on those caught violating the Act. In 1800, Congress increased fines and prohibited American crews from serving on slave ships.

In 1803, Congress added new fines for Americans caught while engaged in the Atlantic slave trade. These measures cost American slavers nothing and appeared to regulate at least the international trade of slaves. In 1808 Congress closed the Atlantic slave trade to Americans and mandated fines, jail terms and other punitive provisions. But a conundrum existed. What to do with slaves found on ships violating the Act? Should the federal government sell them, let the states in which they were found sell them, or free them? In the South there was no sentiment to free the slaves or transport them back to Africa. In a catch-22, the Act let the states in which they were found sell them. So, the Act meant to end the trade did not free the slaves who were cargo in the illicit trade; it made sure they remained slaves, and it increased the slave population in the South.

In 1818, Congress changed the burden of proof in cases alleging violations of the anti–slave trading law. The burden of proof was now on the defendant to show he was not violating the Act, and fines and other penalties were increased. The enforcement of the ban changed in 1819 when Congress required the return of the cargo, the slaves, to Africa, and authorized the President to send naval vessels (the African Squadron) to Africa to enforce the Act. U.S. Naval forces enforced the Act until 1824. Some slaves were returned to Africa, but after that there was no naval enforcement by the United States until 1843. It is unknown how many slaves were returned to Africa because of the United States Navy's efforts.

In 1823, another act became law which made the Americans who still engaged in the slave trade pirates, subject to a sentence of death. Two captains were charged under the law, one a notorious Baltimore slaver, and the other a crew member of a slaver. In *United States v. Gooding*,[17] the defendant was caught clearly violating the Act and convicted, but when Justice Story of the Supreme Court decided the indictment was defective,

3. The Law of Slavery

the government dismissed the case. In *United States v. Battiste*,[18] another case where the government sought the death penalty for a crew member of an American ship transporting slaves, Story wrote, "the mere transportation of a negro slave, as a passenger for hire" was not as morally wrong as kidnaping slaves for sale. Despite the "ending" of the Atlantic trade by these acts, the slave population of the United States doubled from 1810 until 1860. The disease was quarantined but continued to spread. No one was ever convicted of being a pirate.

The South did not need an international slave trade. There were enough slaves and limits on supply to make the domestic slave trade lucrative. Ending the international trade meant nothing when it came to abolition or the safety of free Blacks in the United States. Free Blacks were often kidnapped in states where they had been living in relative freedom.

> [Last night] about ten o'clock at night, five or six men went to the house of a colored man by the name of John Wilkinson, broke open the door, knocked down the man and his wife, and beat them severely, and seized their boy, aged fourteen years, and carried him off into Slavery. After the father of the boy had recovered himself, he raised the alarm, and with the aid of some of his neighbors, put out in pursuit of the kidnappers, and followed them to the river; but they were too late. The villains crossed the river and passed into Virginia. I visited the afflicted family this morning. When I entered the house, I found the mother seated with her face buried in her hands, weeping for the loss of her child. The mother was much bruised, and the floor was covered in several places with blood. I had been in the house but a short time, when the father returned from the chase of the kidnappers. When he entered the house and told the wife that their child was lost forever, the mother wrung her hands and screamed out, "Oh, my boy! Oh, my boy! I want to see my child!" and raved as though she was a maniac. I was compelled to turn aside and weep.[19]

In 1842, the Supreme Court was dominated by Southerners. In a case challenging a state's failure to enforce the Fugitive Slave Act, *Prigg v. Pennsylvania*, 41 U.S. 539 (1842), the conviction of a slave owner's agent for kidnaping by a Pennsylvania Court was appealed to the Supreme Court. Margaret Ashmore, a Maryland resident and slave owner, claimed to own Margaret Morgan, a slave. Morgan's original owner, Ashmore's father, had permitted her to live on part of his Maryland property without the usual fetters of slavery. Margaret eventually met and married a free Black man from Pennsylvania and moved there with him. While in Pennsylvania, Ms. Morgan gave birth to several children. After Ashmore's father died, she sent Edward Prigg and three other men to Pennsylvania to find Margaret

Morgan. Prigg found Morgan and her children and took them to a local Pennsylvania magistrate, who refused to hear the case.

Stymied by the inaction of Pennsylvania authorities, Prigg kidnapped Morgan and her children and returned them to Maryland by force. The Pennsylvania Personal Liberty Act of 1826 was the basis of kidnaping charges against Prigg and his collaborators, and a Pennsylvania jury found Prigg guilty. The case ended up in the U.S. Supreme Court. In deciding the case, Justice Story wrote of the clause in the Constitution that was the basis for the Fugitive Slave Act, "Its true design was to guard against the doctrines and principles prevailing in the non-slaveholding States by preventing them from intermeddling with, or obstructing or abolishing, the rights of the owners of slaves." The Supreme Court found for the slave holder, deciding she exercised a constitutional right to recover her slave and no state could deprive her of that right. Story also found the Court duty-bound to enforce the Act, since state judges had not. The Constitution, according to the Court, provided a right to own people as slaves. "The act of the Legislature of Pennsylvania upon which the indictment against Edward Prigg is founded is unconstitutional and void."[20]

The Letter of the Law

The third branch of government—the federal courts—aided, abetted, and protected slavery. Alexander Hamilton in the *Federalist Papers* described the Supreme Court as the "least dangerous" branch of government. Many at the Constitutional Convention resisted the creation of a federal court system. The colonies, now states, had developed a robust system of local courts. The anti-federalists argued that a national court system created by the Constitution gave too much power to federal courts. Despite their concerns, the Constitution as adopted created the Supreme Court and empowered Congress to create such inferior courts as it deemed necessary. The Judiciary Act of 1789 defined the number of judges to serve on the Supreme Court, established federal district courts in each state, and created a federal appellate court system that was composed initially of three courts, Northern, Middle, and Southern.

In addition to their usual docket as the nation's court of last resort, the justices of the Supreme Court were required to ride circuit in the states to man the three circuit courts. Two Supreme Court judges and one local district judge would constitute a U.S. Court of Appeals panel.

3. The Law of Slavery

The federal courts were to enforce and interpret federal law. They also had jurisdiction in other matters involving citizens and the states. Their federal jurisdiction to enforce federal fugitive slave laws came from many sources, including the laws Congress passed and the Commerce Clause in the Constitution.

The antebellum Supreme Court was not a busy court. At first, nominees to the Court did not want the job. The Court did not seem important and riding circuit throughout the states was an arduous task. But as time went by, the Court, through the management and decisions of Chief Justice John Marshall, established itself as a powerful branch of government. Before Marshall's tenure as Chief Justice, the Court's most important decision was *Chisholm v. Georgia*. In *Chisholm*, the Court found Georgia had to pay a creditor who had sold military supplies to Georgia during the Revolution. Many states had failed to pay or repudiated their Revolutionary War debts. Within weeks of the decision Congress passed the Eleventh Amendment, to protect the states through the doctrine of sovereign immunity from suits by private persons.

Marshall's first and most important decision was *Marbury v. Madison*, 5 U.S. (1 Cranch) 137 (1803), where he established the Supreme Court's right to review acts of Congress to determine their constitutionality. The significance of this decision establishing judicial review was far-reaching, and still results in much spilled ink today. *Marbury* made the Court a powerful branch of government, and the Marshall Court decided over thirty cases. Marshall changed the way decisions were written and the Court issued majority and dissenting opinions. The Marshall Court decided cases increasing the Court's power and making it important in the context of the development of American law in the new republic. Its decisions defined the relationship between the branches of the national government and the state governments.

Marshall owned between seven and sixteen household slaves at any one time.[21] He also bought and sold slaves. While he was the first Richmond president of the American Colonization Society, John Marshall, like many other founders, embraced slavery despite his privately stated beliefs, and sometime dicta in his Supreme Court decisions that the institution was morally indefensible.

The Marshall Court decided four freedom petition cases between 1806 and 1813, all in favor of the person claiming ownership of the slaves. In *Queen v. Hepburn*, 11 U.S. (7 Cranch) 290 (1813) Marshall wrote he believed that such suits could not be maintained on the basis of hearsay testimony. Dissenting, Justice Duvall asserted such suits could not be brought without hearsay testimony, and such testimony had supported them for years in Maryland. Ruling that hearsay was unavailable to the plaintiff meant that practically, such suits could not be brought because there would be no evidence to support the slave's claims.

"That it [the slave trade] is contrary to the law of nature will scarcely be denied," said John Marshall in the case of *The Antelope*, 23 U.S. 66 (1825). The *Antelope* was a Spanish slaver captured by an American privateer, the *Columbia* (*Arraganta*), sailing off the coast of Africa on behalf of Uruguayan rebels. Eventually, the captain and crew of the privateer appropriated the cargo of the slaver, comprised of nearly 300 souls whose average age was probably less than 14. The *Columbia* was wrecked, and the crew transferred its cargo of slaves to the *Antelope*. She was found off the coast of Florida in 1820 by the U.S. revenue cutter *Dallas*, and taken to Savannah, Georgia, because the vessel appeared to be violating the 1807 Act forbidding importation of slaves.

Legal claims arose between the privateer, the United States, Spain, and Portugal as to the ownership of the slaves on board. The United States sought to return the slaves to Africa, but Portugal and Spain sought return of the slaves to them. The federal admiralty court in Georgia decided that the slaves should be restored to Portugal and Spain, and a number repatriated to Africa. Marshall wrote in his review of the admiralty court's decision, "A distinction is taken between men, who are generally free, and goods, which are always property...." The slaves were property. Marshall then applied international law to find that the slave trade was still legal in other jurisdictions, and despite his moral compunctions, the law should prevail, and the slaves would be returned to their rightful owners because they were property.

Roger B. Taney from Maryland followed John Marshall as Chief Justice. Taney was the son of a tobacco farmer and a supporter of Andrew Jackson, who had named Taney as the U.S. Attorney General during his presidency. When Jackson then nominated him as Secretary of the Treasury, Taney became the first cabinet nominee to be rejected by the Senate. Twice nominated to the Supreme Court, he was first rejected as too radical by the Senate, but he was eventually confirmed. Taney owned slaves and even freed them, but he was a pro-slavery Southerner who believed the government had no power to end slavery.

Dred Scott was a Black man born into slavery in Virginia. In the early 1800s he was sold to an army officer, John Emerson. Emerson took Scott

3. The Law of Slavery

with him when assigned to various Army posts and they lived in territories and states where slavery was illegal. During his travels with Emerson, Scott married and had children. When Emerson died, Scott sued Emerson's widow for his and his family's freedom in a Missouri state court. Scott's argument was that they had been taken to free soil by his owner and this residence in free states and territories made them all free.

Scott had sued Emerson's widow in Missouri state court in St. Louis. After many years of legal maneuvering, the Missouri state trial court found for Scott. Such personal freedom lawsuits by slaves were not unheard of and sometimes were successful even in southern states. By this time, Widow Emerson had moved and left her brother, John Sanford, in charge of the Emerson estate that claimed Scott's ownership. Sanford appealed the trial court's ruling to the Missouri Supreme Court, which reversed the finding of the trial court liberating Scott and his family. Scott, with help from former owners, went to federal district court, and eventually his case reached the U.S. Supreme Court.

The Court of nine justices found in a 7–2 ruling, authored by Taney for Sanford, that Blacks were property, not citizens of the United States, and that the Missouri Compromise was unconstitutional, in *Scott v. Sanford*, 60 U.S. 393 (1857).

Taney admitted in his decision that Blacks could be citizens of states and might be able to vote in those states, but he denied that the Constitution permitted them to be citizens of the United States. Taney based this conclusion on his belief that the founders never considered the slaves to be anything but property at the time of the Revolution and the writing of the Constitution. He wrote that because Blacks could not be citizens of the United States, they could not be heard in federal courts. Logically, this meant that Taney should have dismissed the suit for want of jurisdiction. He did not. In a long and rambling opinion, full of historical errors and lapses in logic, Taney found Scott to be property without any legal rights and the Missouri Compromise to be unconstitutional. Taney wrote:

> The Government of the United States had no right to interfere for any other purpose but that of protecting the rights of the owner, leaving it altogether with the several States to deal with this race, whether emancipated or not, as each State may think justice, humanity, and the interests and safety of society, require. The States evidently intended to reserve this power exclusively to themselves.

The *Dred Scott* decision, finding slaves were property and that Congress could not pass an act like the Missouri Compromise in derogation of this principle, did as much to bring on the Civil War as any other act of government. This callous and emphatic disregard of Blacks as humans by the Supreme Court is mirrored in post–Civil War America, where the Constitution has been the shield and sword to protect the racism that resulted in segregation and Jim Crow, left the criminalizing of lynching to state courts, and made Black voter suppression constitutional.

More Land, More Slaves

The supporters of slavery held the Republic hostage until the Civil War. The Missouri Compromise of 1820, found unconstitutional by Taney, was the result of a fight over whether Missouri was admitted as a slave or free state. There were eleven free states and eleven slave states in the Union in 1819 when Missouri, a part of the Louisiana Purchase, applied for admission to the United States as a slave state. Northerners, led by Senator Rufus King of New York, sought the admission of Missouri as a free state. After much divisive acrimony a compromise with southern Senators was eventually reached in the Senate, by which Maine—which had been part of Massachusetts—would be admitted as a free state, Missouri as a slave state and slavery would be prohibited north of latitude 36° 30'. The "Missouri Compromise" patched the Union together over the issue of slavery until 1850.[22]

The United States went to war with Mexico in 1846. The war was seen by many Americans as a land grab, and a way to provide more land for the expansion of slavery. President Polk sent U.S. troops as an Army of Observation to the then-border of Texas with Mexico. It was clear that it was more an Army of Provocation. After a skirmish with Mexican forces, President Polk demanded a declaration of war, claiming American blood had been shed on American soil. A young congressman from Illinois, Abraham Lincoln, opposed the Mexican War and demanded in Congress, through his "spot resolution," to know the exact spot where American blood had been shed on American soil.

The war was a way for Texas to increase its territory. The conflict was made convenient by the formation of the Texas Republic and its subsequent efforts to join the Union. Other lands beyond Texas were at stake, and Southerners saw all these lands as being possible fertile ground for cotton and slavery.

The Mexican War was a training ground for northern and southern soldiers who would later lead military forces in the Civil War. More

3. The Law of Slavery

Americans died from disease than Mexican bullets. The American Army eventually captured all of the major cities in Mexico, including Mexico City. Ulysses S. Grant, who fought in Mexico, later said, "For myself, I was bitterly opposed to the measure [war] and to this day regard the war, which resulted, as one of the most unjust ever waged by a stronger against a weaker nation."[23]

Crushing Mexico by defeating its army and capturing Mexico City, the United States doubled the size of Texas, obtained California and the land that would become Arizona, and bought New Mexico. The peace treaty settled all Spanish and Mexican claims north of the Rio Grande in favor of the United States.

Some two scant years after the war ended, in 1850, California sought admission to the Union. California's population had been swelled by the gold rush, and its application caused Southerners to resist its admission because it would upset the balance between slave and free states in the Union. It was always clear to members of Congress, North and South, that California would never seek admission as a slave state. Another crisis like the conflict over admission of Missouri consumed Congress and the nation. Henry Clay came to the South's rescue and proposed the "Compromise of 1850," although he was opposed by another Southerner, John C. Calhoun, who believed no restrictions should be made on the spread of slavery.

The "compromise" of 1850 had several parts. California would be admitted as a free state, but another compromise was made in Congress to appease Southerners. Texas would give up its claims to land in what is now New Mexico, in return for which the United States would give Texas ten million dollars to pay debts it owed Mexico. The territories of New Mexico, Nevada, Arizona, and Utah, once they were organized, could decide by popular vote if they wanted to be admitted as slave or free on application for admission to the Union. These territories were for the most part south of the Missouri Compromise line, and they had been obtained by conquest and purchase after the Missouri Compromise. The idea of letting the populations of these territories decide their status regarding slavery became known as the "doctrine of popular sovereignty." Slavery was not barred from the new territories, even though Utah and Nevada were clearly north of the line established in the Missouri Compromise banning slavery.

In this bargain, Northerners got the slave markets in Washington, D.C., closed, but only because they had become an embarrassment. The

The Constitution and American Racism

sale—and only the sale—of slaves was forbidden in the nation's capital. Finally, as part of the Compromise of 1850, to get Southerners to agree to the admission of California, a new fugitive slave act was passed by Congress.

The Fugitive Slave Act of 1850 required private citizens to assist in capturing runaway slaves. It created a force of federal officers to help find and return runaway slaves, and it denied a jury trial to a slave on the question of whether he or she was a slave. The Act also compensated special commissioners for hearing fugitive slave cases and paid them twice the minimum fee for their services when they found the victim to be a runaway slave.

Fugitives

By the 1850s, thousands of runaway slaves had managed to reach free states. Many Northerners actively supported these escapes through the Underground Railroad and other means. The Underground Railroad was its most active in the 1850s, and now fugitives were helped to get to Canada, outside the jurisdiction of the United States and the Fugitive Slave Act.

Shadrach Minkins was a Black Boston waiter who escaped slavery in Virginia in 1850. The Fugitive Slave Act required local law enforcement to help apprehend and return Minkins to slavery. On February 15, 1851, Minkins was arrested by two Boston policemen and taken to court. Local anti-slavery forces consisting of Black freedmen and white abolitionists gathered at the courthouse to protest Minkins' arrest. Abolitionists and Black supporters gathered in the courtroom where Minkins had been turned over to federal marshals and rushed them, spiriting Minkins out of the courthouse and eventually to Canada and freedom. Because of this incident, President Millard Fillmore authorized the use of federal troops to capture fugitive slaves.[24]

Anthony Burns, a slave in Alexandria, Virginia, fled to Boston in 1854. His owner followed Burns to Boston and had him arrested for robbery. After his arrest Burns was taken to the federal courthouse and held by authorities. Freedmen and abolitionists in Boston met immediately to decide what to do about Burns' arrest. The freedmen, joined by white abolitionists, decided to liberate Burns at the jail. A crowd of 2,000 Bostonians, freedmen and white abolitionists, gathered in front of the federal courthouse and charged it, battering down its door. During the struggle to

3. The Law of Slavery

get in the courthouse, a deputy was killed, and Burns' would-be liberators were unable to free him. President Fillmore sent Marines and artillery to Boston to escort Burns to the Boston Navy Yard, where he was placed on a naval ship and sent back to Virginia. Fifty thousand Bostonians lined the streets along the way to the Navy Yard to show their opposition to Fillmore's orders. Burns was later purchased out of slavery by anti-slavery supporters.[25]

In 1855, in response to the federal removal of Anthony Burns from Boston, public sentiment pushed support in the legislature for the Massachusetts Personal Liberty Act that was meant to thwart the onerous provisions of the Fugitive Slave Act of 1850. The Massachusetts law placed the state in direct conflict with the federal government on the issue of enforcement of the Fugitive Slave Act. The Massachusetts Personal Freedom Act called for removal of any state official who aided in the return of runaway slaves. The Act called for the use of the writ of *habeas corpus* by state courts in such cases; required people claiming custody under the Fugitive Slave Act to set out in writing their claims; barred testimony at trial by the claimant or the putative slave; and placed the burden of proof on the claimant.

The Massachusetts Personal Freedom Act called for fining and imprisoning those who removed or tried to remove runaway slaves; it forbade issuance of warrants by state officials to aid in the arrest of runaway slaves; it banned state officials from issuing certificates of ownership as required by the Fugitive Slave Act; and it provided that any state official who did so would be considered to have vacated his office immediately and be forever banned from further state office. It provided for the immediate disbarment of any attorney assisting a claimant slave owner under the Fugitive Slave Act.

The Personal Freedom Act provided that state judges who acted as federal commissioners under the Act would be deemed to have "violated good behavior" and would be subject to immediate impeachment. Any law enforcement person or militia member (it forbade use of militia to pursue runaways) who arrested a putative slave would be punished by fine and imprisonment. It prohibited the use of any jail to hold "a person accused ... or convicted of obstructing, resisting any process, warrant or order issued under or in aid of said [Fugitive Slave Acts], or rescuing or attempting to rescue, any person arrested or detained under any of the provisions of ... said acts."[26] There is no record of any runaway slave being removed from Massachusetts after passage of the law.

The Constitution and American Racism

The years from ratification of the Constitution until the Civil War had been marked by the efforts of white Southerners to protect and expand their peculiar institution. Although the Constitution never used the word slave, it clearly provided legal protection for slavery. The pro-slavery forces used the law—state law, the Constitution and acts of Congress—to protect slavery and disrupt any efforts to abolish the institution. All three branches of the federal government aided slave owners in protecting the system of slavery. The Atlantic slave trade was ostensibly ended in 1808, but was continued by those in the South who sought to evade federal law ending the international trade.

In 2018, a wreck of a slave ship was discovered in the tidal areas of Alabama. The owner of the ship, a wealthy Alabama planter, had bet in 1860 that he could get a slave ship safely into harbor despite the federal law banning the Atlantic slave trade. Those who applauded the end of the Atlantic slave trade by the federal government thought it would make abolition easier. It did not. It fed the demand for more slaves by those who were moving west and southwest into United States territories gained by purchase or war. New lands meant new cotton culture and a continuing southern demand for slaves. People were bred for servitude and a vigorous slave trade continued.

After 1850 the issue of slavery haunted the admission process for each territory seeking statehood and admission to the Union. The federal government through Congress compromised time and again to protect slavery. While the Missouri Compromise bought some peace, it was eventually tossed aside by the Compromise of 1850 and Supreme Court decisions. Each Congressional act regarding runaway slaves proved the power of southern Congressional delegations to assert their demands for recovery of their property and protection of the "peculiar institution." Each Congressional compromise extended the reach of the pernicious institution and continued the racial assault on Black men and women held in bondage. And it was all constitutional.

The Kansas-Nebraska Act was driven by slavery and financial interests in the United States in favor of the construction of a transcontinental railroad. One of those keenly interested in the construction of a transcontinental railroad was Senator Stephen A. Douglas. Douglas, from Illinois, wanted the railroad to travel through Chicago, and across land he owned, benefitting his state, and his pocketbook. The Nebraska Territory contained a large swath of the plains and mountain states. The territory was north of the Missouri Compromise line, and

3. The Law of Slavery

therefore slavery was illegal in the territory and any states carved from it.[27]

Southerners in Congress were against this territory being organized as free states. Douglas and his supporters pointed out there had been no such prohibition placed on New Mexico and land obtained through the Mexican War. Northerners and abolitionists were outraged at Douglas's self-dealing and adamantly opposed his "compromise," spreading slavery into areas where it had been prohibited by the Missouri Compromise. In 1854, Douglas was able to engineer a deal with pro-slavery forces by which the Missouri Compromise would be repealed, and the Nebraska Territory would be reformed into the Kansas and Nebraska Territories. The settlers in the territories of Kansas and Nebraska would vote on admission whether to be slave or free.

The Kansas-Nebraska Act effectively repealed the Missouri Compromise, leaving no practical bar to slavery in the territories. This Act resulted in "bleeding Kansas" with two separate state governments, one slave and one free, and a new attitude among abolitionists and Southerners alike that would result in no more compromises on the issue of slavery.

Noise-some, Squat, and Nameless Animal

On May 19, 1856, Senator Charles Sumner, Republican anti-slavery advocate and longtime abolitionist, rose in the Senate to address the issue of the admission of Kansas as a free or slave state. Sumner had a long professional and public record as an attorney and as a Senator opposing slavery. He had bitterly opposed Stephen A. Douglas in his efforts to have the Kansas-Nebraska Act ratified in the Senate. Sumner's "Crime Against Kansas" speech was an attack on slavery and on Douglas, author of the Kansas-Nebraska Act, and South Carolina Senator Andrew Butler. Sumner spoke directly to Douglas on the floor of the Senate, calling him a "noise-some, squat, and nameless animal ... not a proper model for an American senator."

Sumner's characterization of Senator Butler, who was absent from the Senate, was that he was taking "a mistress ... who, though ugly to others, is always lovely to him; though polluted in the sight of the world, is chaste in his sight—I mean, the harlot, Slavery." Two days later, Preston Brooks, a distant Butler cousin and member of the House of Representatives from South Carolina, waited until the Senate business was done for the day, entered the chamber and found Sumner seated at his desk. He attacked Sumner while he was seated, repeatedly striking him with a gold-tipped cane on the head and body until he broke the cane. A colleague of Brooks, also a representative from South Carolina, restrained those trying to come to Sumner's aid. Sumner could not rise from his seat and eventually pulled it from its hinges while trying to resist the blows. A Northern representative finally restrained Brooks.[28]

Despite his badly injuring Sumner, the House of Representatives, rigged by the three-fifths rule and the inflated representation of southern states, shamefully could not muster enough votes to censure Brooks. He was fined $300 by a federal court in the District of Columbia, a fine paid by his supporters. Brooks resigned his seat in Congress and then was re-elected. It took Sumner three and a half years to recover from his injuries. Southerners sent Brooks replacement canes. The conflict over slavery was no longer defused by "great compromises." It was now a full-blown shooting war in Kansas and a matter of beatings in Congress. The Constitution had failed repeatedly to avoid the conflict over slavery because it compromised away democracy and control of the federal government in favor of slavery.

With the passage of the Kansas and Nebraska Act thousands of "free-soil" advocates and pro-slavery forces poured into Kansas. Neighboring Missouri provided transient pro-slavery forces, who went to Kansas to vote and then went home. Intimidation and murder became the order of the day. A small stone church constructed of white prairie limestone stands today in Wabaunsee, Kansas, at the corner of Chapel and Elm streets. It was built by Abolitionists and, after four years, dedicated in 1862. Ely Thayer and Henry Ward Beecher sent the Abolitionist immigrants in Wabaunsee "Beecher Bibles" (Sharps rifles), and so the Church is known as the Beecher Bible and Rifle Church. John Brown went to Kansas and began his own personal war on slavery, killing pro-slavery forces when he could, often hacking them to death with a saber. After elections marked by coercion and violence, a pro-slavery and a "free soil" government both claimed legitimacy.

President Fillmore sent federal troops to Kansas to keep the peace, unsuccessfully it turned out. Elections were marked by Missourians—"border ruffians"—committing voter fraud by illegally voting in Kansas and intimidating "free soil" voters living in Kansas. Despite both apparent and obvious fraud, President Buchanan recognized the pro-slavery government. Although a Congressional investigating committee found widespread

3. The Law of Slavery

abuse and fraud by pro-slavery forces and concluded that the free-state government represented the real will of the people, the President refused to recognize it as the legitimate government of Kansas. In 1859, Southerners in the Senate blocked the application of Kansas for admission to the Union as a "free soil" state.

The Southerners didn't like popular sovereignty when it meant a state voted to be free. The hypocrisy of the South and the failings of the Constitution are evidenced by the fact that Kansas was not admitted to the Union until after the South had seceded in 1861. All of this occurred in the name of protecting slavery and was made lawful by the actions of the federal government created by the Constitution. Even if a majority of Americans were in favor of abolition, slavery could not be abolished short of secession and war.

4

States' Rights as Revisionist History

They lied. History is the record of all that has passed. It is not only a collection of facts but it is a record of cultures, ideas and events. It is about kings and generals but is also a tableau of the common person. All too often history is what we make of it. It is often weaponized and used in ways that are inconsistent with the historical record. A factual record would be a truthful record. And a fact according to Webster's Collegiate Dictionary is "something that has actual existence; an actual occurrence."[1]

Ambrose Bierce was a nineteenth-century American writer and satirist. He was born in Horse Cave Creek, in Meigs, Ohio, one of thirteen children. He was a Union soldier who fought in several major engagements in the Civil War before being badly wounded at Kennesaw Mountain, outside of Atlanta, in 1864. He lived during a time of unprecedented growth and excess for the United States. The years after the Civil War were characterized by "Robber Barons," "Muckrakers," massive immigration, steel, oil and railroads. It was a time known as the "Great Barbecue" and the "Gilded Age."

Bierce believed a dictionary was needed for the time and wrote *The Unabridged Devil's Dictionary*. He defined history as "An Account mostly false, of events mostly unimportant, which are brought about by rulers mostly knaves, and soldiers mostly fools."[2] The history of the Civil War as told and written by Southerners was an effort to help Southerners feel better about being losers. To tell this history, its advocates had to invent a story that revised the facts. It was a revisionist history of the Civil War told to justify a war that killed more Americans than all of our other wars combined.

The South lost the Civil War. It went to war to preserve slavery.[3] Southerners could have blocked any constitutional attempt to stop the

4. States' Rights as Revisionist History

abolition of slavery but instead they took up arms against the government of the United States. The South fired first on federal forces. It then prosecuted a war that it could not win, resulting in utter military and political defeat. All of its leading generals wasted southern lives with a profligacy seldom seen outside the borders of a Europe frequently drenched in blood. Its heroes, memorialized in marble, were thoroughly defeated by Union forces. The men who led the South and southern armies, the men who did the actual fighting were all traitors by the very definition of "levying war against" the federal government.

Mitch Landrieu, born and raised in Louisiana, was elected mayor of New Orleans in 2010. He was the son of a mayor and the brother of a sister who had been a U.S. Senator. He was elected mayor by a majority of white and African American voters when New Orleans was still struggling with the effects of Hurricane Katrina. His leadership helped the city recover from Katrina and reform its government. In 2015 he decided four statues needed to be removed from the streets of New Orleans. Three of the statues were of rebel leaders and one was honoring the White League. In 2017 he removed the statues of Robert E. Lee, Jefferson Davis, P.G.T. Beauregard and the White League. Landrieu spoke passionately in defense of his actions. "There are no slave ship monuments, no prominent markers on public land to remember the lynchings or the slave blocks," he said, adding that the defenders of Confederate monuments "are eerily silent on what amounts to this historical malfeasance, a lie by omission" (*New York Times* May 23, 2017, Frank Bruni). Mayor Landrieu had to decide whether to remove a statue of a rebel general and after a little research concluded such statues were propaganda.[4] The "Lost Cause" is a myth.[5]

Born in Ohio, William Tecumseh Sherman was a graduate of the United States Military Academy at West Point. He was a veteran of the Mexican War, and like many of his contemporaries left the Army after that war in 1848. Sherman tried banking, reading law, and farming before rejoining the Union Army and becoming one of its premier commanders. During the secession crisis in 1860 he was in Baton Rouge, Louisiana, as Superintendent and Professor of Engineering at the Louisiana State Seminary of Learning and Military Academy (today's LSU). A Northerner, Sherman knew he would have to leave Louisiana after it seceded, but before he went, he told a friend and faculty member on Christmas Eve, 1860, "You people of the South don't know what you are doing. This country will be drenched in blood and God only knows how it will end. It is all folly, madness, a crime against civilization!"[6]

The Constitution and American Racism

After the Confederacy attacked Fort Sumter, both the North and South organized armies of amateurs led by former professional soldiers, serving officers, and elected officers who came with little or no training. Many newly minted officers had no idea how to lead and maneuver troops in the field, let alone under fire. The level of violence began slowly in April 1861 with the attack on Fort Sumter by the rebels. In the beginning, each raid, skirmish, and battle was fought with the belief the war would be over in a trice. Later in the summer of 1861, Bull Run, in Virginia, and Wilson's Creek, in Missouri, saw thousands of men deployed by both sides in fumbling efforts to kill one another.[7]

In April 1862, 40,000 Confederates and 35,000 federal troops met at Shiloh, Tennessee, on the banks of the Tennessee River near Pittsburgh Landing. Shiloh established a record for deaths in a single battle at this stage of the war when it was fought. Much worse was to come.[8] The Union Army at Shiloh, led by Ulysses Grant, a man who had resigned from the Army and failed at almost every civilian job he had, killed the Confederate commander, held its ground, and after reinforcement counterattacked. Grant forced the Southerners to retreat. After two days of fighting, the field resembled an abattoir. Confederate and Union losses, dead and wounded, totaled over 24,000 men. The casualties exceeded those for the Revolution, War of 1812, and the Mexican War combined. In some places the survivors could walk across the battlefield on corpses, without touching the ground.[9]

Federal forces in the East, the Virginia theater, were commanded by another West Point graduate who had left the Army after the Mexican War. George McClellan had been a successful engineer building railroads after leaving the Army, but in 1862 he was leading the Army of the Potomac in the Peninsula Campaign trying to capture Richmond. McClellan was a brilliant organizer but no fighter, although his Union forces greatly outnumbered his opponents on the Peninsula.[10] Joe Johnston, another West Pointer and career soldier, led the rebel forces on the Peninsula until he was wounded at the battle of Seven Pines. Robert E. Lee replaced Johnston and renamed the southern forces on the Peninsula and around Richmond, the Army of Northern Virginia.[11]

Lee took the initiative in a series of battles near Richmond, and despite being outnumbered, attacked until McClellan withdrew his massive army. Thousands of dead and wounded Confederates and Federals were the devil's harvest on the battlefields around Richmond. With each battle, casualties mounted. In the first six months of 1862, not only had

4. States' Rights as Revisionist History

thousands been killed but tens of thousands wounded, many disabled for life. These first major battles of the war employed tactics dominated by frontal assaults by large formations armed with rifles trying to get close enough to the other side to break their opponent's lines and then kill and capture them. While the rifles used by both sides had a range of several hundred yards, most battles were stand up affairs of regiments and brigades blazing away at each other over a few hundred yards of distance.[12]

The ammunition for these rifles, the Minié ball, made them more lethal and inflicted terrible wounds, especially when it hit arms or legs. These wounds frequently caused doctors treating the wounded to resort to amputation. Infantry attacked artillery head on in ill-considered ground assaults and were killed, wounded, and maimed by canister fired at close range. During the war, one in four Union soldiers was killed or wounded, and one in three Confederates. The ratio of Confederate dead to Union dead was three to one. Historians now believe over 750,000 Americans died in the war from all causes.[13] Poor camp and field hygiene, disease and exposure to the elements accounted for many of the dead. These large armies—some numbering above a hundred thousand—had to be fed, clothed, and moved from place to place. Eventually, Northern armies would number over two and a half million men.

The Union navy would blockade the Atlantic and Gulf coasts and make possible the conquest, by ironclads supported by infantry, of all the great rivers and their tributaries, including the Mississippi, Missouri, Ohio, and Tennessee rivers.[14]

After the South fired on Fort Sumpter, Lincoln faced a multitude of challenges that demanded his immediate attention. He needed an army, he needed money for an army, he needed to deal with traitors surrounding Washington, D.C., he needed effective military leadership and a plan to suppress the rebellion, and he needed to hang onto the border states and mobilize Democrats and Republicans to fight a civil war. He made decisions and acted to save the Union in ways that would later be criticized as unconstitutional and dictatorial, beyond the scope of his constitutional presidential powers.[15]

Lincoln relied on the War Powers Clause in the Constitution as the source of his authority for many of his actions. He called for volunteers, spent money, suspended the writ of *habeas corpus* without Congressional approval, and tried to find effective military leadership.[16] There was no question at this point of compromise. Lincoln's first cause was the nation, the Union. He saw the American Republic as a beacon of democratic ideals for all the world. It was in his mind the "last, best hope" for democracy. Lincoln sought to protect the Union regardless of the Constitution.

Lincoln had to deal with the issue of what to do with slaves seeking the protection of the Union military forces in the field. Wherever Union forces went, slaves appeared. Lincoln and his generals realized that the slaves who stayed on the plantations were a powerful manpower source available to aid the Confederate armies. The slaves constructed military projects for the rebels and tended fields growing commercial crops for export to support the Confederate War effort, and food for the troops, thus freeing white Southerners to fight.

Contraband

On May 24, 1861, three slaves working on nearby Confederate fortifications sought protection at Union Fort Monroe at the tip of the James Peninsula in Virginia. Major General Ben Butler commanded the fort and had a unique view of their status. A Confederate officer under white flag asked Butler to return the runaways. Butler himself confronted the rebel and told the Confederate his escaped slaves were "contraband of war" and he was not getting them back. After this incident the slaves who fled to Union military forces became "contraband." Confiscated military supplies and "contraband" soon meant "freedmen."[17]

In August 1861, Congress adopted Butler's policy and by legislation, fugitive slaves were declared "contraband" and were not to be returned to their masters. A second Confiscation Act in 1862 provided that anyone who committed treason and was found guilty would forfeit all his slaves, who would be declared free. Then Congress passed legislation forbidding the return of fugitive slaves, even to loyal masters. What to do with the "contraband?" A Militia Act passed by Congress gave freedom to any slave who joined Union forces and permitted Union forces to hire Blacks as laborers for wages set at $10 a day.

In August 1862, Union Secretary of War Stanton authorized the recruitment of 5,000 Black soldiers.[18] This happened as abolitionists supporting the war pressed for emancipation of all the slaves. Lincoln had personally and politically opposed slavery before the war, but now he had to balance his interest in keeping border states loyal with political interests demanding immediate emancipation. Lincoln declared that if he could save the Union and free the slaves he would, and if he could save the

4. States' Rights as Revisionist History

Union and keep slavery, he would.[19] Now that war had come, emancipation of the slaves was a difficult proposition, militarily and politically. Most war Democrats, Democrats who supported the Union, were opposed to emancipation, and many others including some Republicans opposed the idea.[20]

Many soldiers who had volunteered to save the Union opposed freedom for the slaves. But Lincoln had a strong base within his own party in favor of emancipation, composed of abolitionists and Radical Republicans, and inexorably all these forces moved toward the idea of emancipation. In the summer of 1862, Lincoln saw that emancipation was not inimical to his war aims and that it would damage the South militarily. Hoping for military victories to soften the blow, he began to discuss freeing the slaves with his cabinet.[21]

The summer of 1862 was a disaster for Union troops and disabused everyone of the idea that there would be a quick victory by either side. Lee, before taking command of the rebel army, had turned Stonewall Jackson loose in the Shenandoah Valley, and Jackson wrecked Union forces there, capturing millions of dollars in war supplies and thousands of federal soldiers. Then Lee and Jackson joined forces on the old Bull Run Battlefield and defeated the Army of the Potomac, recently returned from the Peninsula with a new commander who was unable to concentrate his forces to beat the Army of Northern Virginia. Because of this string of defeats, Lincoln decided to wait for a Union victory before acting on emancipation.

Having fired "Little Mac" McClellan after the debacle on the Peninsula, Lincoln turned again to him to reinvigorate Union forces in the East, which had been on a long losing streak and needed a steady hand to reorganize them and restore their confidence. Unfortunately, McClellan came with baggage. He had always opposed emancipation and did and said many things that militarily and politically undercut Lincoln's positions on fighting the rebels and emancipating the slaves. McClellan criticized Lincoln in the harshest terms and was not always the obedient soldier.[22]

In September 1862, Lee, hoping to divert federal attention and military operations away from Virginia and Richmond, took the Army of Northern Virginia north across the Maryland line to invade Pennsylvania. Lee's plan was a complicated movement meant to concentrate his Army in Western Maryland and threaten Philadelphia and Washington, D.C. The plan had many moving parts. In one of those happenstances that could have changed history, Lee's written plan fell into the hands of George McClellan. A copy of the plan was found, wrapped around three cigars, by

The Constitution and American Racism

Union soldiers near Harpers Ferry, Virginia. Essentially Lee had detached various units from his main Army to conduct raids and attack isolated Union forces and then planned to bring them all back together.[23]

The separate parts of Lee's army, even if united, totaled only 55,000 men. Lee's opponent, the Army of the Potomac, numbered 120,000 men.[24] Having Lee's orders, McClellan had an opportunity to defeat the separated parts of Lee's Army and end the war. But McClellan always estimated Lee's army at two to three times its actual number and then he always moved with the pace of a slow turtle. Lee calculated that McClellan would move slowly, and despite being outnumbered, he decided to concentrate his army and make a stand at Sharpsburg, Maryland, on the banks of Antietam Creek. As Lee's army concentrated at Sharpsburg, McClellan predictably dawdled.

On September 16, 1862, Lee had only 15,000 soldiers at Sharpsburg and by this point they were a sad lot, many being shoeless, and all being exhausted from marching throughout Virginia and Maryland. The Union forces numbered 60,000 and despite their 4–1 superiority they did nothing but watch Lee and wait for McClellan and more men.[25] As the day wore on, Lee's forces increased to 35,000 men and the federal forces to over 87,000 soldiers.[26] The next day, September 17, as more Union troops poured onto the battlefield, McClellan finally attacked Lee. The Civil War could have ended that day in September with a resounding defeat of Lee and the destruction of his army.[27]

George McClellan pulled stalemate out of the jaws of victory and made piecemeal and uncoordinated attacks up and down the rebel line. Despite overwhelming numerical superiority, he failed to drive home his attacks by taking advantage of his numbers. At one point the situation was so desperate for the Confederates that General James Longstreet manned a cannon in the center of the rebel line.[28] The Union attacks were unsuccessful in breaking the rebel lines, and the commanders lacked any real knowledge of the land's topography and so failed to use its peculiarities to their advantage.

Union General Burnside, when ordered to attack Lee's troops on the other side of Antietam Creek, ordered his men to attack across a narrow stone bridge spanning Antietam Creek, and saw them massacred by 400 rebels waiting at the other end, until sheer weight of numbers overwhelmed the Confederates. The creek could have been safely crossed at other places along its meandering, narrow, shallow course, avoiding a bloody, direct assault on a narrow front, into the mouths of cannons.[29]

4. States' Rights as Revisionist History

As the day wore on the Federals continued piecemeal attacks that because of their numbers sometimes pressed the rebel lines to the breaking point. During the afternoon's fighting, at the last desperate minute, the troops of rebel General A.P. Hill arrived on the battlefield. Hill's arrival stabilized the rebel line. The day's combat ended, and the Confederate Army stayed on the field through the next day and still, despite having a considerable advantage in numbers, McClellan did nothing to press his advantage with further attacks.

Lee, unmolested, retreated to Virginia. Nearly 23,000 men were killed, wounded and captured on that September day. Because of the extraordinary casualties incurred, Antietam is the bloodiest day in American military history.[30] Every single Confederate unit had suffered significant casualties, while on McClellan's side there were over 30,000 Federal troops who never fired a shot on September 17. But, because of Lee's retreat, the Union could claim a victory, and Lincoln could issue the preliminary emancipation proclamation.

Lincoln argued his authority to issue the preliminary emancipation proclamation came from Article II, Section 2, the War Powers Clause of the Constitution, and he viewed the proclamation as a military order. If the Confederates did not lay down their arms by January 1, 1863, slaves in those areas not yet occupied would be free, but the proclamation did not affect slaves in the border states or areas already occupied. On New Year's Day 1863, after meeting holiday visitors at the White House, Lincoln signed and issued the final Emancipation Proclamation.[31]

There was significant resistance to the proclamation in the Union. Despite admitting the war was about slavery, many in the Union Army declared they joined to fight for the Union and not the slaves. Those soldiers who had fought or been stationed in the South had observed slavery firsthand and believed it to be an evil, pernicious institution. The Commander of the 120th Ohio wrote "since I [came] here I have learned and seen more of what the horrors of slavery was than I ever knew before.... I am [in] favor of doing away with the accursed institution.... I am [now] a strong abolitionist."[32]

Union soldiers recognized that freeing the slaves would have two profound military effects on continued fighting. Freeing the slaves would eliminate a resource that the South relied on for military labor and cultivation for food supplies for the armies. Eliminating this resource put the Southerners on a level with the Union men who had left their farms and homes with no one save their wives and children to carry on. The liberated slaves also represented a manpower resource for the Union armies. One Union soldier was a Kentucky Lieutenant who had threatened resignation with emancipation but came to write, "the inexorable logic of events is rapidly making practical abolitionists of every soldier. I am afraid that [even] I am getting to be an Abolitionist. All right! Better than a Secessionist."[33]

Both the massive Union Armies in the East and West were Lincoln's armies. Some of these soldiers, particularly the Westerners, never saw Lincoln, but all the soldiers viewed him as one of them and his causes as theirs. Like "Father Abraham" they came to acknowledge that this War was about freeing the slaves and that the Union was about liberty, and so the slaves must have their freedom. The Emancipation Proclamation, written as a military order, authorized the recruitment of Black soldiers. White soldiers who had been fighting for two years realized that Black soldiers could also kill and be killed. Despite skepticism, as the numbers of Black troops increased until almost 180,000 served the Union Army, white Union soldiers acknowledged the bravery and effectiveness of Black soldiers.[34]

A tribute to the ordinary soldier's devotion to Abraham Lincoln came in 1864. When he promised a constitutional amendment to abolish slavery as part of his Presidential platform for re-election, he received 80 percent of the soldiers' vote.[35] "Once let the Black man get upon his person the brass letters U.S.; let him get an eagle on his button, and a musket on his shoulder, and bullets in his pocket, and there is no power on earth or under the earth which can deny that he has earned the right of citizenship in the United States," wrote Frederick Douglass.[36]

From Kansas to South Carolina, former slaves and freedmen flocked to the colors and enlisted in what for them was truly freedom's cause. These former slaves were organized as the United States Colored Troops, generally in regimental sized units, typically composed of ten companies. Their officers and NCOs were mostly white. In the beginning, Black Troops were paid less than their white comrades received for the same service, "ten dollars per month and one ration, three dollars of which monthly pay may be in clothing."[37] The argument of the government for this disparity was that the pay had been set by the Militia Act, which had intended Black recruits would serve as laborers. White soldiers received thirteen dollars a month, which included the three-dollar uniform allowance.[38] Many Black soldiers, because of this disparity, refused to take their pay. In Massachusetts, the governor convinced the state legislature to make up the difference for the 54th and

4. States' Rights as Revisionist History

55th Regiments Massachusetts Colored Infantry. It took until December of 1863 for Congress to end this difference in pay.[39]

The Confederacy's reaction to the enlistment of Blacks was to issue the "Black Flag" order.[40] White officers serving with Black units were to be tried for inciting insurrection and executed, and captured Black soldiers were to be returned to a state of slavery. As a practical matter the white officers and Black enlisted soldiers understood these orders to be "no quarter" orders—"that it meant the bayonet." President Lincoln responded that "for every soldier of the United States killed in violation of war, a rebel soldier shall be executed, and for every one enslaved by the enemy or sold into slavery, a rebel soldier shall be placed at hard labor on public works and continued at such labor until the other shall be released and receive the treatment due to a prisoner of war."[41] A prisoner exchange program had operated for most of the war, trading captured rebels for Yankees regardless of rank. Now because of this rebel policy and for other reasons the process stopped in 1863.[42]

Among the massacres of Black troops by rebel troops was the 1864 battle at Fort Pillow, Tennessee, an isolated post 40 miles North of Memphis. Fort Pillow had been built by Confederate forces in 1861 and was captured by Grant in 1862. In January 1864, General Sherman, at the beginning of his Atlanta Campaign, ordered the Fort abandoned, but his orders were ignored. Rebel General Nathan Bedford Forrest, a former slave trader and co-founder of the Ku Klux Klan, attacked the post with some 1,500 men on April 12, 1864. The Fort had been badly sited by the rebels on the banks of the river in 1861 and had insufficient fortifications constructed to properly defend the place. Its garrison of 500 federal troops including Colored Infantry was quickly overrun. Forrest's men showed no quarter to the Black troops and killed around 270 of them, most after the fighting had stopped when they tried to surrender. The massacre soon became a rallying cry for Colored and white troops.[43]

Lincoln had to manage multiple military disasters before the 1864 election. The two main armies of the Union forces were positioned in the East, in the D.C. and Virginia area, and in the West in a huge theater of operations that included the Mississippi River Valley, the Deep South, and the trans-Mississippi West, consisting of Western Louisiana, Texas, Arkansas, Missouri and the Indian Territories.

In the East, a succession of mediocre and incompetent generals at the helm of the Army of the Potomac, all West Pointers, plagued Lincoln. The first was Irwin McDowell who foundered at Bull Run and was replaced by McClellan. McClellan was an able organizer but an egomaniac averse to fighting, and he was an anti-emancipation Democrat prone to grandiose plans badly executed, who consistently misjudged his main antagonist Lee, even when he held Lee's plans in his hands. McClellan always inflated the strength of the Confederate Army to delusional levels to justify his lack of aggressiveness and demands for reinforcements.

After the Peninsula Campaign, Lincoln tried on John Pope, newly arrived from the Western Army, and made him commander of the Army of Virginia. Pope was badly beaten by Lee at the Second Battle of Bull Run. Then Lincoln recalled McClellan, who despite having in his possession Lee's orders for the rebel invasion of Maryland, and despite an overwhelming superiority in men, managed only a draw at Antietam.

Next was Ambrose Burnside, who connived among the generals of the Army of the Potomac for the appointment as commander. In a few days in December, in his first and last battle as Commander of the Army of the Potomac, he lost thousands of veteran soldiers in suicidal frontal attacks on entrenched rebels at Fredericksburg, Virginia. Then, "Fighting" Joe Hooker, loud-mouthed and profane, on record as saying a dictator was needed to save the Union, gave Lee his greatest victory at Chancellorsville despite outnumbering him over two to one. After Hooker left, George Gordon Meade said he didn't want the job but got it in time for Gettysburg. The litany of defeat was long: Bull Run, and the Shenandoah Valley—where the Union general Banks was called Commissary Banks by Confederates because of the amount of supplies they captured from him—the failed campaign on the Peninsula, Second Bull Run, Fredericksburg, and Chancellorsville. The disasters finally stopped in July 1863 with the Union victories at Gettysburg and Vicksburg.

In the West, another general from Ohio by the name of Ulysses Grant seemed unstoppable. After destroying a series of Confederate positions in the Mississippi Valley and stopping a Confederate offensive at Shiloh, he conducted a brilliant campaign that captured the rebel fortress at Vicksburg, freeing the Mississippi River all the way to the Gulf of Mexico and cutting the Confederacy in two. He then moved against rebel forces in Eastern Tennessee and set up Sherman's campaign against Atlanta. In 1864, Lincoln believed he finally had a fighting general and called Grant back to the East, naming him commander of all Federal armies.

Grant didn't wear plumes and shiny swords; he was modest and always tried to get at the enemy. He was a consummate horseman but more resembled a private soldier in his appearance and dress. He was a

4. States' Rights as Revisionist History

determined commander who understood that his real objective was the destruction of the enemy army.[44] He was remarkable and unlike any of his predecessors, and he was also a Lincoln man. He was dogged by rumors of his use of alcohol and admitted that he was unable to drink without consequences. But in the end, he was the man more than any other general who destroyed the rebel army and won the war. For the first time he coordinated Union attacks everywhere with one objective: attacking the enemy's army.

In Virginia the war had been conducted in a hundred-mile swath between the nation's capital and Richmond. It was good defensive ground for Lee and favored him with rivers, swamps, and "wilderness" areas that provided natural barriers and fortifications for his army. Because of this terrain Lee was able to use the military strategy of interior lines where he could shift troops from one point to any other along the interior line as military circumstance dictated.

Grant always wanted to be in the field with his army, and so after his appointment as General in Chief he made his headquarters with the Army of the Potomac. Grant left George Gordon Meade, the hero of Gettysburg, known as "that damn snapping turtle," in command of the Army. Grant planned to move on Lee's Army, and in the West, he ordered Sherman to attack Confederate forces guarding Atlanta, a strategic rail center funneling supplies north to the rebel Army. He simultaneously ordered operations against Mobile, Alabama, and in the West against Texas. His strategy was to close the last ports open to blockade runners and attack Confederate forces everywhere at once.

"Ulysses doesn't scare worth a damn."

In Virginia, Grant was just another new commander of an army that had never beaten Lee except at Gettysburg. In May 1864, Grant moved south to get between Lee and Richmond. He attacked Lee in an area where "Fighting" Joe Hooker in May of 1863 fought and lost his first and only battle as commander of the Army of Potomac. The Wilderness, a tangled area of second growth forest with undergrowth, made a fine defensive ground for the rebels. Grant pitched into Lee, fighting the first battle of the Overland Campaign, now known as the Battle of the Wilderness. In a war where the fighting became more desperate with each new battle, the fighting in and among a tangled undergrowth was at point blank range where smoke and fire obscured the opposing sides. Wounded were lost in the woods and underbrush and burned to death when the leaves and fallen branches caught fire. Soldiers said afterwards that it must be what hell looked like. After two days fighting, the armies were awash in a sea of blood. There were 11,000 Confederate casualties and 17,500 Federal casualties.[45]

Grant had only begun. In one of the great turning points of the war, he ordered another move around Lee's left flank. The Army of the Potomac had retreated after the battles on the Peninsula, retreated after Second Bull Run, retreated after Fredericksburg, and retreated after Chancellorsville. It did not retreat now. Grant ordered the Army to again move by Lee's left, trying to get between Lee and Richmond. When they realized it was moving to fight again and not retreat, the Army of the Potomac found a new fighting spirit and cheered Grant.[46]

Grant's Army next pitched into Lee at Spotsylvania Courthouse on the edge of the Wilderness. More desperate fighting at point blank range with bayonets and rifle butts. More extraordinary casualties on both sides and once again at battle's end, more movement to the South. Grant was supposed to be supported in these attacks by the Army of the James commanded by Ben Butler. Butler was a political general who was promoted because he was a War Democrat. Butler moved so slowly as to draw no response from Lee and managed to let his Army be bottled up on the Peninsula by a force a tenth the size of his army. Butler had enough troops to capture the rail center at Petersburg or the capital Richmond but did neither, missing two chances to end the war a year earlier and save thousands of lives.

Grant attacked Lee again at a road junction named Cold Harbor and lost thousands of men in a failed frontal attack. He later admitted he should never have made the attack. The Overland Campaign had cost the Army of the Potomac 55,000 men and the Confederates 35,000 casualties.[47] Grant could make up these losses, but the ineluctable logic of numbers made the Army of Northern Virginia a wasting asset. This campaign gave rise to the accusation that Grant was a butcher, that he won only because of having a superiority in numbers that made his success inevitable. Grant managed to pen Lee up in Petersburg, and even Lee admitted if it became a siege, it was only a matter of time until the end of the fight for the Army of Northern Virginia.

Grant's success was never inevitable. McClellan had far outnumbered Lee on the Peninsula and at Antietam but had failed to aggressively

4. States' Rights as Revisionist History

attack him and end the war at either place. Analysis of the battles fought by Grant, save Cold Harbor, shows that Lee consistently lost more men in each battle than Grant based upon the percentage of men lost compared to the percentage engaged in the combat. As for Cold Harbor, all of Lee's apologists seem to have forgotten the battle of Malvern Hill in 1862 on the Peninsula, where Lee lost 5,565 men in a frontal assault on trenches and artillery that should never have been made. At Gettysburg on the third day, Lee ordered Pickett's charge, an attack on entrenched Union troops holding the center of the Union line. The attack began a mile from their objective and cost his army over 7,000 men. Lee was aggressive and a risk taker, but often the butcher's bill for his audacity were losses the South could not replace, and he had never fought a general like Grant, nor did he ever successfully invade the North or achieve a knockout blow.

Various politicians, the press and the peace movement criticized Grant because of the combat losses and pressured Lincoln to get rid of him and end the war. But Lincoln stayed the course and did not give up the general who would fight for the cause of the Union. Lincoln faced something that had never happened before, an election in the middle of a civil war. Lincoln was challenged by Democrats who nominated George McClellan for President. McClellan promised to end the war on terms favorable to the South. Atlanta fell that fall, and Lincoln could rightfully claim the North was finally winning the protracted conflict. Public opinion, the Republican Party, the press and the Army coalesced around Lincoln.

Lincoln by this time had lost any reservations he had about emancipation and supported the passage of the Thirteenth Amendment, forever ending slavery. Lincoln and others were concerned that since the Emancipation Proclamation was a military order its terms would lapse with the end of the war. There was by then substantial and broad support for an amendment to the Constitution ending slavery. Thinking had changed from the issue of slavery being a matter of state law to being one of national scope, demanding national action. Even politicians from the border states recognized that abolition's time had come. With over a hundred thousand Black men in Union blue, Lincoln knew it was time for them and their families and descendants after hundreds of years in bondage on American soil to be permanently free, free at last.

In April 1864, the Senate, by a two-thirds majority, passed the proposed amendment, but it failed in the House of Representatives. However, once Lincoln weathered the election of November 1864, he went back to the lame duck House in January 1865. The Amendment passed with just

The Constitution and American Racism

enough votes and by the end of 1865 had been ratified nearly unanimously by the states still in the Union. There had not been an amendment to the Constitution in over 40 years, and this one changed the Constitution in a way that more closely represented the ideal of liberty and justice for all that the Declaration of Independence proclaimed.

The war sadly continued. It was clear to everyone that the South was defeated, and the end was a matter of time. When Petersburg fell, Richmond would fall. Lee's Army of Virginia was wasting away in a siege that could have only one outcome. It lost men every day as they were killed and wounded in combat defending the lines around Petersburg, and desertion became a problem. The very old and the very young now appeared more frequently on the battlefield for the rebels. The rebel army was poorly fed and poorly clothed, supported by tenuous supply lines under attack by Federal forces at all points.

In the West, William Tecumseh Sherman had defeated Joe Johnston's rebel army and John Bell Hood and captured Atlanta. The one-armed Texan John Bell Hood took over after Johnston was dismissed by Jefferson Davis and managed to destroy what was left of the Confederate Army by ill-advised and hopeless counterattacks attempting to distract Sherman. After capturing Atlanta, Sherman embarked on his march to the sea, tearing out a huge swath of the Confederacy and destroying any military forces near his army and any places, supplies, or anything else that could help the Confederate armies.

The forts on Mobile Bay had fallen to Admiral Farragut after he damned the torpedoes. While the occasional blockade runner made landfall, the business of smuggling war supplies into the southern states from the sea was almost undone. Foreign powers had rejected any idea of giving aid to the Confederacy and did business with Confederates only on a cash basis. But the dying went on to little or no purpose from the South's standpoint and because it had to from the Union standpoint. There would be only one outcome, unconditional surrender.

By Christmas of 1864 Sherman had made it to Savannah on the Georgia coast. Resupplied and reinforced, he moved north into the Carolinas to destroy military forces that rallied around rebel General Joe Johnston. In Virginia, Lee knew he had to escape Petersburg before his Army dissolved. When he left the long lines of trenches around Petersburg, in April 1865, Richmond fell. The Army of Northern Virginia was in its death throes but its soldiers tried to escape to someplace where they could be fed and perhaps fight another day. The Union forces pursued them to ground at

4. States' Rights as Revisionist History

Appomattox. Lee asked for terms on Palm Sunday, April 9, 1865. Grant gave the same terms, unconditional surrender, but softened them with provisions for paroling the rebel troops, permitting officers to keep sidearms and permitting those who had horses and mules to keep them. Joe Johnston down in North Carolina asked Sherman for terms and the military game was up.

Lincoln visited Richmond on April 4, 1865. Lincoln never believed the states could legally or constitutionally secede. He never believed the Confederacy was a nation. But now he had captured the capital of treason and the end was in sight because his armies had destroyed rebel armies wherever they could be found. The war for the Union had become the war for the freedom of the slave. Lincoln and hundreds of thousands of dead Union soldiers, Black and white, did what the Constitution could not do, ended slavery and tried to live up to the promise of a "new nation, conceived in liberty, and dedicated to the proposition that all men are created equal."

On April 14, 1865, John Wilkes Booth snuck into the President's box at Ford's Theater and shot Abraham Lincoln. Lincoln died the next morning and joined his Union soldiers who had given their last full measure of devotion to the Union and to Lincoln's vision of a democratic Union without the curse of slavery. The great emancipator now belonged to the ages.

Unreconstructed Rebels
Oh, I'm a good old Rebel,
Now that's just what I am;
For this "fair land of Freedom"
I do not care a damn.
I'm glad I fit against it—
I only wish we'd won.
And I don't want no pardon
For anything I've done.

I hates the Constitution,
This great Republic too;
I hates the Freedmen's Buro,
In uniforms of blue.
I hates the nasty eagle,
With all his brag and fuss;
But the lyin', thievin' Yankees
I hates 'em wuss and wuss.

We got three hundred thousand
Befo' they conquered us.
They died of Southern fever

The Constitution and American Racism

> And Southern steel and shot;
> And I wish it was three million
> Instead of what we got.
>
> I can't take up my musket
> And fight 'em now no mo',
> But I ain't a-goin'to love' em,
> Now that is sartin sho';
> And I don't want no pardon
> For what I was and am;
> And I won't be reconstructed,
> And I do not give a damn.[48]

As more southern territory fell into Federal hands, something had to be done to politically reorganize these areas and provide not only some kind of government but protection and services for the freedmen. At some point the states of the Confederacy would once again participate in the Federal government. Lincoln had argued states could not secede so that there never was a Confederacy.[49] Others, Radical Republicans, argued seceded states had to be formally readmitted to the Union. The Radical Republicans were on the left of the party, had always been for abolition, and strongly supported the war. Their vision of Reconstruction was different from Lincoln's and envisioned protections for the freedmen and punishment for the South.[50]

There were three periods of Reconstruction: Presidential Reconstruction, Congressional Reconstruction, and Military Reconstruction and Redemption. For the whites, redemption occurred when the fight for equality was given up by the North and "white redeemers" came back to power. The "Redeemers" adopted segregation as Southern policy, with all its cultural and political implications for African Americans.[51]

Lincoln had thought about Reconstruction as early as 1863, and in his December 1863 Proclamation of Amnesty and Reconstruction he offered a full pardon and restoration of rights to all who took an oath of loyalty and pledged to accept the abolition of slavery. When the number of oath-taking reconstructed rebels equaled 10 percent of the votes from that state in the 1860 presidential election, the state could re-establish a government. Any new state constitution must abolish slavery, but the proclamation remained silent on the issue of suffrage for Blacks and issues of equality before the law.[52]

The Radical Republicans were not nearly so generous in the terms they thought acceptable for reconstruction of the states. The Wade-Davis Bill in July 1864 required that a majority of a state's white males must have

4. States' Rights as Revisionist History

pledged support for the federal Constitution before reconstruction could begin.[53] Only those who took the "Ironclad Oath," swearing that he had never voluntarily aided the Confederacy, could vote.

> I, A. B., do solemnly swear (or affirm) that I have never voluntarily borne arms against the United States since I have been a citizen thereof; that I have voluntarily given no aid, countenance, counsel, or encouragement to persons engaged in armed hostility thereto; that I have neither sought nor accepted nor attempted to exercise the functions of any office whatever, under any authority or pretended authority in hostility to the United States; that I have not yielded a voluntary support to any pretended government, authority, power or constitution within the United States, hostile or inimical thereto. And I do further swear (or affirm) that, to the best of my knowledge and ability, I will support and defend the Constitution of the United States, against all enemies, foreign and domestic; that I will bear true faith and allegiance to the same; that I take this obligation freely, without any mental reservation or purpose of evasion, and that I will well and faithfully discharge the duties of the office on which I am about to enter, so help me God.[54]

Lincoln exercised the pocket veto to keep the bill from becoming law. Clearly Lincoln leaned toward leniency in bringing the states back into the constitutional fold. But equally clear there were those in Congress who wanted citizens of the states to repudiate their secessionist governments in larger numbers. Both Lincoln and the Radical Republicans agreed that any new state governments must abolish slavery. The elephant in the room was suffrage for the freed slaves, and none of the proposals took a position on establishing equal rights for them. The Confederate states would have near Black majorities in many areas and did not want Black suffrage, let alone any requirement that Blacks be afforded equality of the law.

The first experiments in Reconstruction began in occupied Louisiana and did not bode well for those expecting the South to be repentant or willing to embrace abolition, suffrage and Black rights.

In 1863 the Union War Department created the American Freedmen's Inquiry Commission to offer support and guidance for the freed slaves in the South. The Commission was composed of three abolitionists who went South to study the problem. Ultimately, they recommended to Congress the establishment of the Freedmen's Bureau. Congress established the Bureau in March 1865 by way of creation of the Bureau of Refugees, Freedmen and Abandoned Lands. The Bureau was to provide clothing, food, and fuel to assist destitute freedmen and aid them in their transition to freedom. The Bureau could also provide small plots of land, 40 acres for rental and eventual sale if the United States could obtain title to the land. The Bureau's efforts included providing education, assisting freedmen with employment, mediating contractual disputes arising from work contracts with planters and other challenges, including the political and legal treatment of the freedmen.[55]

There were many issues involving the employment of former slaves by their masters with employment contracts that were one-sided and amounted to fraud, simply substituting a fictitious wage system for slavery. The Bureau as representatives of freedmen was often at the center of disputes arising from these contracts because of its efforts to counter white exploitation of available Black labor.

At the end of the war, whites who went south to invest in economic opportunities were soon labeled "carpetbaggers" by their Southern neighbors. The Southerners wanted neither abolition nor Northern entrepreneurs. They particularly wanted to retain political control at the state level to limit or deny Black participation in the political process, and that meant denying freedmen suffrage. They also wanted no part of Southern-born white Republicans who wanted to help Blacks; these whites were named "scalawags" by their Southern brethren.[56]

The freedmen were acutely aware that economic freedom and the right to vote were keys to their survival within the white southern political structure. Many former southern states unashamedly sought to deny them suffrage and even refused to acknowledge the abolition of slavery. As the war entered its final stages there was economic and political dislocation throughout the South. As southern soldiers came home there was resistance to anything that smacked of Reconstruction or equal treatment of the former slaves.

The second phase of Reconstruction policy began with Lincoln's assassination, when Presidential Reconstruction fell into Vice President Andrew Johnson's hands. Presidential Reconstruction meant Johnson would set the terms for entry of the states into the Union, deciding when there were enough loyal Southerners and when they could have their own local governments.

"Andrew Johnson was the queerest character that ever occupied the White House."[57] Part of his legacy on the American political landscape was that he was the first President to be impeached. His political history during the war suggested that as a pro–Union Democrat his Reconstruction policies would be punitive. He told Blacks during the war that "I will indeed be your Moses and lead you through the Red Sea of war and bondage, to a fairer future of liberty and peace."[58] Johnson's

4. States' Rights as Revisionist History

Reconstruction Proclamations in May 1865 required participants in the rebellion to pledge loyalty to the Union and support for emancipation as a path to amnesty and pardon. These proclamations also required certain classes of rebels, former Confederate officials and large-scale property holders, to apply individually for Presidential pardons.

The war ended in a total Union military victory with the South prostrate and economically ruined. Many Southerners now claimed that they had been reluctant rebels, forced by events to cast their lot with secession. However, when it appeared that Johnson was not going to be the radical Reconstructionist that his pre-presidential rhetoric reflected, there was less denial and more defiance by former white rebels. Johnson handed out pardons like candy and showed an inclination to policies that were more forgiving and helpful to the re-establishment of white rule.[59]

With Johnson as President there were no mass arrests of rebel traitors. There were no trials, with two exceptions. Lee, Johnston, Longstreet, Forrest, all the Confederate generals went home—despite the fact that their wartime service was precisely the definition of treason in the Constitution. Only two Confederate officers were arrested and tried. The Swiss-born commander of Andersonville prison was tried for the cruel and indifferent treatment of Union prisoners that resulted in the deaths of thousands. Another Confederate officer was arrested in North Carolina by federal forces for the same reasons but acquitted. Former Confederate civil officials fared about as well. Although Jefferson Davis was held in a federal prison in Florida, he was never tried for treason and went home after two years. Alexander Stephens, the Confederate vice-president, was held briefly in a federal prison, and he too went home and later showed up in Congress with former rebel generals Joe Johnston, Wade Hampton, John B. Gordon.[60]

"Their whole thought and time will be given to plans for getting things back as near to slavery as possible."[61]

President Johnson was able to appoint governors for the former states of the Confederacy to manage the formation of new governments. State legislators were elected, along with Congressional representatives. The men Johnson appointed were a mixed bag of those who had claimed not to be complicit in secession or swore they were reluctant Confederates. But all proved to be reactionaries on the issues of emancipation, abolition, and suffrage and equal rights for Blacks. Johnson also interfered in the work of the Freedmen's Bureau and tried, with success, to remove Black soldiers from the South as soon as possible.

Johnson's policies emboldened unreconstructed rebels who sought to reassert white authority and control the Black population by limiting their civil rights in fundamental ways.

Blacks sought independence in their dealings with whites on labor issues. The whites wanted to reassert some form of control to thwart Black economic freedom. Labor contracts were oppressive because of their terms, and often enforced through legislation. State law required Blacks to be employed or they were treated as vagrants who could then be arrested and jailed. These jailed Blacks were rented out to white southern planters. The states passed "Black Codes" that, while they permitted Blacks to own and rent land, marry, make contracts and sue or be sued but not to testify against whites, regulated employment contracts and provided punishment for those who were allegedly in breach of such contracts.[62]

States made it illegal for Blacks to own weapons, imposed hunting restrictions and taxes on those who owned dogs and guns, outlawed hunting on Sundays, and made it illegal to take timber, berries, fruit or anything of value from private property. Enforcement of these rules and regulations lay in the hands of white men, not Blacks. The southern criminal justice system made no effort to enforce the law equally among whites and Blacks.

Congressional testimony revealed that hundreds of freedmen in Texas were assaulted and killed from 1865 to 1868. Many indictments were made but no one was convicted. The reaction by Union generals charged with the occupation of some states was to suspend the "Black Codes" and attempt to enforce the law equally.[63]

Before war's end only five northern states, all in New England, had given Blacks the right to vote. The right to vote is an essential basis for democratic government; it is the essential mark of citizenship. Only by voting can a citizen hope to change his government and hold it responsible for its direction and policies. Here the deck was stacked against the freedmen. Unreconstructed rebels adamantly opposed Black suffrage. Before his death it was clear that Lincoln favored Black suffrage as a component of Reconstruction. But President Johnson helped reinforce white southern opinions on Black suffrage when he said it would result in "a tyranny such as this continent has never witnessed."[64]

The Radical Republicans were men in the Senate like Charles Sumner, Ben Wade, and Henry Wilson, and in the House, Thaddeus Stevens, George W. Julian and James M. Ashley. All these men had a long-standing commitment to abolition and the Union. They all believed that slavery and the rights of Blacks were of paramount concern over other political

4. States' Rights as Revisionist History

considerations. All, to some extent, had been conditioned by a belief in natural rights, civil rights, political rights and equal rights.

Senator Sumner believed natural law required equality in civil rights. He also believed the southern states had committed "suicide" when they seceded and that their status at war's end was akin to their being territories. In a speech before the Senate, Sumner referred to the Constitution's guarantee of a republican form of government and maintained that any government that denied citizens equality before the law was not a Republic. This was not President Johnson's idea of government and it was not a white Southerner's idea of a government. It was clear to Radical Republicans that Johnson was abandoning protection of the natural rights, equality, suffrage, and other political rights, in favor of a white Reconstruction that would deny these rights to freedmen. So began the struggle that was Congressional Reconstruction, which led to Johnson's impeachment.

The Thirteenth Amendment was brief:

Section 1.
Neither slavery nor involuntary servitude, except as a punishment for crime whereof the party shall have been duly convicted, shall exist within the United States, or any place subject to their jurisdiction.

Section 2.
Congress shall have power to enforce this article by appropriate legislation.[65]

Section 2 of the Amendment was the enforcement provision. In 1866, Senator Lyman Trumbull, a moderate Republican Senator from Illinois, brought two bills before Congress. Trumbull thought he could reconcile Johnson's Reconstruction efforts with the Radical Republicans' demands for equality for the freedman. He had two ideas. The first was an act extending the life of the Freedmen's Bureau, providing pay for its employees and giving it enforcement authority to punish white officials seeking to deny Blacks "civil rights belonging to white persons."

The second idea resulted in the Civil Rights Act of 1866, meant to enforce the Thirteenth Amendment. The Civil Rights Act was unprecedented. It defined as national citizens any persons born in the United States. The Act also defined a bundle of rights all national citizens were to enjoy: the right to make contracts and bring lawsuits, and the right to guaranteed equal benefit of the laws for the protection of life and property. The Act was necessary because with little more than a year since the end of the Civil War, southern governments and law enforcement had acted to discriminate against Blacks. The Act authorized federal attorneys, marshals, and Freedmen's Bureau employees to bring actions on behalf of Blacks in federal court. It provided penalties for violation of the Act to include fines and imprisonment. Johnson vetoed the Act and a Congress, still composed of Union men, for the first time in its history, overrode a presidential veto.[66]

Following in the footsteps of the Civil Rights Act of 1866, Congress wrote, debated and passed the Fourteenth Amendment. It made all persons born or naturalized in the United States, citizens of the nation and the state where they resided:

> All persons born or naturalized in the United States, and subject to the jurisdiction thereof, are citizens of the United States and of the state wherein they reside.[67]

The amendment also protected the rights that accompanied citizenship and prohibited states from abridging these rights, "nor shall any state deprive any person of life, liberty, or property, without due process of law; nor deny to any person within its jurisdiction the equal protection of the laws."

The three-fifths clause had caused southern states to be over-represented in Congress before the Civil War. The Radical Republicans and others realized that counting the southern population for Congressional representation and the Electoral College would include freed slaves as a whole person. Counting them without giving them suffrage would increase southern representation in Congress. Because of southern resistance to Black suffrage the drafters and backers of the Fourteenth Amendment added Section 2, which provided a penalty when states failed to enfranchise Blacks (or other citizens). States that did not recognize suffrage for Blacks and other citizens would have their representation reduced in the Electoral College and Congress by the percentage of the population disenfranchised by the states.

> Representatives shall be apportioned among the several states according to their respective numbers, counting the whole number of persons in each state, excluding Indians not taxed. But when the right to vote at any election for the choice of electors for President and Vice President of the United States, Representatives in Congress, the executive and judicial officers of a state, or the members of the legislature thereof, is denied to any of the male inhabitants of such state, being twenty-one years of age and citizens of the United States, or in any way abridged, except for participation in rebellion, or other crime, the basis of representation therein shall be reduced in the proportion which the number of such male citizens shall bear to the whole number of male citizens twenty-one years of age in such state.[68]

4. States' Rights as Revisionist History

Section 3 of the 14th Amendment prohibited service by anyone as an elected official of the national or state governments—Senator, Congressman, President or Vice President, elector, civil or military office holder—who had taken an oath to the Constitution, but then later engaged in insurrection or rebellion or giving aid and comfort to the Confederacy. This was Reconstruction by way of disqualifying former rebel officials, civilian and military, who prior to their Confederate service, had taken an oath to the U.S. Constitution. Unfortunately, there was a provision that permitted such person to serve if a two-thirds majority of each house of Congress removed the disability. Many former rebels would serve in the federal and state governments.

The military was tapped to implement Congressional Reconstruction. Radical Republicans believed that Presidential Reconstruction had been such a failure that Congress passed the Reconstruction Act of 1867, which divided the South into five military districts and authorized the military commanders of these districts to use force to protect lives and property. The former states of the Confederacy were required to write new constitutions providing suffrage for Blacks, which had to be approved by a majority of voters, and they had to ratify the 14th Amendment. Additional legislation authorized military commanders to register voters and hold elections. A *Habeas Corpus* Act passed by Congress permitted citizens to remove cases to federal court to avoid racist local courts and abolished the system where planters could hold freedmen to labor until a debt was paid, thus striking at a system that was tantamount to economic peonage. These provisions did result in control of many of the southern states by Union men who supported Black suffrage and equal treatment.

Using the powers of the Reconstruction Act, General Philip Sheridan removed the governor of Texas, as well as numerous other officeholders. New constitutions were written by Blacks and their white supporters, called by their southern enemies "scalawags" and "carpetbaggers." These state constitutions guaranteed Blacks civil and political rights. The whites continued to attack Blacks at the polls, and Congress in 1869 approved the 15th Amendment, which on its face forbade the federal or state governments from denying the right to vote on racial grounds.

Violence against the freedmen had begun during the war and continued after the defeat of the rebel armies. First, men called "white regulators" intimidated and murdered freedmen for no reason but to show that they could, hoping thereby to terrorize the Black population. The Ku Klux

The Constitution and American Racism

Klan organized violence and murdered Blacks, burned their churches, schools and homes to terrorize and intimidate them. The level of violence was appalling, and Congress finally responded with the Ku Klux Klan Act of 1871. The Act made attempts to prevent Blacks from voting, holding office, and serving on juries federal crimes enforceable in federal courts. The Act could have been enforced by federal troops and the writ of *habeas corpus* could have been suspended, but the violence continued. The Klan had been founded in 1866 in Pulaski, Tennessee. Its first leader was the former rebel general Nathan Bedford Forrest. The Klan spread quickly across the South and was an instrument of intimidation, and terror. They lynched Black men and women everywhere in the South and were committed to restoring white power and eliminating Republican efforts to reconstruct a South with racial equality.

As the years passed, federal commitment to civil rights declined until in 1876 another presidential election was contested. In 1876 Samuel J. Tilden ran for President on the Democratic ticket and Rutherford B. Hayes on the Republican ticket. For the third time in the Republic's history there was a disputed election, with Tilden winning a majority of the popular vote and just one vote short of an Electoral College victory. But there were disputes as to the authenticity of the Electoral College votes from Oregon, South Carolina, Louisiana, and Florida, all states but Oregon with white and Reconstruction governments that nominated electors who voted differently. An independent commission decided that the Republican votes should be counted. These results could be overturned by Congress. Southerners in the Senate threatened to filibuster any vote and Hayes, the Republican, agreed to withdraw federal troops from the South. The Southerners withdrew their threat.

As Congressional Reconstruction began to collapse, federal troops were removed from the southern states, and white-only "Redeemer" governments replaced Reconstruction governments that had Black and white elected officials and legislators who were pro–Reconstruction. In 1876, only Florida, South Carolina and Louisiana still had Reconstruction governments and federal troops there to keep the peace. Among other compromises with Southerners, President Hayes agreed to remove federal troops from those three states in return for their electoral votes. He thus became President in March 1877. Reconstruction was dead and with it any hope of Black equal rights in the South. "When the bayonets shall depart ... then look out for the reaction. Then the bottom rail will descend from the top of the fence."[69]

4. States' Rights as Revisionist History

The "White Redeemers" were a coalition of ex-rebels and political strains of all kind, mostly Democrat, but all united in ensuring white power and segregation would be the main policies of the South. No good would come of any of this. The federal government created by the Constitution and saved by Lincoln would fail to enforce his promise of a "new liberty." The Constitution had endorsed and protected a system of slavery that was inconsistent with all the professed values of the founding fathers. It protected that system with a clause that did not count slaves as free men but as three-fifths of a person, so the South could control the destiny of the country. It insured there would be no President elected by a majority of Americans but rather by an obscure panel known as the Electoral College, subject to manipulation in terms of its membership and graft as shown in the election of 1876.

The three branches of government had acted before the Civil War in concert to protect slavery. The deadlock was only broken by the moral outrage of Americans and the election of Lincoln. The South unwisely seceded to protect their peculiar institution and insanely, in Sherman's words, attacked the Union at Fort Sumter. Over 750,000 Americans died over slavery, not states' rights. Once the war began, slaves were no longer an abstraction for most of the Union, and certainly its soldiers who viewed slavery up close in the South. Lincoln acted to emancipate and then free the slaves through the abolition of slavery by the Thirteenth Amendment. The Fourteenth Amendment made the freedmen citizens and gave Congress the authority to protect them. The Fifteenth Amendment was meant to guarantee Black voting rights by prohibiting federal and state governments from depriving any citizen the right to vote on racial grounds.

None of these amendments would have been possible if the South had not seceded. While an admirable attempt to guarantee freedom, suffrage and equal rights for the former slaves, the amendments merely made "Redeemer" governments in the South more imaginative in the ways they denied Blacks the right to vote. Intimidation, poll taxes, reading tests, recitations of local state constitutions and many more contrived tests were designed to exclude Blacks from the polls. After the election of 1876 the federal government totally withdrew all troops and support from the South. This put the fate of the former slaves into the hands of men who had been buying, selling, and whipping them a few years before. The Constitution continued to provide a framework for national government that ignored segregation and worse. The promise of a republican form of government made by Madison in the Constitution failed again to make "all men created equal." Racism became the driving force in southern politics and continues to survive under the protection of the government created by the Constitution.

5

"The Constitution is colorblind"

Redeemers

The Constitution failed as a governing document for the people of United States because it recognized and protected slavery and was impossible to amend to abolish slavery. "Slavery was the Constitution's original sin. The Framers had not merely tolerated slavery but had enshrined it in the Constitution."[1]

Once slavery was abolished by a civil war, millions of slaves were cast upon the shores of southern benevolence. Southerners rejected the idea that slavery was abolished and that the freedmen could ever be their equal.[2] White Southerners set their minds to reestablishing a society and economy where, despite abolition, they were in charge. "Redeemers, the indigenous white business class, and what remained of the old planter class"[3] sought by violence and manipulation of state politics and the legal system to reestablish an unreconstructed South by depicting the Republican state governments as being "wastefully corrupt regimes dominated by ignorant former slaves acting as dupes for vicious scalawags and greedy carpetbaggers."[4] This effort was based on racism, the same racism that perpetuated and justified slavery. "Reconstruction was a tragedy … followed by an era when racism became more deeply embedded in national politics and culture."[5]

Racism was the legacy of slavery and inequality was fostered and perpetuated by the rule of law. Despite the Constitution's guarantee of a republican form of government in Article IV, the federal government for almost 100 years after the Civil War and the abolition of slavery did nothing to prevent southern states from terrorizing Blacks to keep them from voting and exercising fundamental liberties guaranteed all citizens by the Constitution, the Civil Rights Act of 1866 and the Fourteenth Amendment. The Constitution protected racism.[6] Racism became the political issue that elected and perpetuated southern governments that made segregation and discrimination legal.

After 1876, the federal government failed to act when the South legalized segregation and unequal treatment of Blacks at all levels of government and society. None of the southern states had republican forms of government when they sanctioned terrorism, suppressed Black voters, and legalized segregation. We know the southern governments had no republican form of government because a Southerner, James Madison, defined a republican form of government in *Federalist* No. 39 as one "which derives its powers from the great body of the people.... It is essential to such a government that it be derived from the great body of the society, not from an inconsiderable proportion or favored class of it...."

The Thirteenth Amendment abolished slavery. The Fourteenth Amendment defined a citizen as a natural born person, therefore clearly making the freedmen citizens, and the Fifteenth Amendment made it clear that Blacks were not to be deprived of the right to vote. The campaign of terror and other policies contrived to deprive Blacks of their political rights as citizens were clearly in violation of the Constitution and any definition of equality of law. Any southern state that deprived Blacks of the right to vote deprived a considerable portion of its population of their basic rights. Any southern state that did this was not a republican form of government by Madison's definition.

By the 1890s every southern state government had devised a way to eliminate Black voter participation in elections. The percentage of Black participation in elections went from sixty percent to two percent.[7] Using the test formulated by the architect of the Constitution, none of the southern state governments had republican forms of government when they disenfranchised Blacks.[8]

The rule of law is based on the idea of equality. The government's citizens are not above the law.[9] There must be equality in the way the law treats all men and women. Equal justice before the law. There must be equality in the way the legislatures make the law and the way courts interpret the law to protect all men and women. The judges selected to administer and enforce the law must be composed of men and women beyond any kind political or cultural bias. There can be no rule of law without equality regardless of race, money or class.

The pre–Civil War Constitution gave the South too much power through the three-fifths compromise for determining representation in

5. "The Constitution is colorblind"

the House of Representatives and in the Electoral College. The Constitution stopped the amendment process dead in its tracks by requiring super majorities for change. The Senate became a roadblock to prevent abolition and civil rights from becoming national law. Any one of these provisions made the Constitution undemocratic and the Civil War inevitable if slavery was to be abolished.

Once the South seceded the only way for Lincoln to save the Union, free the slaves and abolish slavery was to ignore the Constitution. The first hundred days of Lincoln's presidency saw one calamity after another, which Lincoln could only respond to by expanding his executive powers through the war powers given the President in Article II of the Constitution. This reliance on the War Powers Clause would have a legacy of unforeseen consequences for future presidents and future conflicts. Emancipation was accomplished by a military order, and the Thirteenth Amendment abolishing slavery was possible only because the southern states had seceded and could not block it. Once the slaves had been freed and Lincoln was dead, the only protection the freedmen had was the federal government.

Racism and vestiges of the pro-slavery "compromises" in the Constitution thwarted recognition of Black emancipation and equal protection of the law. After the beginning of Congressional Reconstruction and Grant's election as President, the federal government endeavored through the Fourteenth and Fifteenth Amendments, the Civil Rights Acts, and Enforcement Acts to require the states to acknowledge Black voting rights and protect Black civil rights. It was a diminishing effort because as time passed the North grew weary of the task, and the federal government politically moved to a tacit acknowledgment that white Southerners would retake control of state and local governments.[10]

While the executive branch and Congress tried to suppress white violence and political fraud during Reconstruction, the Supreme Court's record protecting Black lives and liberties was abysmal. The white terrorism in the South was unworthy of a democratic society or any political system. The violence was meant to suppress Black voting and the exercise of Black civil liberties. It was meant to encourage Black exodus from the South. The brutality and horror of lynching was the victory of lawlessness and evil over the idea of equality, and after the withdrawal of federal troops the federal government did nothing to stop the inhumanity.

Lynching and other coercive tactics employed by white Southerners are the current definition of terrorism used by the federal government in the "war on terror," "the unlawful use of force and violence against persons or property to intimidate or coerce a government, the civilian population, or any segment thereof, in furtherance of political or social objectives" (28 C.F.R. Section 0.85).

"Northern Aggression"

In the beginning, no one thought much of the Supreme Court. It didn't have a home—it moved from New York to Philadelphia to Washington—and nobody seemed to want the job of Chief Justice. Within months of his appointment, John Jay resigned as Chief Justice to become governor of New York, and Alexander Hamilton when offered the job respectfully declined it to go home to New York and practice law.[11] At the Constitutional Convention the argument was that the new federal government should have its own court system because "a check on the legislature is necessary," and "the courts of the states cannot be entrusted with the administration of the national laws."

Some delegates were suspicious of how a federal court system would fit in with existing local and state courts and were opposed to judicial review by the Supreme Court. Hamilton in his brief in support of the federal courts, *Federalist* No. 78, famously said that the judicial branch was the "least dangerous" and "weakest of the three departments of power." In its first years the Court did little to draw attention to its workings.

The first judiciary act created local federal trial courts in each state, courts of appeal staffed by two Supreme Court judges, and a local district judge.[12] This lack of permanently staffed courts of appeal meant that the Supreme Court justices had to "ride circuit" in the appellate courts.[13]

The only real decision by the Supreme Court that aroused any passion was *Chisholm v. Georgia* in 1793.[14] In *Chisholm* a creditor of the State of Georgia, a private citizen, sued Georgia to collect Revolutionary War debts incurred for the sale of military equipment to the state. Nearly all the states had gone deeply into debt to local merchants and foreign governments to prosecute the war. Despite the confiscation of loyalist property, the states had no money to repay their debts. *Chisholm* was heard by the Supreme Court and resulted in a judgment that ordered Georgia to pay the creditor, and within months the Eleventh Amendment was passed by the states in Congress making it impossible for private citizens to sue them. Justice Wilson wrote in *Chisholm* that the people were the supreme sovereignty and not the state. The states justified their action in passing

5. "The Constitution is colorblind"

the Eleventh Amendment by an ancient common law doctrine meant to protect the king from suit. After fighting a revolution to get rid of a sovereign who acted arbitrarily and without restraint, the states decided to adopt the doctrine of sovereign immunity to protect themselves from their creditors and later citizens whose rights they violated.

A Southerner, John Marshall, became Chief Justice of the Supreme Court in 1801 and molded and reshaped it into an important branch of government so that, contrary to Hamilton's argument, it was dangerous. Marshall was a staunch Federalist and relied on the doctrine of judicial review in *Marbury v. Madison*[15] to establish the Court's power. In *Marbury* he determined that the Court had authority through the doctrine of judicial review to decide whether the acts of Congress and the executive were constitutional. Judicial review "is the essence of judicial duty."[16]

Marshall was a slave holder who bought and sold slaves all his life. He protected those who owned slaves because he believed slaves were property and their owners deserved to have their ownership rights in human beings protected like any other kind of property.[17] In *Adams v. Woods*,[18] Marshall interpreted a federal statute providing payment of informants in slave trade cases to make it more difficult for them to recover payment for their information; in *Scott v. Negro London*,[19] he reversed a lower court that freed a slave because of the owner's failure to follow the provisions of a Virginia law meant to limit the importation of slaves into Virginia; and in *Scott v. Negro Ben*,[20] he reversed a lower court's finding that a slave was free because his owner failed to comply with a Maryland law that required registration of slaves brought into the state. In *Mima Queen and Child v. Hepburn*,[21] Mima, a slave, sued for her freedom, claiming she was descended from a relative who been brought to the colonies free. Because she could prove this only by hearsay testimony, Marshall rejected the proposition that hearsay could support her claims of freedom. In *Brig Caroline v. United States*,[22] Marshall ruled the government could not seize a ship that had originally been fitted for the slave trade in a U.S. port, thus setting up a precedent to hinder enforcement of the federal act prohibiting American ships from participating in the slave trade.

In *The Antelope*,[23] a slave ship whose owners claimed foreign registry had been seized in U.S. waters for violation of the act prohibiting slave trade by ships with American crews. It had 212 Africans aboard, and ownership of the slaves was claimed by various parties. The case had a long procedural history but was finally decided in 1825. Marshall admitted that slavery was "contrary to the law of nature," but he found it was consistent with the law of nations recognizing the right of foreigners to engage in the slave trade.[24] The slaves were divided among the various litigants, with some being returned to Africa.[25]

Marshall reformed the Supreme Court, making it the institution we know today, and his decisions are still important and sometimes controversial, particularly those that invoked judicial review by the Court of the acts of the other branches of government. He worked hard to make an effective court, one that had power within the context of the constitutional idea of separation of powers. This development of the Court made it more a branch of government and less an afterthought proposed to protect federal law.[26] Both Justices Marshall and his successor Roger Taney stated during their careers that slavery was either an "abomination" or a "blight on the national character," but saw their jobs as interpreters of the Constitution, and both believed the Constitution protected property and that slaves were property. To be sure, the rule of law according to Marshall was that slavery was legal and slaves were property with no rights.

Marshall was followed by another Southerner, Roger Taney, who had freed his slaves and once condemned slavery. But with age Taney hardened his position on slavery, eventually calling abolitionism "northern aggression."[27] As the author of the *Dred Scott*[28] decision in 1857, he did as much to bring on the Civil War as any "fire-eating" Southerner by his finding that Blacks were property, not people, and had no rights, and slavery could not be limited by Congress. His opinion swept away the Missouri Compromise and other attempts made after it to limit the spread of slavery as unconstitutional.

After the Civil War began, Taney found Lincoln's suspension of the writ of *habeas corpus* to arrest traitors after the firing on Fort Sumpter unconstitutional, but Lincoln ignored him. This was ironic because the man who appointed Taney to the Supreme Court, Andrew Jackson, had ignored Chief Justice Marshall's orders in the Cherokee removal cases. Taney's tenure as Chief Justice was framed by his belief that the Constitution recognized and protected slavery, and he in turn protected it in his opinions. This belief was based on an interpretation of the Constitution as a pro-slavery document from its inception. There would be no constitutional way to end slavery. The South could prevent a constitutional amendment in Congress, and the Court could find unconstitutional any law trying to limit or abolish slavery. In the Taney Court the rule of law was slavery.

5. "The Constitution is colorblind"

The post–Civil War Supreme Court proved itself no friend of the Black man and aided and abetted the spread of Jim Crow and the return of white supremacy in the South through its decisions. The antebellum Supreme Court had found only two acts of Congress unconstitutional, while the post–Civil War Court found twelve acts unconstitutional between 1865 and 1872.

After the Confederacy collapsed, the South was in a state of legal and economic ruin. Returning rebel soldiers and other whites turned violently on the Black population and their white supporters, blaming them for their misfortune. The enabling/enforcement clause of the Thirteenth Amendment provided that "Congress shall have power to enforce this article by appropriate legislation."[29] Pursuant to this clause, Congress passed the Civil Rights Act of 1866. The Act provided:

> That all persons born in the United States and not subject to any foreign power, excluding Indians not taxed, are hereby declared to be citizens of the United States; and such citizens, of every race and color, without regard to any previous condition of slavery or involuntary servitude ... shall have the same right, in every State and Territory in the United States to make and enforce contracts; to sue, be parties and give evidence, to inherit, purchase, lease, sell, hold, and convey real and personal property, and to full and equal benefit of all laws and proceedings for the security of person and property, as is enjoyed by white citizens....[30]

The 1866 Civil Rights Act was vetoed by President Andrew Johnson, but Congress overrode Johnson's veto, making it the law of the land. It survives today as 42 U.S. Code, Section 1981.

Johnson had in part argued that the Constitution did not give Congress power to regulate acts of the states. This argument ignored the enabling clause of the Thirteenth Amendment. Senator Lyman Trumbull, one of its authors, said in support of the Civil Rights Act of 1866, "To be a citizen carries with it some rights.... They are those inherent, fundamental rights which belong to free citizens or free men in all countries, such as the rights enumerated in this bill, and they belong to them in all the states of the Union."[31]

There were a few victories in the Supreme Court for freedmen in the immediate aftermath of the Civil War. In the *Matter of Turner*,[32] a federal court of appeals case, Chief Justice Salmon P. Chase of the U.S. Supreme Court, sitting as a Court of Appeals judge, wrote that where a state law required that the employer teach an indentured servant apprentice to read, he must also provide that education for a Black indentured apprentice, and in 1872, the Civil Rights Act was the basis for a decision that a Black woman who had bought a first-class ticket on a train had a right to ride in the first-class section (*Stevens v. Richmond, Fredericksburg, and Potomac R.R. Co.*).

The Congressional authors of the Thirteenth, Fourteenth and Fifteenth Amendments and Civil Rights Acts had intended them to apply to the states. Presidential Reconstruction led by Johnson had required the former Confederate states to ratify the Thirteenth Amendment before readmission to the Union, and Congressional Reconstruction required them to ratify the Fourteenth Amendment as a prerequisite to rejoin the Union. There was legal authority for the Supreme Court to act to protect Blacks in the North and South, but as time passed it wholly abandoned civil rights in the South and Black citizens throughout the United States.

At the Constitutional Convention in 1787, Madison and Hamilton argued that a Bill of Rights was unnecessary. However, both were proved wrong. During the ratification process there was great interest in adding a bill of rights to the Constitution. Madison and the Federalists committed to drafting a Bill of Rights in the First Congress despite Madison's comment that it was a "nauseous project of amendments." In the pre–Civil War history of the Republic, the assumption was based on the understanding of the delegates to the First Congress, and the Federalists, that the Bill of Rights, the first ten amendments to the Constitution, were a check on the federal but not state governments. The Supreme Court adopted this position in 1833 in *Barron v. Baltimore*,[33] where Chief Justice Marshall wrote that the Constitution limited the power of the national government, and this limitation extended to application of the Bill of Rights to the states. The Fourteenth Amendment was passed by the Republican Congress in 1866 to enable the federal government to define citizenship to include the freedmen and to intervene in the former Confederate states to protect Black Americans. The "privileges and immunities" clause in the Fourteenth Amendment was one of the rationales for the argument that the Bill of Rights could be enforced against the states. The privileges and immunities clause stated:

> All persons born or naturalized in the United States, and subject to the jurisdiction thereof, are citizens of the United States and of the state wherein they reside. No state shall make or enforce any law which shall abridge the privileges or immunities of citizens of the United States; nor shall any state deprive any person of life, liberty, or property, without due process of law; nor deny to any person within its jurisdiction the equal protection of the laws.[34]

5. "The Constitution is colorblind"

The drafter of this clause, Representative John A. Bingham of Ohio, had been clear that the language was meant to give Congress the power to enforce the Bill of Rights in the states.[35] The Constitution guarantees each state a republican form of government. While a "Republican Form of Government" is never defined by the Constitution, a government that terrorizes citizens to deprive them of their vote and basic civil liberties is clearly not one.

In 1873, the Republican state government of Louisiana gave a monopoly for the slaughtering of all animals in the City of New Orleans to one slaughterhouse, owned by Louisiana Republicans and supporters who were pro-reconstruction. In one of history's ironies, independent butchers, for the most part Confederate veterans and Democrats, challenged the monopoly, claiming it enslaved the butchers and was therefore a violation of both the Thirteenth Amendment because it was tantamount to slavery for those who did not benefit from the monopoly, and the Fourteenth Amendment because the state law creating the monopoly violated the privileges and immunities clause.

The butchers were represented by New Orleans lawyer, John A. Campbell, who had been a justice on the Supreme Court before the Civil War but resigned to serve the Confederacy as assistant secretary of war. Supreme Court Justice Miller dismissed both claims, finding that the amendments' "pervading purpose" was to protect the "freedom of the slave race." In a decision that had far reaching consequences for civil rights for Black Americans, Miller rejected the idea that the Fourteenth Amendment had been meant to apply the Bill of Rights to the states. Regardless of this finding it was clear that the Reconstruction Congress in the Fourteenth Amendment intended for the federal government to recognize the rights of all citizens and to protect them when states deprived them of these rights. In fact, the Civil Rights Acts and Amendments had been necessary because "unreconstructed rebels," "regulators," the Klan and "redeemers" sought to crush Black political power through Black Codes, terror and other means of voter intimidation and suppression. The federal government was the only recourse for protection from the terror sanctioned and the segregation imposed by the southern state governments, as they began to replace reconstruction governments with all white governments. The violence was so bad in Georgia during the 1870 election that some in Congress proposed punishment of Georgia, but a five-day filibuster in the Senate defeated the resolution.[36]

White Terror and Reconstruction

Lynching is an ugly chapter in American history that gets little public attention and no ownership by the perpetrators and the governments who did nothing to stop or punish it. In a country that glorifies the rule of law, Reconstruction was a period of white racist anarchy. Lynching was meant to suppress Black participation in politics and minimize their economic opportunities.[37] The "regulators" and organizations like the Klan sought to ensure the return of white power throughout the South, and to do this they intimidated, tortured, shot, hung, and burned publicly and in secret Black men, women and children. The South had been economically crippled by a self-inflicted wound, secession. By seceding and prosecuting a civil war that resulted in the deaths of hundreds of thousands of white Southerners and destruction of hundreds of millions of dollars in property, the secessionists had ruined the South. After the guns fell silent there were southern whites who told the freedmen that there was no Emancipation Proclamation or Thirteenth Amendment. By intimidating Blacks, white Southerners sought to create a labor pool very similar to slavery.

Historian Eric Foner has written: "[the] wave of counterrevolutionary terror that swept over large parts of the South between 1868 and 1871 lacks a counterpart ... in the American experience or in that of other Western Hemisphere societies that abolished slavery in the nineteenth century."[38]

Major General George Armstrong Custer (brevet) told Congress in 1866 that in Texas more than 500 former Confederates had been charged with murdering Blacks or white unionists, but none had been convicted.[39] The Freedmen's Bureau and the Union Army reported many lynchings that occurred in this period. Men and women were killed for not performing one sided labor contracts; not taking off their hats as a symbol of respect for white persons; not giving way to a buggy occupied by whites; trespass; and quarrels over livestock. Many lynching victims were raped, castrated or whipped.[40]

In 1871, ten Blacks were taken from a jail in South Carolina and shot and killed[41]; in the same year nine were lynched in Georgia.[42] Two hundred Blacks were killed in election violence in Louisiana in 1868 by the "White League."[43] Nearly one hundred fifty Blacks were killed in Colfax, Louisiana, in a massacre in 1873.[44] Estimates of Black and white Americans murdered during Reconstruction ranged from Union General Philip Sheridan's 3,500 during the period 1865–1875,[45] to Dorothy Sterling, who concluded that 20,000 were killed from 1868 to 1871.[46]

5. "The Constitution is colorblind"

Ida Wells-Barnett, a Black anti-lynching activist, estimated 10,000 Blacks were lynched from 1865 until 1890.[47] The numbers are elusive because of the chaos and unlawfulness in the immediate aftermath of the surrender at Appomattox, and because white authorities and governments weren't interested in keeping records of blatant lawlessness, which included crimes against Black Americans. Many Black people just disappeared.

Union Army officers, medical officers and Freedmen's Bureau personnel reported various atrocities perpetrated in 1865, after the end of the war:

1. Nancy, colored woman, ears cut off by a man by the name of Ferguson, or Foster, an overseer.
2. Mary Steel, one side of her head scalped, Died. She was with Nancy.
3. Jacob Steel, both ears cut off.
4. Amanda Steel, ears cut off.
5. Washington Booth, shot in the back while returning from work by William Harris of Pine Level, without provocation.
6. Sutton Jones, beard and chin cut off.
7. Robert, servant of Colonel Hough, was stabbed while at his home by a man wearing in part the garb of a Confederate soldier.
8. Ida, was struck on the head with a club by an overseer, died of her wound at this hospital.
9. James Monroe, cut across the throat while engaged in saddling a horse.

A Freedmen's Bureau Assistant Superintendent reported in July 1865:

1. Three Negroes were killed in the southern part of Dallas County; it is supposed by the Vaughn family. I twice tried to arrest them, but they escaped into the woods.
2. Mr. Dermot started to Selma with a Negro having a rope around his neck. He was seen dragging him in that way but returned home before he could have reached Selma. He did not report at Selma, and the Negro has never been heard of.
3. A Negro was killed in the calaboose of the city of Selma, by being beaten with a heavy club, also by [being] tied up by the thumbs clear of the floor, for three hours, and by further gross abuse, lasting more than a week.

4. At Bladen Springs, a freedman was chained to a tree and burned to death.
5. About two weeks later, and 15 miles from Bladen, another freedman was burned to death.
6. About the first of June, six miles west of Bladen, a freedman was hung. His body is still hanging.
7. About the last of May, a planter hung his servant (a woman) in presence of all the neighborhood. Said planter had killed this woman's husband about three weeks before.
8. About the last of April, two women were caught near a certain plantation in Clark County and hung. Their bodies are still suspended.
9. On the 19th of July, two freedmen were taken off the steamer Commodore Ferrand, tied and hung, then taken down, their heads cut off and their bodies thrown in the river.
10. July 11, two men took a woman off the same boat and threw her in the river. This woman had a coop with some chickens. They threw all in together and told her to go to the damned Yankees. The woman was drowned.[48]

This sad litany of violence and depravity is but a bare glimpse into crimes that continued throughout the South during Reconstruction in a war on largely defenseless freedmen. As the years passed more federal troops were withdrawn until there was no protection for the former slaves who were now citizens. State and county governments were wrested from Republican control by terror and fraud at the ballot box and in the legislatures and state courts. Considering this violence, Grant's administration requested and Congress passed three "Enforcement Acts" whose purpose was to protect the Black men and women of the South. They were to protect voter rights, oversee elections, fight the Klan and impose martial law if necessary.[49]

The last Enforcement Act resulted in the indictment and trial of several hundred Klansmen and the presidential suspension of *habeas corpus* in nine South Carolina counties.[50] Without federal troops, marshals, federal prosecutors and federal Courts, there would have been no justice, and when the marshals and troops were gone there was none. In 1875 Congress passed a Civil Rights Act prohibiting discrimination in public places: hotels, theaters, and public conveyances. This Act was the culmination of Congressional Reconstruction. The election of Rutherford B. Hayes in the

5. "The Constitution is colorblind"

disputed election of 1876, where southern states agreed to support Hayes if he would withdraw all federal troops, resulted in Blacks in the South losing almost any advocacy in the national government and all influence in the southern state governments. Terrorism won.[51] Terrorism was the rule of law.

Equal Rights

The Civil Rights Act of 1875 sought to enforce equality in public accommodations. The law provided "That all persons within the jurisdiction of the United States shall be entitled to the full and equal enjoyment of the accommodations, advantages, facilities, and privileges of inns, public conveyances on land or water, theaters, and other places of public amusement; subject only to the conditions and limitations established by law, and applicable alike to citizens of every race and color, regardless of any previous condition of servitude." The second part of the law provided those who had been discriminated against could bring an action in federal court for damages.

The Civil Rights Act of 1875 was declared unconstitutional in the *Civil Rights Cases* of 1883.[52] Five cases from the North and South were combined by the Supreme Court. Dealing a fatal legal blow to the Act, Supreme Court Justice Bradley found that it could not be enforced because it was intended to correct private, not public, conduct, which the Constitution never intended. Bradley wrote that it was time for Blacks to no longer think of themselves as "the special favorite of the laws...." The only dissent was penned by Justice John Marshall Harlan, who wrote if the Constitution could protect slavery it could protect the rights of former slaves. Harlan argued that the Thirteenth Amendment was written to provide freedom throughout the United States and this freedom included equal access to public facilities.[53] The decision in these cases set the Supreme Court on a course that would take decades to correct and effectively abandoned Black men and women to segregation and Jim Crow. "The whole South, every state had got into the hands of the very men that held us as slaves."[54] As for the effect of the constitutional abandonment of the Black men and women, "They are to be returned to a condition of serfdom—an era of second slavery."[55]

After Hayes's election and the removal of federal troops from the South, lynching became public spectacle. The United States claimed to be a country of laws not men, but between 1877 and 1964 it abandoned a whole population to lawlessness and terror. The southern white power structure sought to intimidate Black voters, destroy Black independence, and force a Black exodus from the South. The terrorism used by white Southerners was not a secret, it was a matter of public knowledge and was a subject of newspaper coverage throughout the nation. It was a public spectacle of brutal violence conducted and witnessed by hundreds and sometimes thousands of white terrorists.

After 1876 until the 1950s the constitutional government of the United States did almost nothing—not the President, not Congress and not the Supreme Court—to protect Blacks and live up to the promise of the Civil War amendments and the Declaration of Independence. Over 200 anti-lynching bills were introduced in Congress, but all failed. In June 2005, the Senate, long after the dead were buried and their graves lost, apologized in a late-night session for its failure to enact any federal anti-lynching legislation. Before the vote Senator Mary Landreau from Louisiana said: "There may be no other injustice in American history for which the Senate so uniquely bears responsibility." Only 80 Senators supported and voted for the measure. The Senators from Mississippi, where the greatest number of Black men and women were lynched, were nowhere to be found. The Senate had three times been presented with bills passed by the House to outlaw lynching and three times Southerners in the Senate filibustered the bills to death. Seven Presidents had recommended such bills, but none was ever passed. In December 2019 the House passed the Emmett Till antilynching act, but Rand Paul blocked it in the Senate.

Strange Fruit[56]

Lynching was in no way about crime. It was a public act of terrorism meant to oppress Black community members. Many victims were accused of rape or murder and killed without evidence that would have persuaded a jury. Some were lynched for asking for a drink of water, or sassing a white woman, and an eight-year-old boy was lynched for nothing.[57] Sometimes the cause was a dispute over wages or working conditions.[58] These Black men and women suffered their fate because of hate and racism. There are magnificent statues to rebel soldiers, many of whom became members of the Klan (see 1866 Report of the Joint Committee on Reconstruction, Report of the Joint Committee on Reconstruction, 39th Cong., 1st Sess., pt. ii

5. "The Constitution is colorblind"

at 228, pt. iii at 80 [1866]) which encouraged and participated in lynchings throughout the South in the aftermath of Appomattox. If we believe in the rule of law, none of the victims of white terrorism deserved their fate. Lynching eventually moved from the streets and became capital punishment in southern courts, and legal proceedings that bore no resemblance to due process were substituted for extra-legal lynching.

Lynching was possible because the law enforcement officials did nothing. The law condoned the crimes by doing nothing even when it knew the names of the perpetrators. Most troubling, these acts of terror typically involved hundreds and sometimes thousands of people in horrific acts of violence. As time went by the terrorism became public spectacle. Terrorism moved from acts committed in the dark of the night by masked men to public lynching. The perpetrators and spectators took pictures and made post-cards of their deeds, whose raw ugliness and heartlessness are unsurpassed in American history.[59] The participants cut body parts from their victims as souvenirs or to auction them to the highest bidder.[60]

The practice of lynching was so widespread in the nineteenth and early twentieth centuries that Mark Twain wrote an essay titled the "United States of Lyncherdom."[61] According to most recent research nearly 5,000 Black persons were lynched in the United States from 1882 until 1968. It is now believed that thousands more were lynched in the South from the end of the Civil War until 1875, and that for various reasons their deaths were unaccounted for.[62]

In the tales of white Western justice, plot lines end with the public lynching of a scofflaw, once again showing the power of the people. The truth is much harder to imagine. American Indians, Mexicans, Chinese and white "outlaws" were lynched in the "Old West," but at nothing like the levels of violence in the South. The extant lynching records don't include the Black man or woman taken into custody in the morning, tried by midday, and hung by sundown. In the South, in the immediate post-war period, the intimidation of the enemies of the conservative white resurgent political class also included white Republicans who had sought to help Blacks, and many of them were lynched. Contrast the efforts of post–Civil War white Republicans to help and protect Blacks with the conduct of today's Republicans in response to the Charlottesville anti–Semitic white power march in 2017, which resulted in not only violence but the death of a young white woman protesting racial injustice. The post–Civil War violence led to the Fourteenth Amendment and various federal enforcement acts trying to protect Black Americans from white terrorism.

The Constitution and American Racism

According to the Tuskegee Institute and the Equal Justice Initiative, from 1877 until 1950, thousands of Black men and women were lynched. The Equal Justice Initiative has confirmed 4,084 African Americans lynched during this period in twelve southern states. During the same period whites were lynched in the United States, but at nowhere near the numbers of Blacks, and their deaths were not racially motivated. In Alabama 361 African Americans were lynched; in Florida 311; in Tennessee 223; in Texas 335; in Georgia 589; in Mississippi 654; and in Virginia, North Carolina and South Carolina, hundreds more.[63]

Without federal intervention, the white South continued its war on Blacks. In 1893 Henry Smith was a Black resident of Paris, Texas. Smith was known to many as mentally disturbed, perhaps suffering from schizophrenia, but nevertheless, the occasional part-time laborer for residents. He was arrested for public intoxication by a local deputy who was known for his cruelty. The deputy beat Smith. A few weeks after this incident, in January 1893, the four-year-old daughter of the deputy was found dead. The deputy believed his daughter must have been killed by Smith as revenge for his beating. A local Methodist bishop of the Southern Methodist Church, a former president of Emory College, proclaimed that the girl had been viciously raped and demonically torn apart. Those who had seen the body said the bishop was wrong. Smith fled Paris when he heard the deputy was looking for him, but his stepson was lynched because he would not reveal his whereabouts. He was eventually arrested in Hope, Arkansas, and transported back to Texas on a train.

The train stopped briefly in Texarkana where 5,000 local citizens had gathered at the train station. When the train arrived in Texas, on February 1, 1893, it was met by over 10,000 people, some from as far away as Dallas. Smith allegedly admitted the crime and asked to be killed quickly. Instead the deputy tore Smith's clothes from him and tossed them to the crowd, who fought over them for souvenirs. The deputy and his 12-year-old son then tortured Smith with red hot irons that were placed first on his feet then all over his body until his eyes were burned out. The pokers were then pressed down his throat. Kerosene was thrown over his body and he was set alight. At one point Smith's body rolled out of the fire and he was pulled back into it by the crowd. His bones were taken by crowd members as souvenirs.[64]

On July 5, 1893, two white sisters went to pick berries near their home in Bardwell, Kentucky. The family dog came home without them and a search was begun that found their bodies. Both had their throats slashed,

5. "The Constitution is colorblind"

and both had been raped. At first a local Black man named "Glass eating Joe" was a suspect but he was exonerated. Despite testimony by neighbors that they had seen a strange white or mulatto man near the scene of the crime, the investigation centered on a Black man in Sikeston, Missouri, who had been arrested for hitching a ride on a freight train. His name was C.J. Miller and he was wearing blue clothes that matched a blue coat found at the murder scene. It was also claimed he had two rings that belonged to the girls and a razor with dried blood on it.

The girls' father and the local sheriff went to Sikeston to "interview" Miller. They discovered he did not look like the man who had been seen near the crime and the rings did not belong to the girls. Regardless, the sheriff took Miller back to Bardstown where a crowd had been gathering all day and night. The father appealed to the crowd to let the sheriff finish his investigation and then they would burn Miller. Miller addressed the crowd and made an impassioned plea for his life, setting out in detail his whereabouts and where he lived. The sheriff tried without success to verify Miller's story, but then the mob took over. They dragged Miller with a log chain around his neck to a telegraph pole, hoisting him and then dropping him, breaking his neck. They continued hoisting him and dropping him all the time shooting the corpse. They then burned and dismembered the body for souvenirs. Later, Miller's story checked out and a white Missourian was found to be the rapist and murderer.[65]

In April 1899, Sam Hose was a laborer in Coweta County, Georgia, outside of Atlanta, and was employed by Alfred Cranford on his plantation. Hose and Cranford got into an argument over unpaid wages and Cranford pointed a gun at Hose. Hose had been chopping wood and threw his ax at Cranford, killing him. Hose fled, and false rumors were soon circulated that Hose had assaulted and raped Cranford's wife and assaulted their infant child. The *Atlanta Constitution* published an article suggesting Hose should be burned at the stake. Hose was captured and returned to Coweta County where he was taken off a train by several hundred local citizens. They cut off his fingers, ears, genitals and skin from his face. The mob then tied him to a tree and burned him alive. Parts of Hose's body were sold as souvenirs. An investigation by a Pinkerton detective concluded later that Hose had acted in self-defense.[66]

In 1904 Luther Holbert and his wife were brutally murdered in a small town in Mississippi. Holbert killed a white planter in an argument over wages where both men were armed. Holbert and his wife, who had nothing to do with the killing, were pursued over 100 miles across country. When apprehended they were turned over to a mob, which used corkscrews to tear pieces of flesh from them, cut their fingers and ears off and then burned them alive.

> When the two Negroes were captured, they were tied to trees and while the funeral pyres were being prepared, they were forced to hold out their hands while one finger at a time was chopped off. The fingers were distributed as souvenirs. The ears of the murderers were cut off. Holbert was beaten severely, his skull was fractured and one of his eyes, knocked out with a stick, hung by a shred from the socket. Some of the mob used a large corkscrew to bore into the flesh of the man and woman. It was applied to their arms, legs and body, then pulled out, the spirals tearing out big pieces of raw, quivering flesh every time it was withdrawn.[67]

Mississippi led southern states in lynchings. In 2018 one of Mississippi's Congressmen wrote: "The destruction of these [Confederate] monuments, erected in the loving memory of our family and fellow Southern Americans, is both heinous and horrific. If the, and I use this term extremely loosely, 'leadership' of Louisiana wishes to, in a Nazi-ish fashion, burn books or destroy historical monuments of OUR HISTORY, they should be LYNCHED! Let it be known, I will do all in my power to prevent this from happening in our State."[68] Lynching is not dead, nor the hate that supported it and helped it flourish.

Federal intervention was rare in cases involving lynching, but in January 1906 when a white girl was raped in Chattanooga, Tennessee, the federal courts stepped in. Based on one item of evidence the sheriff arrested Ed Johnson, a Black man who supposedly had been seen with a black leather strap and who the victim later said looked like the man who raped her. At trial Johnson protested his innocence and testified he was at a saloon when the raped occurred, a story that many witnesses corroborated. The jury nevertheless found Johnson guilty on February 9, 1906, and the judge sentenced him to be executed on March 13, 1906.

After procedural shenanigans by the trial court, Johnson's lawyers appealed to the Tennessee Supreme Court, which declined to postpone his execution. Johnson's attorneys next sought a writ of *habeas corpus* in federal court, which was denied, but the court postponed the execution to give the lawyers time to file a writ in the United States Supreme Court. Johnson's lawyers then filed an emergency writ in the Supreme Court. The judge who heard the emergency writ in the Supreme Court was Justice John Harlan. Harlan met with other justices at the Chief Justice's home, and the Court issued an order staying Johnson's execution.

The day after the Court issued the stay, a mob broke into the jail and

5. "The Constitution is colorblind"

took Johnson to a nearby bridge where a noose was placed around his neck and he was thrown off the bridge's deck and hung. The Attorney General of the United States charged the sheriff and 20 other members of the lynch mob with contempt of the Supreme Court. Ultimately, the Court found the sheriff, the jailer, and four members of the lynch mob in contempt, and sentenced three of them, including the sheriff, to 90 days in jail, and the rest to 60 days in jail.[69]

In August 1914, Germany attacked France, Belgium and Russia in hopes of gaining European hegemony. For three long years French, British and German soldiers killed each other on the Western Front in France by the hundreds of thousands. In May 1917, the United States declared war on Germany and entered the war on the side of France, Britain and Italy. Hundreds of thousands of Americans enlisted, including Black Americans. Black Americans served bravely overseas, and many served with French combat troops.[70] Blacks went to war in Europe to fight for Wilson's "14 freedoms" but came home to America to face lynching, segregation and racism.

Charles Lewis enlisted to fight in the Great War and was honorably discharged. He still had his uniform on when he was singled out by a deputy for a search in Tyler Station, Kentucky. An argument ensued, and Lewis was arrested for assault and taken to the local jail. In the middle of the night a masked mob took him out of the jail, hung him and left his body for all to see.[71]

The *True Democrat*, a Louisiana paper, published an editorial in 1918 entitled, "Nip it in the Bud":

> The root of the trouble was that the negro thought that being a soldier he was not subject to civil authority, the editorial read. The conditions of active warfare and the regulations of army life have probably given these men more exalted ideas of their station in life than really exists and having these ideas they will be guilty of many acts of self-assertion, arrogance and insolence which will not be borne with, in the South at least, and which will be followed by consequences to them, more or less painful.[72]

This was not an isolated incident and many more Black veterans who had fought to "make the world safe for democracy" were beaten, bludgeoned, shot, tortured, hung and burned by masked men in the dark of the night and in broad daylight by proud citizens. Lynchings increased in the immediate aftermath of the war.

After the Japanese attack on Pearl Harbor, Black men again volunteered by the hundreds of thousands, with eventually 1.2 million serving in the war against fascism and imperial Japan. Isaac Woodward was a veteran of combat in the Pacific and received his discharge at Fort Benning, Georgia. He boarded a bus to go home to New York. In South Carolina he asked to go to the bathroom when the bus stopped, and after Woodward used the bathroom, the bus driver claimed he had taken too long. The driver radioed ahead that he had a troublesome Negro aboard and at Batesburg, South Carolina, Woodward was ordered off the bus by the local police chief. He was then taken to an alley by the chief and a deputy and almost beaten to death and permanently blinded.[73] Many more Black veterans were killed and harmed and terrorized as their reward for fighting for freedom.

Lynching rolled forward with the times in the South, with James Meredith shot by ambush, four beautiful Black children killed by cowardly white men in the bombing of the 16th Street Baptist Church in Birmingham, and civil rights workers Chaney, Goodwin and Swerner buried in a dam. Instead of holding Robert E. Lee up as a paragon of white male virtue, Americans should recognize the damnable history of terrorism inflicted on Black men, women and children. Racism will continue until Americans acknowledge this abominable history and work to purge it from their institutions and politics.

The Great Dissenter

Supreme Court Justice John Harlan was a Kentucky lawyer who volunteered for the Union Army and was loyal to the Union throughout the Civil War. Harlan was born into a slave holding family and in his early years was opposed to abolition. During the Civil War he was against secession and became a colonel in the Union Army. He opposed emancipation and the Thirteenth Amendment but changed his position on these matters in the lawless aftermath of the war where lynchings, floggings and other terrorism were used to oppress the freedmen. Harlan came to believe that only federal intervention could restore the rule of law. In 1877 President Hayes appointed Harlan to the United States Supreme Court. He was the lone dissenter in various decisions restricting civil rights in a long career on the Court, which earned him the sobriquet the "great dissenter."[74]

Homer Plessy was a light-skinned octoroon who lived in New Orleans and worked as a shoemaker and later an insurance agent. Plessy, with the aid of the *Comite des Citoyens*, a New Orleans Black organization,

5. "The Constitution is colorblind"

challenged Louisiana's laws requiring separate accommodations on public transportation for white and Black passengers. Plessy bought a first-class ticket on the East Louisiana Railroad. When Plessy boarded the train and sat in the whites-only car, and he was asked to move to the car reserved for Blacks. He refused and was thrown off the train and arrested, charged with and convicted of violating the Louisiana segregation statute of 1890.[75] The case finally made it to the U.S. Supreme Court and Justice Brown, writing for eight of the Court's justices in 1896, found that the Fourteenth Amendment was intended to establish an absolute equality of the races before the law but "it could not have been intended to abolish distinctions based upon color or, to enforce social, as distinguished from political equality, or a commingling of the two races unsatisfactory to others."

While this case effectively legalized "separate but equal," the phrase is used nowhere in the opinion. Justice Harlan dissented vigorously. He wrote that legislation that imposed criminal penalties for use of public transportation was not only "inconsistent with equality of rights which pertain to citizenship ... but with personal liberty." Harlan concluded that the Constitution is "color blind" and that "the destinies of the two races ... are indissolubly linked together, and the interests of both require that the common government of all shall not permit the seeds of race hate to be planted under the sanction of law." By an 8–1 decision in *Plessy v. Ferguson*,[76] the U.S. Supreme Court sanctioned and made lawful segregation based on racism. The decision would stand until 1954 on the fiction that separate but equal was fair or just, and constitutional. But separate Black facilities were never equal. The rule of law was segregation.

The Constitution, despite the Thirteenth, Fourteenth, and Fifteenth Amendments, failed because it did not ensure equality before the law. In a nation that claimed to be governed by the rule of law, the Supreme Court, charged with the administration of justice, did little until the 1950s to protect Black Americans and reject segregation and the myth of separate but equal. For over fifty years, except in some criminal cases that came before it from southern state courts, all of which involved egregious violations of legal principles regarding due process and the trials of Black men, the Supreme Court did little to ensure the rule of law for all Americans. While lynching continued in the streets, injustice moved to the courtroom where expedited trials occurred with little formality.

In 1931 nine Black teenagers, aged 13 to 19, were accused of raping two white girls on a freight train in Alabama. The nine "Scottsboro Boys" were all tried in one day and all but one were sentenced to death in the electric chair. Because Alabama law required appointment of counsel, the judge appointed lawyers to represent the boys. But the lawyers refused to meet with their clients and refused to represent them. When the judge appointed the local bar as counsel for the Scottsboro Boys, the lawyers all left the courtroom. Two lawyers who finally did appear for the defendants never investigated the case and met with their clients only 30 minutes before the trial.[77]

The U.S. Supreme Court in *Powell v. Alabama*[78] ruled that the lack of effective counsel did violate the defendants' rights to due process as required by the Fourteenth Amendment and to counsel as guaranteed by the Sixth Amendment. When the case went back to Alabama, the Scottsboro Boys were tried again, and found guilty and sentenced to prison terms by an all-white jury. One, Ozie Powell, escaped to Michigan, where the governor refused to send him back to Alabama. After the retrial of the case in rural Alabama with an all-white jury, the Supreme Court in *Norris v. Alabama*[79] found that race could not be used when selecting a jury. One of the alleged female victims later said she was sorry for all the trouble she had caused the Scottsboro Boys. Eventually, they were all pardoned by Alabama, but not until 2013 and only after they were all dead.[80]

Finally, in 1941, the Court, because of changes in the justices appointed by Franklin D. Roosevelt, began a perceptible move from separate but equal to recognition of the real purpose of Jim Crow, racial segregation. In *Mitchell v. United States*,[81] the Court found that a railroad involved in interstate commerce (it crossed state lines) could not discriminate by race. Arthur Mitchell, the only Black member of the U.S. House of Representatives, bought a first-class ticket for a train trip from Chicago to Hot Springs, Arkansas. Once the train entered Arkansas, which had a separate but equal law for public accommodations, he was asked to move from his first-class sleeper car to a substantially substandard "colored" car, and threatened with arrest if he did not move. Mitchell filed a complaint with the Interstate Commerce Commission for violation of the Interstate Commerce Act, which found the Arkansas law calling for segregation was consistent with its regulations. Breaking with the *Plessy* decision and finding against the railroad and ICC, the Supreme Court held unanimously that the Interstate Commerce Act forbade segregation in interstate commerce and that Black passengers were entitled to the same accommodations as white passengers.

The Supreme Court was still not an advocate for Blacks whose rights and lives dangled by the slenderest thread in southern states. Robert Hall

5. "The Constitution is colorblind"

was a thirty-year-old Black man who owned a pearl-handled pistol and was known to the local sheriff in rural Newton, Georgia, as a "biggety negro" because he was looked to as a "leader of sorts." M. Claude Screws, the local sheriff, ordered a deputy to seize Hall's pistol. Hall personally requested Screws to return his pistol, and eventually sought the help of a lawyer to get the pistol back. On the night of January 23, 1943, Screws sent two deputies to Hall's house to arrest him. The deputies took Hall to the town square where in plain sight they brutally beat him senseless while he was handcuffed. Hall died, but the local Georgia authorities would not bring charges against Sheriff Screws and his deputies.[82]

The U.S. Attorney brought charges though, claiming Screws had deprived Hall of his federal constitutional rights. It was alleged that Screws had deprived Hall of his life without due process of law by using a Civil War–era statute. Sheriff Screws and the deputies were convicted in a jury trial. Screws appealed, and the 5th U.S. Circuit Court of Appeals affirmed the conviction. In a 5–4 decision the U.S. Supreme Court in *Screws v. U.S.*,[83] Justice William O. Douglas wrote that the statute was vague and that the killers had not acted under color of state law. The three killers were retried and found not guilty. Sheriff Screws was later elected to the Georgia State Senate.[84]

Restrictive covenants are rules that are attached to and run with real estate. They are usually part of deeds of dedication that are used by developers when they develop real estate for residential purposes and sale to the public. It is argued that they make real estate more valuable by limiting its uses. Covenants restrict a buyer's use of the property, prohibiting things like using the property for commercial purposes, posting signs, burning trash, or grazing farm livestock on residential property.

Throughout the United States covenants were used to restrict sale and resale of primarily residential real estate property to Blacks. They were just another tactic in the toolbox of segregationists and another way to discriminate against Blacks. The use of these covenants had far-reaching results for Blacks by limiting choices for residential living and further proscribing economic rights that are part of every citizen's bundle of rights. In two companion cases decided in 1948, the Supreme Court held that such covenants were unenforceable by the courts. In *Shelley v. Kraemer*[85] the Court found that racial discrimination might be enforceable but enforcement of such covenants by the states was in violation of the Fourteenth Amendment and therefore the covenants were unenforceable. In *Hurd v. Hodge*[86] the Court found the use of such covenants in the District of Columbia violated the 1866 Civil Rights Act. In both cases the Court concluded that enforcement of covenants by a court constituted discriminatory governmental action.

Separate but Equal Has No Place

In the 1950s segregationists opposed admission of Blacks to law school. In two unrelated cases, Ada Lois Sipuel sought admission to Oklahoma University's Law School and Heman Marion Sweatt sought admission to The University of Texas College of Law. Sipuel was denied admission in Oklahoma because state law prohibited admission of Blacks to the law school. The Court in 1948 ordered Oklahoma to provide Sipuel a legal education "in conformity with the equal protection clause of the Fourteenth Amendment and provide it as soon as it does for applicants of any other group."[87] Despite faculty and student protests, Oklahoma circumvented the order by creating a separate law school with three professors. Sipuel eventually graduated from the Oklahoma University Law School.

When Heman Sweatt applied to the University of Texas law school, a local judge ordered the state to open a law school at all-Black Prairie View University, which did not have equal facilities for Black Texas law school students. The President of the University of Texas spoke out in favor of ending segregation and was fired and replaced by a dedicated segregationist. Texas went the Oklahoma route and tried to establish an all-Black law school that was a fiction in all but name. Sweatt went to court, and for the first time the United States Department of Justice filed a brief asking the Supreme Court to overrule *Plessy v. Ferguson* and the separate but equal doctrine. The Court did not overrule *Plessy* but instead found that the Texas plan to create a separate law school was inadequate.[88] In 1950 for the first time ever the Court ordered a Black man, Sweatt, to be admitted to The University of Texas School of Law.

After the Japanese attack on Pearl Harbor on December 7, 1941, war hysteria gripped the West Coast of the United States. The war in the Pacific had a dimension that did not exist in the U.S. war effort in Europe. Racism had long been a component of American relations with the Chinese and Japanese, and the Japanese were immediately hated for the infamous nature of the attack and their race. The success of the Japanese attack, crippling the American Pacific fleet, coupled with racism, resulted in a war

5. "The Constitution is colorblind"

hysteria that the Japanese were about to attack the West Coast. The Attorney General of California, Republican Earl Warren, sought the removal of the Japanese population from California. Bowing to political pressure, President Franklin Roosevelt authorized by executive order, without due process or any criminal charges, the removal of all Japanese from the West Coast to interior "camps."[89] Thousands of Japanese-American men, women and children were uprooted from their homes and moved to concentration camps far inland. In one of history's ironies, the most highly decorated Army unit in the history of the Second World War was the 442d Infantry Regiment manned by Japanese-American volunteers from these camps. The Regiment earned over 9,400 purple hearts and 21 Medals of Honor and incurred a 93 percent casualty rate.[90]

In 1943 Earl Warren successfully ran for governor of California. After he agreed to help Eisenhower win California in the 1952 Presidential election, Eisenhower appointed Warren Chief Justice of the United States Supreme Court in 1953. All the justices but Warren had been appointed by Democrats Roosevelt and Truman and shared the ideals of the "New Deal." There was nothing in Warren's background that gave anyone pause to think that he would act differently than he had as a Republican Attorney General and Governor of California once he was appointed to the bench. But Earl Warren surprised everyone and became a foil for conservatives, racists and opponents of civil liberties everywhere in the United States. Schools in the South and the North deemed "separate but equal" were for the most part deplorable fictions created by the segregationist mind, and Warren was happy to acknowledge as much.

In 1953 several cases involving "separate but equal" schools came to the Supreme Court of Earl Warren. The cases were consolidated into one involving a nominally northern school district, *Brown v. Board of Education of Topeka*. Warren believed it was time to end segregation and a way to do that was through education. *Brown* broke down the barrier but invited further briefs and arguments on the issue of enforcement. The opinion was only 11 pages long because Warren wanted people to read it. "In approaching this problem, we cannot turn the clock back to 1868 when the [Fourteenth] amendment was adopted, or even to 1896 when *Plessy* was written." Warren believed that public education must be considered in the light of its full development and its present place in American life throughout the nation. Education was the key to preparing citizens to make choices in democratic societies, and the law required the state to make choices based on equality.

The Constitution and American Racism

Segregation of white and colored children in public schools has a detrimental effect upon the colored children. The impact is greater when it has the sanction of law, for the policy of separating the races is usually interpreted as denoting inferiority of the Negro group.... Any language in contrary to this finding is rejected. We conclude that in the field of public education the doctrine of "separate but equal" has no place. Separate educational facilities are inherently unequal.[91]

A beginning, not an end. On that day, in that courtroom, for Black children the Constitution was "color blind" and the rule of law was equal.

6

Tyranny of the Republic

"No-one is deprived of freedom that I know about."
—Strom Thurmond

James Madison represented Virginia in the House of Representatives of the First Congress in 1789. He was initially consumed with drafting a Bill of Rights promised during the ratification debates.[1] But other matters also took up his time: the organization of the government; the proposal for a bank of the United States; the necessity to fund the Jay Treaty with Great Britain; and funding of national improvements.

Madison's Congress, the Constitution's legislative branch, was composed of the House of Representatives and the Senate, both established by Article I of the Constitution. The House is popularly elected, its representation based upon a state's population as counted by the census. Article I, Section 2 requires a census to determine the population of the states and calculate their representation in the house. The census is to count the whole number of "free Persons" in each state. The number of representatives and Senators of a state is also equal to the number of electors to the Electoral College for the state.

The Senate was to be composed of two persons from each state, selected by the state legislatures.

Congress was a battleground for slavery in the years before the Civil War. While abolitionist sentiment increased in Congress and the United States, there was no constitutional remedy to end slavery. The truth was that Congress could not abolish slavery because abolitionists could not muster the votes to do so. The slave states could block any attempts at abolition by votes in both houses of Congress and by filibuster in the Senate, veto by the President, and even if Congress somehow voted for abolition, amendment was impossible because of the requirement of super majorities in the Congress and among the states. There could be

The Constitution and American Racism

no amendment to abolish slavery while the southern states were there to block it.

The three-fifths clause in the Constitution meant that in the early years of the Republic, from 1792 until 1802, the South got twelve congressmen they would not have had without the compromise. From 1802 until 1811, they got fifteen more and from 1811 to 1822, eighteen additional seats.[2] Every time an increase in the slave population added a seat to Congress, it added a vote to the Electoral College. Washington, Jefferson, Madison and Monroe, four of the first five Presidents, were all slave holding Southerners. A southern president was appointing members to the Supreme Court affirmed by Southerners in the Senate. There was abolitionist sentiment among Northerners who resented this overrepresentation of a slave South in the government but in the face of the Constitution there was little they could do but publicly attack slavery.

Early in the Republic's history, in 1790, Quakers in Pennsylvania petitioned Congress to end the international slave trade. The Pennsylvania Abolition Society filed a petition signed by Benjamin Franklin urging "the restoration of liberty to those unhappy men."[3] Southern representatives responded with threats of "civil war" and claimed slavery was a "palladium sanctioned by the Bible."[4]

The first legislation passed by Congress that addressed slavery was the First Fugitive Slave Act. In 1793, the Act made possible the interstate capture and rendition of slaves. The owner of a slave, or his agents, could seize a fugitive slave and take that unlucky person before a federal judge or local magistrate or judge in that state and by affidavit or testimony prove he was the owner. The putative slave could not give testimony in his or her defense unless the judge permitted such testimony. The Act provided criminal penalties for those who might help the runaway.[5]

In response to the Fugitive Slave Acts, some states passed personal liberty laws. These laws were deemed unconstitutional at the federal level because they conflicted with the federal Fugitive Slave Acts. Eventually many private persons and northern states defied the federal government and aided the escape of fugitive slaves. Not only were the Fugitive Slave Acts used to capture and send escaped slaves back to the South, they punished private citizens who provided help to run-aways.

In 1794, in response to petitions by a Pennsylvania abolitionist society, Congress did pass an act making it illegal to fit out a ship or sail from an American port to engage in the international slave trade. Abolitionist

6. Tyranny of the Republic

societies also mounted freedom suits to secure the freedom of Black persons.[6]

South Carolina reopened its international slave trade in 1803. Northerners in Congress were critical of the South Carolinians for reopening the trade when there was a provision in the Constitution for its abolition by Congress in five years. Tens of thousands of slaves were brought to the United States from 1803 to 1808, when Congress finally ended the trade. Jefferson made the Louisiana Purchase in 1803 and by treaty owners of existing slaves there could keep them. A whole vista of new land opened up to the contest between slavery and abolition. Americans who moved to the Purchase could take their slaves with them if they had been brought to the United States before May 1798. "You cannot prevent slavery—neither laws moral or human can do it—men will be governed by their interest, not the law."[7]

The international slave trade was declared illegal by Congress in 1807, but there was no strict American enforcement of the ban and there was a thriving and prosperous internal slave trade. It is estimated that over 54,000 slaves were brought illegally to the United States after 1807.[8]

Congress was consumed by the crisis that developed over the admission of Missouri to the Union. The country had managed to keep the balance of slave and free states equal until territories from the Louisiana Purchase began to apply for admission to the Union. The Purchase was criticized as early as 1804 because it would increase southern membership in Congress by introducing slaves into territories that would become states. "Slave representation has governed the union."[9] Representative James Tallmadge of New York had tried to keep new territories from becoming new slave states. He introduced an amendment to the Missouri enabling bill that would have effectively prohibited "the further introduction of slavery" in Missouri. One of the surviving members of the Constitutional Convention, now a Senator, stated in a Senate speech that Congress could limit slavery as a condition of admission. Finally, after much dissembling by Southerners and half-reasoned constitutional arguments to justify the protection of slavery, it was agreed. Maine would be admitted free, and Missouri slave. Slavery would be limited in the territories to a line south of 36° 30'—Missouri's southern border.[10]

Abolitionist work intensified in the 1830s to include mailing circulars to Southerners demanding abolition and presenting petitions to Congress calling for an end to slavery. Southern Congressman and Presidents tried to censor the mails and forbid consideration of abolitionist petitions.

The Constitution and American Racism

New territories opened and more debates began over the march of slavery across the continent. Texas was annexed; the border of Oregon was finalized by treaty with the British; the Mexican Cession added territory; the Gadsden Purchase added territory; and all of this land exceeded the size of the Louisiana Purchase. Pro-slavery forces wanted more, they wanted slavery everywhere. "The South can never consent to be confined to prescribed limits.... She wants and must have space."[11] In 1850 a new Fugitive Slave Act amended the first, and its enforcement pushed the country closer to armed conflict. The Kansas-Nebraska Act made certain that popular sovereignty in the territories over the issue of slavery would result in bloodshed.

Finally, in 1857, when Chief Justice Taney of the Supreme Court in *Dred Scott*[12] wrote that Blacks free or slave could not be citizens of the United States, that slaves were not persons but property, and that Congress had no power to outlaw slavery because it was sanctioned by the Constitution, the impasse was clear. The South would never agree to the voluntary abolition of slavery. In one of the great ironies of American history, the South seceded when it could have continued to thwart the abolitionists in Congress through constitutional means. Had they not seceded, slavery could not have been abolished.

The Civil War resulted in the Emancipation Proclamation, a military order issued by the Commander in Chief, President Abraham Lincoln. The proclamation freed only those slaves who were in areas then in rebellion. In 1864 Lincoln, having embraced the idea of abolition, ran for re-election, promising an amendment to the Constitution abolishing slavery. Without an amendment to the pro-slavery Constitution not all of the slaves would be free, and no one really knew what the effect of a military order would be after hostilities ended. The Thirteenth Amendment was first rejected by Congress but eventually passed in 1865. This Amendment could not have been adopted without secession.

The Fourteenth and Fifteenth Amendments were also possible because of secession. When the South seceded, the Constitution was no longer a protection for slavery. When the Confederate soldiers returned home most had not accepted abolition or the results of the Civil War. A reign of terror began in the South to coerce the freedmen and their white allies, whether Freedmen's Bureau employees, carpetbaggers or scalawags. The central issues were equal rights and voting rights. White Southerners did not accept the former slaves as free men deserving equal treatment or voting rights.

6. Tyranny of the Republic

Without Congressional Reconstruction and the Thirteenth, Fourteenth and Fifteenth Amendments, no former Confederate state would have recognized abolition and Black voting rights. Federal troops and marshals were required in the South to protect Blacks from white terrorism and enforce basic civil liberties. The South sought to suppress voters' rights for Blacks and coerce the former slaves into a new economic system that amounted to economic peonage.

The election of 1876 resulted in the withdrawal of federal troops from the South and insured the supremacy of white governments acting to segregate and discriminate against Blacks. The national government turned its back on the continuing terrorism in the South. The Constitutional efforts to protect and integrate Black Americans into the fabric of American politics and society went unfulfilled and a reign of terror and segregation walked hand in hand into the twentieth century.[13]

After President Hayes was elected, Congress refused to do anything to stop the terrorism or check and reverse segregation. After 1876, every time someone brought the issue of lynching before Congress the southern delegates blocked the question, leaving Congress without power on an issue that brought death to Blacks and shame to the country.[14]

One hundred fifty-four Blacks have served in Congress since the Civil War. In 1870, the first Blacks became members of Congress. Twenty-two served from 1870 until the beginning of the twentieth century, but this service was not continuous and there were periods during the twentieth century when no Blacks served despite their population representing substantial numbers in many southern states.[15] Black men in the South fought endemic racism and voter suppression to be elected. It was a struggle that was doomed, without federal intervention, to stop southern tactics meant to eliminate Black participation in politics.

There were two Civil Rights Acts passed during Congressional Reconstruction—the last in 1875. The bill outlawed discrimination in almost all aspects of American life. It was found unconstitutional, and there was virtually no enforcement of the Civil Rights Act of 1866 between 1883 and the turn of the century. It took almost a hundred years before another Civil Rights Act would be passed by Congress. The Congress, between 1877 and the turn of the century, was consumed with the economic issues of the growth of the American Republic. This was the period referred to many as the "Great Barbecue."[16] It was the era of mega-trusts and unfettered capitalism.

The Homestead Act of 1862 opened the West to any American who was willing to move and take up the cultivation and improvement of 160 acres. The Homestead Act encouraged railroad growth, further opening the West by granting railroads vast tracts of right-of-way across the country. Controversies over the federal government's economic policy, including whether the country's economy should be gold or silver based, and industries regulated, marked the trajectory of Congressional business. Tariff policy, paper money, and labor reform took up much time in Congress.

In the first Congress elected after the Compromise of 1877 all eleven of the southern states of the Confederacy were seated in both houses. President Hayes had believed he could rebuild the Republican Party in the South by appealing to the better nature of southern white voters by pursuing a conciliatory strategy and abandoning Radical Republican policies that had sought protection of Black citizens by federal troops and U.S. marshals.[17] This strategy of course abandoned the Black voters who had supported the Republicans in the South.

The white South embraced the Democratic Party and its delegations began chipping away at Northern enforcement of voters' rights and civil rights. After the Civil Rights Act of 1875 had been found unconstitutional, a first-time Black member of the House, James O'Hara, proposed an amendment to an interstate commerce bill that would prohibit discrimination on railroads based on color. His original effort at amending the bill would have re-established the equal accommodations provision of the Civil Rights Act of 1875, but it was killed in the House.[18]

The voting on the O'Hara amendment to the interstate commerce bill was 137 Republicans and 97 Democrats in favor of it. All the Republicans had voted yes, and all the northern Democrats had voted yes. But, ultimately after much lobbying, inter-house politicking, and consideration of several amendments to the proposal which would allow railroads to classify passengers as they saw fit, the bill went to the Senate where the language was changed to a vague acknowledgment that it would be unreasonable for a railroad to give a passenger a preference or advantage.[19]

Congress would vote along party lines, and the racial bias of the Southerners had swung the support of northern Democrats. It was also clear that Republicans would support Southerners on race issues in a Faustian bargain to protect their economic agendas. Another attempt at reform, proposing a sweeping education bill that would have benefited Black schools by focusing on education as a tool of progress, was defeated.

In the last decade of the nineteenth century a Federal Election Bill

6. Tyranny of the Republic

was proposed that would have called for federal election supervisors to watch over state elections. The southern delegations pounced and managed to bargain for votes to defeat the bill, and it died in the Senate.[20] Civil rights, despite a 1957 Civil Rights Act, was done in the Congress until 1964.

Southern block voting and other House and Senate procedural rules gave Southerners the means to protect segregation and Jim Crow. Congress joined in the white South's suppression of Black rights by ignoring violence, fraud, poll taxes, literacy tests, restrictive and arbitrary voter registration practices and white primaries. Mark Twain wrote: "It could probably be shown by facts and figures that there is no distinctly American criminal class except Congress."[21]

In the 1890s southern delegates to Congress succeeded in repealing parts of Radical Reconstruction–era Enforcement Acts that protected Blacks in the South by using federal troops and marshals. This paved the way for continued attacks by southern state legislatures on Black voting rights, and a more rigidly segregated society. While it occurred to some Republicans that limiting the franchise of Black voters would limit southern seats for them in Congress, the Southerners fought attempts at the Congressional level to protect Black voting rights.

In the early Republic, indeed until the twentieth century, the Senate was not popularly elected by the citizens of the states it represented. Article I, Section 4 of the Constitution gave the state legislatures the right to choose the times, places and manner of holding elections for Senators. Until the adoption of the Seventeenth Amendment in 1913, Senators were chosen by the state legislatures. In the late nineteenth century, the Populists and Democrats joined in arguing the Senate should be popularly elected. The change was prompted by concerns that the Senate had become a millionaires' club whose agenda was often driven by graft and corruption, power and money.[22] That tradition continues today even though they are popularly elected, as most Senators are millionaires.

After Woodrow Wilson's election in 1912 the Democrats took control of Congress for six years. The Democrats continued the war on Black civil rights. In 1912, a Georgia House member proposed an amendment to the Constitution prohibiting interracial marriage. Despite the hideous crimes committed, anti-lynching legislation was blocked in Congress between 1918 and 1922, and 1930 and 1940. In February 2020 the House of Representatives finally passed the Emmett Till Antilynching Act. The Senate remains silent.

The Constitution and American Racism

The two world wars caused mass migrations of Blacks out of the old South and into the North. This changed voter demographics and by the 1950s both Republicans and Democrats in the North had new voters to appeal to for their election and re-election. In 1952, the first Republican elected President in twenty years, Dwight Eisenhower, recognized that Black voters would make an impact in elections. Despite this it was the Supreme Court that began to push the Civil Rights movement into the public forum, and to lend the weight of the Court and the federal government to the cause of simple justice for Black children, when it reversed *Plessy v. Ferguson* in *Brown v. Topeka Board of Education.*

In 1953, the Supreme Court of the United States stood up for the cause of justice. The Supreme Court and federal courts of appeals like the Fifth Circuit Court of Appeals began to attack segregation. The elected Congress had failed to do the right thing and make the United States of America the place where Jefferson's words mattered on more than the Fourth of July. Eisenhower was later supposed to have said that he regretted his nomination of fellow Republican Earl Warren to be Chief Justice more than any nomination he ever made.[23]

In March 1956 southern senators and congressmen announced the "Southern Manifesto," which declared southern opposition to *Brown* and claimed that the desegregation of schools was a matter of states' rights. It was signed by 19 Senators and 82 members of the House, all representatives of states from the former Confederacy. The authors, Strom Thurmond and Richard Russell, declared that *Brown* was an abuse of judicial power. Democratic Senators Al Gore, Estes Kefauver of Tennessee and Lyndon Johnson of Texas, then Senate majority leader, refused to sign the manifesto.[24]

Congress in 1957 did pass a Civil Rights Act that created a civil rights division in the Justice Department and a national commission on civil rights. The Act was burdened with a southern amendment that required a jury trial for anyone accused of violating someone's voting rights. The amendment would mean that a white person accused of having violated the voting rights provision would get a jury trial before his or her white neighbors.[25] Dixiecrat South Carolina Senator Strom Thurmond unsuccessfully filibustered the Act. The legislation was the first Civil Rights Act passed since 1875. Regardless, across the South segregationists in and out of public office obstructed justice by illegal acts and terrorism, including shootings, lynchings, and bombing and burning Black churches, to stop efforts to desegregate the South and turn back Jim Crow. Well-documented

6. Tyranny of the Republic

beatings and police violence were used to punish and discourage civil rights workers.

During Kennedy's administration there was little progress on civil rights. Ninety-nine Democrats in Congress were from eleven southern states. Standing committees in the House and Senate were chaired by Southerners. Given the reality of these numbers Kennedy believed a fight he could not win over civil rights would jeopardize the rest of his legislative program. Congress made no progress on civil rights until after Kennedy's death.[26]

Desegregation, Black activism and civil rights activists gained momentum with persistent work by Black activists and a powerful new news tool—television. Now Americans could watch hate in action when they turned on their televisions and saw white segregationists beating civil rights workers and attacking them with water cannons and dogs. TV journalists also reported the cowardly acts of dynamiting high schools, burning churches and other senseless hate crimes.

In November 1963 Lyndon Baines Johnson became President after the assassination of John F. Kennedy, and adopted a civil rights agenda that called for Congress to pass a Civil Rights Act. After much arm-twisting and lobbying, Johnson got the Civil Rights Act of 1964 passed. In 1965 he was able to get a Voting Rights Act passed. But it had taken Congress almost a hundred years to do something about Jim Crow and the injustice of segregation.

In the 1970s, civil rights legislation began to disappear from the work of Congress. Nixon used the "Southern Strategy," appealing to supporters of George Wallace and other racists for election. Carter, Clinton, Obama and the Democrats faced a Republican Party that had embraced the idea that less government was better. That idea was not theirs alone, it was the principle of white southern politics. Less government meant less busing, less affirmative action, fewer voting rights, and reduced economic opportunities for Blacks. The Republican presidents, Reagan, the Bushes and Trump, used the strategy, and it worked for them.

Before the ink was dry on the Constitution that boogeyman of Madison, political factions, had formed around those in favor of ratification, and those opposed to a national government. The "compromises" made by Madison and his supporters created a document that was cursed by its protection of slavery. The three-fifths clause made sure the South would have representation in the national Congress completely out of proportion to its voting population. The Electoral College made sure that the southern states were overrepresented in presidential elections. Southern influence in the Congress and provisions in the Constitution resulted in Fugitive Slave Acts.

Creation of the Senate made sure that there was a legislative body that could block abolition. The amendment process made sure the South could block any amendment to the Constitution, making slavery permanently the law of the land. Only after secession could the abolitionists finally succeed in ending a horrible economic system built on blood.

One of the tools used by Southerners in the Senate to block civil rights legislation was the filibuster. The name was first used in the 1850s in a Senate consumed with debates over the issue of slavery. The filibuster, or unlimited debate, was used in the First Senate but was adopted by Senate rule in 1856.[27] The filibuster has been used to block legislation in the Senate coming from the House and the President for consideration. A bill must be passed by both the House and Senate in the same form and signed by the President to become law. For much of its history one Senator could block a vote of the Senate. From the 1920s until the 1960s the Southerners used the filibuster regularly to block civil rights legislation.

For over a hundred years, from 1806 to 1907, the only way the Senate could stop a filibuster was a unanimous vote. After cloture vote rules were changed, from 1927 until 1962 cloture was not invoked once. Both Democrats and Republicans have used the filibuster to block the other party's agendas. There is nothing in the Constitution about the filibuster. While the idea of the Senate itself is anti-democratic because each state gets two Senators regardless of population, a Senate with filibuster is clearly anti-democratic. The filibuster violates the majority rule. One person and forty-one Senators can block any legislation.[28]

The politics of the filibuster are the politics of obstruction. (See Gerard N. Magliocca, Reforming the Filibuster, NW. U.L. REV. 303, 303–04, 2011.) "Forty-one senators, who could represent less than forty-one percent of the population due to the malapportionment of the Senate, can veto most legislation and presidential nominations by refusing to invoke cloture." Cloture today takes a three-fifths vote or 60 senators. The filibuster is a sorry way for the Senate to execute its democratic duty and refuse to act on legislation.

Senator Strom Thurmond of South Carolina holds the record for filibustering, at two days totaling over 24 hours, set in 1957 while trying to

6. Tyranny of the Republic

stop passage of the Civil Rights Act. Thurmond was a lifelong segregationist who ran for President in 1948 as a Dixiecrat opposing segregation. Thurmond never considered racial equality an option.[29]

The Senate today is an undemocratic institution that represents the interests of a minority of Americans. A bizarre math dominates the Senate where Senators who are Democrats, were elected by a greater proportion of the population of the United States than the Republican Senators. The twenty-two smallest states have a population of thirty-eight million people and are represented by forty-four senators. California has thirty-eight million people and only two senators. So much for Madison's belief that the Constitution protected the minority from oppression by the majority. This math discourages compromise and encourages a government by and for the minority of Americans.

This decidedly anti-democratic institution makes most members representatives of not the nation's interest but a minority's interest. Somewhere in Wyoming a cowboy sits on his horse and counts for more than 66 Californians. He can block any attempt at gun control or universal health care and sponsor the nomination and confirmation of a Supreme Court Justice who will vote against unions, gay rights and abortion and the majority of the electorate. In the 2016 election 45.2 million Americans cast votes for Democrats in the Senate and 39.3 million for Republicans.

An autocratic, anti-democratic President can with a compliant Senate make a wreck of presidential norms and the political process. The Electoral College chooses Presidents who have not won the popular vote, and with a Senate controlled by a minority party, democracy is dead in the United Sates. The Republican Party is a parody of the Dixiecrats.

Congress in the federal period and the antebellum period was dominated by slaveholding interests. Factions, parties, coalesced around the issue of slavery. Southerners fought back any attempt to limit or end slavery. Almost every constitutional crisis involved slavery. Southerners became more focused and dedicated to the idea of protecting slavery. Each territorial addition to the United States resulted in a conflict over whether it would enter the Union slave or free. The Constitution's design meant that the South could block by constitutional means the efforts to regulate or end slavery.

The Republican Party was founded by abolitionists to end slavery. The party produced Abraham Lincoln and a score of congressmen dedicated to ending slavery. Lincoln in fact was the "Great Emancipator" who

The Constitution and American Racism

saved the Union. The Radical Republicans dedicated their service in Congress to that end and once the war was over, and Lincoln was dead, they worked for the equality of the freedmen. Lincoln's Republican Party faded away after the Compromise of 1877 and its progeny embraced unfettered capitalism as its agenda. Congress, dominated by Republicans, turned from the hard work of liberty for all to "root hog or die." The rule of law from the ratification of the Constitution until the Civil War had been racism. In those parts of the South in rebellion to the United States government, it was racism. Once the war ended, the shooting never stopped. White Southerners consumed with the onus of defeat, the result of a bad bargain with slavery, motivated by racism, continued by lynching and eventually racist laws to enslave Blacks. The sharecropper system was economic peonage, while Jim Crow and segregation were ways to keep Black Americans down and protect white governments. Any study of the South in the post–Civil War years reveals a system of racism that was an exemplar for totalitarian governments. From the end of Reconstruction until the *Brown* decision the rule of law in America was racism that made segregation and inequality endemic.

The Democratic Party in Congress after the Civil War served the Southerners as its instrument to ensure the status quo. The Democrats had no history as the party of emancipation or Reconstruction. It functioned as a safe harbor for racists and dominated southern politics after the end of Reconstruction. Senator Strom Thurmond, from South Carolina, sometime Democrat/Dixiecrat/Republican; Senator James F. Byrnes, South Carolina; Senator Olin D. Johnston, South Carolina; Senator Theodore Bilbo, Mississippi; Senator Allan Ellender, Louisiana; Senator James O. Eastland, Mississippi; Senator John Stennis, Mississippi; Senator Harry Byrd, Virginia; Senator Herman Tallmadge, Georgia; Senator Richard Russell, Georgia: and Senator Jesse Helms, North Carolina, are but a few men whose racist prose and votes for segregation carved names for themselves into the history of Congressional racism. Russell, Byrd and Thurmond drafted the "Southern Manifesto" in response to *Brown*.[30]

In the 1940s through the 1950s the northern Democrats in the party began a move towards support of civil rights in Congress, made possible because the party had key constituencies that embraced civil rights. The change in attitudes seems to be a product of various coalitions that came about during the 1930s, despite Roosevelt's deplorable record on civil rights. By the 1950s Republicans had been more supportive of white Southerners battling change than northern Democrats. While it has been argued the tipping point was Lyndon Johnson's support of civil rights, there is evidence that prior to 1963 there was already support for change among northern Congressional Democrats.[31]

Regardless, for most of the twentieth century the rule of law in Congress was racism and segregation.

7

The Power Vested in the President

"If the colored people made a mistake in voting for me, they ought to correct it."
—Woodrow Wilson

"It is necessary that the executive magistrate should be the guardian of the people, even the lower classes, against legislative tyranny, against the great and wealthy, who in the course of things, will necessarily compose the legislative body. Wealth tends to corrupt the mind and to nourish its love of power and to stimulate it to oppression."[1] The office of the presidency was conceived of as a super-executive. Edmund Randolph, delegate to the Constitutional Convention from Virginia, argued the chief executive should be a triumvirate with "vigor, dispatch and responsibility."[2] Alexander Hamilton, intrigued by monarchial governments, believed that "men of little character acquiring great power become easily the tools of intermeddling neighbors."[3] Ben Franklin observed that "the first man put at the helm will be a good one. Nobody knows what sort may come afterwards. The executive will be always increasing here, as elsewhere, till it ends in a monarchy."[4]

George Mason argued at the Constitutional Convention in September 1787, that "considering the powers of the President and those of the Senate, if a coalition should be established between these two branches, they will be able to subvert the Constitution."[5] Mason feared that the system of checks and balances could be easily thwarted by the President and the Senate being ruled by the same party. If this were the case, there would be no check on the ambitions of either branch. After the official appearance of political parties, this concert of interests and action of the President and the Senate has occurred frequently in the history of the Republic. Since the President is the person who nominates candidates to the

7. The Power Vested in the President

federal judiciary, including the Supreme Court, and these nominations are approved by the Senate, there are no checks on any branch of the government when the President and the Senate are of the same party.

Because of the Electoral College a President can be elected without a majority of voters. Both the presidency and the Senate in combination can control national politics, and the men or women who occupy those positions can be elected by a minority of Americans. Madison made much of majority factions controlling government and ending a republic, but he was wrong.[6] The end of Madison's Republic is now engineered by a minority party, composed of minority factions, and those factions have no political goals, only cultural prejudices seeking validation and acquisition of money and power. If there is a venal, incompetent man or woman in the presidency, seeking power and using corruption to line his or her own pockets they cannot be removed without impeachment, and there will be no verdict removing them without a Senate willing to vote for such a result.

The Presidents of the United States have seldom used the office to advance the interest of racial equality. For the Republic's first seventy-two years the office was one more branch of government that danced to the tune of slavery. George Washington, John Quincy Adams and Abraham Lincoln stand alone in their public opposition to slavery. Washington, Jefferson, Madison and Monroe, all Virginians and slaveholders, were involved in the creation of the Republic. Jefferson freed few of his slaves during his life and at his death, and then only if they were a male and a Hemings.[7] Madison, the architect of the Constitution, died owning slaves. Of the first seven presidents only John Adams and John Quincy Adams never owned slaves.[8]

George Washington made the institution of the presidency from whole cloth because there was no example to follow and the Constitution lacked detail. An able general, he was also an able administrator. His leadership in all of the public endeavors he undertook marked those institutions with his personal notion of right and wrong. For him, character was everything. His character mattered to him. It is perhaps impossible in our time to understand that for Washington, a man acted with the best intentions, seeking the best outcome in whatever challenge confronted him. His service as commander of the Continental Army was remarkable. He wanted to be a British officer. When the British refused Washington that office, they made a remarkable enemy. The Continental Army was initially composed of men who were at best militia with some smattering of military training. Many men never had any military training until they joined the Continental Army. Washington held that Army together through the sheer force of his will. Those were indeed times that tried men's souls, and few rose to the challenge, but those who did were led by Washington to victory. As President, Washington made the office and its institutions. He worked hard to keep the states in the Union and when it was time to go, he knew it and did it with dignity.

Washington owned slaves for fifty-six years and came to believe abolition was necessary. In 1786 he wrote a letter to John Francis Mercer: "With respect to the first, I never mean (unless some particular circumstances should compel me to it) to possess another slave by purchase; it being among my first wishes to see some plan adopted, by the legislature by which slavery in this Country may be abolished by slow, sure, & imperceptible degrees."[9] Later Washington said, "The unfortunate condition of the persons, whose labour in part I employed, has been the only unavoidable subject of regret."[10]

Washington deplored political factions and his was the only presidency not dominated by party politics. Politics in the country quickly become consumed by those who believed in a strong federal government, the Federalists, and those who favored a less powerful national government, the Anti-Federalists. John Adams and Alexander Hamilton were the leaders of the Federalist faction, and Thomas Jefferson and James Madison led the Democratic-Republicans. Jefferson never publicly spoke out against slavery before or after ratification of the Constitution. The Jeffersonian party became the Democrats by 1828 and would play the race card well into the twentieth century.[11] The Federalists counted abolitionists among their ranks, but the Jeffersonian party did not include abolition in their agenda.[12] Sectionalism and slavery would be at the center of conflicts from the founding through the Civil War.

Thomas Jefferson owned many slaves before and after writing the Declaration of Independence. The Declaration had originally included an attack on slavery, more accurately on King George for perpetuating the African slave trade, but it was struck at the urgings of the Georgia and South Carolina delegations to the Continental Congress. It was not an attack on the institution of slavery.[13] Jefferson, despite the proclamation of equality in the Declaration, was a racist who prospered from slavery. While he found slavery distasteful, he believed its victims to be inferior and even advanced the idea that their blackness might come from the color of their blood.[14] He was a racist who attacked the

7. The Power Vested in the President

intellectual abilities of his slaves, of all Blacks, and wrote they had a "disagreeable odor," were inferior in the endowments of body and mind and that Black women might mate with an "Oranootan." They lacked the "tender delicate mixture of sentiment and sensation."[15] Jefferson did nothing for Black men or women as President. When he died, he freed only one of his male slaves but did not free the man's wife and eight children, who were sold in four separate sales.[16] Historian Gordon S. Wood has written, "If one believed in the natural equality of Blacks, then slavery became impossible, which is why most enlightened thinkers on both sides of the Atlantic came to oppose slavery. Like other slaveholding Southerners, Jefferson sensed this and came to realize Black slavery could ultimately be justified and explained only if Black Africans were considered a different order of beings, different race, one unequal to whites."[17]

Andrew Jackson owned a thousand-acre plantation worked by slaves and hated American Indians. Jackson pursued his runaway slaves with a vengeance by offering rewards and promising that any person who captured a slave would increase his reward by whipping him or her. He permitted confiscation of anti-slavery pamphlets and vilified abolitionists. His presidency was a departure from the norm in that he was a Westerner, a man of the people, the white people, of the more common sort. His objective was a great leveling, for white men. His support came from "slave frontier" states like Alabama, Kentucky, and Tennessee.[18] His agenda included confiscation of Indian land, a war on banks and contempt for institutions. With the Indians forced out of the way, their lands in Georgia, North Carolina, Tennessee and Alabama became a source of new plantations and more slaves producing more cotton.[19]

Roger Taney, Chief Justice of the Supreme Court who wrote the Dred Scott decision, was appointed by Andrew Jackson to the Supreme Court. Jackson's man served on the Court from 1836 and did not leave the bench until his death in 1864. Taney was Chief Justice of a court that mattered. Jackson had ignored John Marshall's decisions at the Supreme Court protecting the Cherokees from removal and wanted a compliant man on the bench. Taney's decisions regarding slavery protected the peculiar institution. The Black man, he wrote, "has no rights the white man was bound to respect."[20]

James K. Polk, a Tennessee slave owner and protégé of Andrew Jackson, became the eleventh President in 1845. This was the age of "Manifest Destiny," the belief that Americans were bound by God and destiny to

The Constitution and American Racism

spread across the Continent, taking democracy and civilization with them. Polk was an expansionist and wanted to add more Mexican land to newly annexed Texas. He sent an Army of Observation to the Nueces River in Texas, one that managed to start a war with Mexico. This was a land grab successful beyond Polk's ambitions, eventually adding California and the Utah and New Mexico territories, adding more land than any other President. Ulysses Grant, a Lieutenant in the Army in Mexico, said later, "I do not think there was ever a more wicked war than that waged by the United States on Mexico," and it was "one of the most unjust ever waged by a stronger against a weaker nation."[21] Manifest Destiny meant more land for more cotton and more slaves. In 1846, David Wilmot, a Pennsylvania Congressman, managed to get a proposal through the House barring slavery in these new lands. The Wilmot Proviso died in the Senate.

"When the time comes, I shall speak…. It is true that, while I hold myself, without mock modesty, the humblest of all individuals that have ever been elevated to the presidency, I have a more difficult task to perform than any one of them,"[22] said Abraham Lincoln, the man who emancipated the slaves, preserved the Union and abolished slavery. Lincoln gave life to Jefferson's words. While criticized as being unqualified, indecisive and slow to embrace abolition, he made freedom real to all of those who labored in servitude as slaves in the American South. He bore the burdens of a bloody civil war that destroyed slavery and fought a Second American Revolution to make Jefferson's Declaration apply to all Americans. Professing a love of the Constitution, he used it to crush the rebellion. He dealt with traitors, dissemblers, and incompetents, but in the face of military defeats and thousands of casualties he never lost sight of the "better angels of ourselves." In the twilight of his administration, he ran for re-election as President in 1864, promising an amendment to the Constitution to abolish slavery and consummate this Second American Revolution, making the slaves forever free. The volunteers who filled the ranks of the Army of the Potomac and the Western Armies who enlisted in 1861 to save the Union re-enlisted in 1864 to free the slaves. The Union Army was Mr. Lincoln's Army and it helped keep him in the White House. On Saturday April 15, 1865, the

> Pale Horse had come. To a deep river, to a far country, to a by-and-by whence no man returns, had gone the child of Nancy Hanks and Tom Lincoln, the wilderness boy who had found far lights and tall rainbows to live by, whose name even before he died had become a legend inwoven with men's struggle for freedom the world over.[23]

7. The Power Vested in the President

When the last rebel surrendered, the Radical Republicans in the Congress, the U.S. Army, and the Freedmen's Bureau defended freedmen. Lawlessness and white reconstruction reigned in the South as defeated rebels returned home and attacked the largely defenseless freedmen. Andrew Johnson was not the man for the hour and talked emancipation until he was President. "Tennessee" Johnson was impeached but not convicted, because of his Reconstruction policies that re-established white power in the former rebel states. He proved to be a huge disappointment to both Radical Republicans and moderates in the Senate. The Senate struggled with Johnson over who was in control of Reconstruction in the South. He had interfered in Army attempts to protect freedmen from white terrorism by withdrawing troops and countermanding military orders. He had waged war on the Freedmen's Bureau, and he opposed the Fourteenth and Fifteenth Amendments. Johnson had proved far too conciliatory and lenient to former rebels, and his language and acts were racist. He vetoed the Civil Rights Act of 1866 and the creation of a permanent Freedmen's Bureau, but the Senate overrode his vetoes.[24]

When Ulysses S. Grant became President, he used federal troops and marshals to protect Black civil and voting rights. He urged adoption of the Fifteenth Amendment granting Blacks the right to vote and signed it in 1870. He used the Enforcement Acts, including the Ku Klux Klan Act, to suppress white terror in the South. At one point he declared martial law in nine South Carolina Counties and sent federal troops to keep the peace. Grant remained faithful in his commitment to Black Americans, but time did not. As the Civil War became more of a memory, those who supported Black rights began to disappear from the political stage. Eventually Blacks were betrayed by President Hayes, who withdrew federal troops from the South and all but ceased enforcement of the Civil Rights Acts and other legislation designed to protect Blacks from white terror. Frederick Douglass said, "That sturdy old Roman, Benjamin Butler, made the negro contraband, Abraham Lincoln made him a freeman, and Ulysses S. Grant made him a citizen." The Civil Rights Act of 1875 was passed by Congress and signed by Grant. It provided wide-ranging protections for Blacks and made discrimination in public accommodations illegal. Unfortunately, the public accommodations protections were found unconstitutional in the *Civil Rights Cases* in 1883.[25] The Court ruled that the Act was unconstitutional because Congress had no power to regulate the conduct of private persons and corporations. In fact, this ruling was at odds with much of Supreme Court jurisprudence and paved the way for the legalization of

The Constitution and American Racism

Jim Crow through state legislation regulating the conduct of private persons and corporations.

President Rutherford B. Hayes had defended fugitive slaves before the Civil War and while he was greatly influenced by his wife's beliefs regarding the abolition of slavery, he never fully embraced the idea of equality. Hayes had served in the Union Army and was wounded three times. The election of 1876 resulted in Hayes agreeing to Southern home-rule and withdrawing northern troops. Hayes considered nominating former Confederate General Joseph Johnston to the War Department, but this idea fortunately faded in the clear light of day.[26] Thinking conciliation would win the day, Hayes appointed Southern Democrat and former rebel officer David Key to head the Post Office.[27] Hayes's administration meant an end to Reconstruction designed to give the Black Southerners legal and civil equality. The withdrawal of federal troops meant there was virtually no protection for Blacks trying to participate in the political process. There was virtually no protection for Blacks trying to live normal lives. Racism won.

When Teddy Roosevelt charged up San Juan Hill, he was accompanied by Black soldiers.[28] Although impressed by their bravery that day, he later claimed that the Black soldiers were unreliable under fire, an opinion unsupported by eyewitnesses. Black Republican voters supported him when he was elected President in 1904, after serving the rest of the assassinated President McKinley's term. Roosevelt invited the first Black person to the White House, Booker T. Washington. The invitation and visit were hotly criticized by segregationists. A Memphis newspaper called the invitation and visit the "most damnable outrage ever perpetuated by any citizen of the United States."[29] Eventually, Black activists who considered the government far too conciliatory on civil rights for Blacks were also critical of Roosevelt's failure to intervene in the South and protect Blacks from white violence. Roosevelt's handling in 1906 of the "Brownsville Affair" signaled a partiality for white justice. Black troops stationed in Brownsville, Texas, were involved in the shooting of a white bartender. A Texas court found no one guilty. Roosevelt waited until after the November midterm elections, and after Black votes had been counted, to dismiss 167 Black soldiers from the Army, "without honor" and "forever barred from reenlistment." Many of those men were long-serving soldiers who lost their pension benefits. Six of them had received the Congressional Medal of Honor.[30]

Woodrow Wilson was a racist. The son of a Confederate soldier and

7. The Power Vested in the President

native Virginian, he had been New Jersey's governor and became the 28th President. As president of Princeton University, Wilson had kept Blacks out of the school.[31] He appointed cabinet members, Josephus Daniels for the Navy, Postmaster General Burleson and William McAdoo at Treasury, who were Southerners and all racists. Daniels said, "the subjugation of the negro, politically, and the separation of the negro socially, are paramount to all other concerns." Wilson supported segregation in the federal workplace, including separate toilets and other measures designed to segregate workers.[32] He was initially supported by Blacks, but when his promises for fair treatment evaporated with the passage of time, Black civil rights leaders asked for a face-to-face. The first meeting resulted in more unkept promises, and the second meeting ended when Wilson threw one of the leaders, William Trotter, out of the White House when he dared to confront Wilson with his record of inaction on civil rights issues.[33]

During Wilson's first term as President, Congress passed a bill making interracial marriage in the District of Columbia illegal and a Southern senator promised repeal of the Fourteenth and Fifteenth Amendments. When America entered the First World War, Blacks enlisted in the armed forces in large numbers and migrated to the North for jobs. Race riots in various U.S. cities marked the white response to these events. Wilson was the first President to condemn lynching, but when pressed for concrete action to help Blacks he said, "We all have to be patient with one another,"[34] and applauded the "great Ku Klux Klan."

For over half of the twentieth century Presidents did little to intervene in the reign of terror in the South. "Smiling Cal," President Calvin Coolidge, flooded predominantly Black communities as the result of the destruction of levees by the Army Corps of Engineers during the "Great Mississippi River" flood. This action displaced thousands of Blacks who were forced into labor camps under the management of the National Guard, which did not protect them from beatings, rapes and lynchings by local whites. Congress passed a racist Immigration Act and Coolidge declared that "America must be kept American."

Herbert Hoover believed in personal initiative to improve Black lives, but not government intervention. W.E.B. Du Bois said that Hoover was an undemocratic racist who saw Blacks as a species of "sub-men" when Hoover began a policy of purging Blacks from the Republican party. This so-called "Southern policy" was meant to attract white Southerners to the party. He wrote in a mining textbook that whites were of a higher mental order and made better workers.[35]

The Constitution and American Racism

While large numbers of Blacks received job training from the Works Progress Administration and hundreds of thousands benefited from literacy and housing programs, Franklin D. Roosevelt was fond of jokes about the "darkies." The press emphasized that Hitler refused to shake hands with Jesse Owens, the 1936 Olympic hero, but FDR never congratulated him. Roosevelt banned Black reporters from his news conferences for eleven years. Fifty-seven Blacks were lynched in the South in his first three years in the White House, but he never supported anti-lynching legislation for fear it would offend white Southern Democrats. The Roosevelt who worked for civil rights was his wife Eleanor.[36] The massive Tennessee Valley Authority project that brought electricity to rural homes all over the South segregated Black employees. When H. Phillip Randolph demanded integration of defense industries in 1942, Roosevelt refused until Randolph threatened to lead a massive demonstration on Washington. Race still drove American presidential politics in the Great Depression and during the Second World War.[37]

Black leaders during the Depression and World War II urged Black voters to cross over to the Democrats during Roosevelt's administration. New Deal programs sustained large numbers of Blacks but did not end racial discrimination. Gunnar Myrdal said that the New Deal "changed the whole configuration of the Negro problem" because "for almost the first time in the history of the nation the state has done something substantial in a social way without excluding the Negro."[38]

"Truman was a complex of ideas and impulses, prejudices and principles."[39] He was from Missouri and had a grandfather who had owned slaves, and his southern colleagues in the Senate believed there would be no change to racial policies when he became President. They were wrong. According to historians, Truman brought an attitude of decency and justice and a sense of fair play to race issues. He condemned the Klan and violence against Blacks; he was the first President to address the NAACP; he created the President's Committee on Civil Rights; he ordered the armed forces desegregated, a move that had no political upside for Truman; and he spoke out on civil rights and put it on the national agenda. In 1948, facing a hard-fought presidential campaign, he endorsed a strong civil rights platform at the Democratic convention. This caused a schism in the Democratic Party, and traditional Southern Democrats led by Strom Thurmond walked out of the convention and formed the Dixiecrat Party.[40]

Dwight Eisenhower's most significant civil rights act was to appoint Earl Warren Chief Justice of the Supreme Court. There was not much in

7. The Power Vested in the President

Warren's background to indicate that he would be a civil rights advocate, but that is precisely what he became on the Court. Historian James F. Simon wrote that "Earl Warren was the very personification of honesty, decency, and fairness.... His moral condemnation of the official practice of racial segregation could not be ignored by his colleagues."[41] Eisenhower told Warren at a February 1954 White House dinner he understood why white Southerners felt "their sweet little girls [are not] required to sit in school alongside some big black buck."[42] Eisenhower had been commander of a segregated army. He confessed to a Black special assistant after his election that he had been guilty of racial prejudice during his military career. He had opposed integration of the armed forces during the Second World War and he refused to meet with Black leaders while courting white Southern segregationists.[43] Eisenhower was the reluctant civil rights warrior. He opposed federal intervention in the South to protect Black civil rights.[44] But pressed by events and Southern arrogance, Eisenhower did send federal troops to Arkansas to force integration of Little Rock Central High School. However, he did this only after making statements that the law could not change personal feelings, and it became apparent that the situation in Little Rock was out of control.[45]

The 1957 Civil Rights Act was a middle-of-the-road measure that created a civil rights division in the Justice Department, called for appointment of a bipartisan civil rights commission, and gave authority to the attorney general to seek judicial enforcement of civil rights violations and protection of voting rights. The bill caused a firestorm in the southern delegations in Congress. A "mere shell of the bill" was passed only after section 3, which gave authority to the Attorney General to prosecute civil rights violations, was dropped from the bill, and section 4 amended to require jury trials for those violating voter's rights.[46]

Senator John F. Kennedy had frequently voted with the southern block on civil rights issues. When Kennedy was elected President, he was reluctant to sponsor any civil rights legislation, because he believed that a fight over civil rights would jeopardize his legislative agenda. He tried to get his civil rights advocate to stop Freedom Rides in the South, and his justice department encouraged civil rights workers to concentrate on voter registration, not segregation.[47] Kennedy believed that he could accomplish more for civil rights through executive order than legislation. Yet he acted slowly, and it took twenty-two months to end discrimination in public housing.

Despite this, there were some accomplishments for Black Americans.

The Constitution and American Racism

Kennedy used his power to appoint the first Black U.S. Attorneys and federal district judges, and he appointed the longtime Black civil rights attorney Thurgood Marshall to the U.S. Second Circuit Court of Appeals. Blacks were named ambassadors and filled positions as executives in the civil service. He banned discrimination in federal employment and appointed the Equal Employment Opportunity Commission to prevent discrimination in the federal workplace. Robert Kennedy, his Attorney General, made civil rights enforcement a priority. He sent hundreds of U.S. Marshals to the South in response to white violence and filed more voters' rights actions. After the violence in Birmingham in the spring of 1963, the President made civil rights his fight.[48]

In 1960 Lyndon Johnson wanted to be the Democratic candidate for President but instead left the Senate to be John Kennedy's vice president. Johnson came from a hardscrabble Texas youth and became a teacher and then a politician. He was the consummate politician and loved the fight. He was a southern Congressman from Texas who refused to sign the Southern Manifesto, but he was not shy about using racial epithets and had a strained relationship with Martin Luther King, Jr. After Kennedy's assassination he took up civil rights as his cause and made possible the passage of the Civil Rights Act of 1964 and the Voting Rights Act of 1965. After the violence in Selma, Johnson went to Congress and made an impassioned appeal for the Voting Rights Act. "Even if we pass this bill, the battle will not be over. What happened in Selma is part of a far larger movement ... of American Negroes to secure for themselves the blessings of American life. Their cause must be our cause too. Because it is not just Negroes, but really all of us, who must overcome the crippling legacy of bigotry and injustice. And we shall overcome."[49]

Richard Nixon used racism in Republican efforts to regain the White House and scooped up Dixiecrats to support him and his party's electoral efforts. The South had been solidly Democratic until 1948. With the advent of the Civil Rights era it turned to the Republican Party in order to slow desegregation. The United States Fifth Circuit Court of Appeals had been managing desegregation in the South through court decisions that struck at Jim Crow and segregation. The Supreme Court under Chief Justice Earl Warren had generally supported these decisions. Nixon offered the Southern Democrats a home port in what they saw as a stormy sea by promising to support "states' rights" (code for slowing or halting desegregation), and appoint only "strict constructionists" to the Supreme Court. The Southerners embraced the Republicans and gave the party a base for

7. The Power Vested in the President

its war against the federal government, which meant for white Southerners a war against desegregation.

Part of Nixon's strategy was to pack the Supreme Court with men who would slow or halt integration. At the U.S. Circuit Court level Nixon promised to dilute the power of the Fifth Circuit Court of Appeals in the South by adding a new federal circuit court of appeals to be filled with conservatives. Thus, the Eleventh Circuit Court of Appeals was born in the South. Nixon used it to attack busing, welfare and affirmative action.

This "Southern Strategy" helped Ronald Reagan, George H. Bush, George W. Bush and Donald Trump get to the White House. The strategy has now appealed not only to Southern white racists but to evangelicals and other Christians on the right who seek a society based on dogma that calls for judgment of those in our society who do not conform to their definition of morality. In 2016 the evangelicals supported a candidate who told them whatever they wanted to hear and decried cultural inclusion and civil rights. A new bargain with the devil dictated Republican policies and politics. All of this was politically possible because of the Constitution that made slavery legal, and its legacy of racism.

The presidency, like Congress and the Supreme Court, is a shell of whatever greatness it once offered the American people. As Franklin said at the convention, the institution will surely go the way of monarchy—or perhaps dictatorship. Since Richard Nixon, racism has been a plank in the Republican platform. Nixon wanted the support of former Dixiecrats and the supporters of George Wallace. The Republicans claimed that they would rein in a big government that had sought to destroy Jim Crow, desegregate schools and offered equality to Black Americans. The mantra was protecting states' rights; it was Republican politically correct speech. To maintain power, Nixon not only engineered felony break-ins, but his vice president was convicted of corruption. Ronald Reagan took on welfare moms and adopted anti-feminism. He not only used race but broadened the party's appeal to attack the poor and women, who wanted to be treated as equals. The Republican party managed the elections of the Bush, father and son candidates, on the backs of all these issues and the party went for the evangelical vote, opposing gay rights, prohibiting abortion and putting religion back into government. Trump used race to unify a base who believes they have been cheated of their American destiny. Nazi and Confederate flags are carried by "some very fine people" who happen to advocate a race war. George Washington would not understand how this was possible. Trump was elected despite three million more votes for his Democratic opponent. All of this has been made possible by the undemocratic government created by Madison's Constitution.

The Constitution made this possible because it failed to protect Black Americans from 1876 until the 1960s. The Senate of the United States was and is the greatest debating society in the world for men who wanted to support and protect segregation and prevent reform. Filibuster became an effective tool. Southern Senators adopted vicious rhetoric for which there are no apologies. They protected lynching and were aided and abetted by Northerners who sought coalitions for their own purposes. Jack Kennedy voted with them on occasion in the Senate. When change finally came it was resisted by the southern Senators. The rule of law in the Senate was racism. Madison's constitutional promise of checks and balances can only break the southern resistance in the Senate if the Democrats in favor of change are able to have sufficient numbers to stop filibusters and pass bills with agreement of the House and President. If the Senate is controlled by one party, it can stop government and the rule of law in its tracks. It hasn't always worked this way but in the twenty-first century, if the presidency and the Senate are controlled by the same party, they can easily thwart the will of the majority of Americans. The House is the only branch of government truly elected by the people, although it too is affected by gerrymandering and voter suppression. In the Senate in 2020, Republicans are a majority, representing 153 million Americans, while the minority party, the Democrats, represent 168 million Americans. The President was elected by the Electoral College in an election he lost by three million popular votes. This is neither a republic nor a democracy.

8

Civil Rights

There were no civil rights in slave America. There were no civil rights for Black persons until after the Civil War and the abolition of slavery. Slaves were property and treated throughout the South as things to be bought and sold, given as gifts, and inherited. They were collateral for loans and payment for debts. The slave codes reinforced the notion that a whole race of people was nothing but chattel. Slaves could be punished at a master's whim, including beatings and sometimes death. They were forbidden the ordinary necessities of life and were chained to a system that was not concerned with their rights or their human qualities. The rule of law in the United States before the Civil War was clearly stated by Chief Justice Taney in *Dred Scott* in 1857: "[Blacks] had no rights which the white man was bound to respect...."

The first Fugitive Slave Act had been passed by Congress in 1793, and some states responded with personal liberty laws to protect escaped slaves and afford due process to them, including the right to a jury trial, the right to appeal and the right to an attorney.[1] In these states the procedural rights attending jury trial were the rights afforded runaway slaves. Those states believed that these rights were necessary to protect the interest of Black persons captured, kidnapped, and claimed by white men to be slaves. These personal liberty laws were deeply resented by Southerners and were attacked in the courts and in Congress. In *Prigg v. Pennsylvania* the pro-slavery Supreme Court found that laws affording minimal due process rights to fugitive slaves were unconstitutional.[2] Regardless, men and women of good will continued to do what they could to thwart what most considered to be kidnapping.

With the Compromise of 1850 came a new Fugitive Slave Act and more pressure from the South to enforce the Act. Federal marshals, troops and more state officials were called on to return Blacks to slavery. States and individual citizens continued to offer sanctuary and relief to runaways. Some states reinforced their personal liberty laws and aided runaways despite decisions in the federal courts enforcing the Act. The harder the South sought to enforce it the more people recognized the evils of slavery, turning public opinion inexorably toward abolition. In Ohio, bordering on slave states and part of the Old Northwest Territory, the state legislature made it harder to return fugitive slaves.[3] Other northern states sought to afford protections to the fugitives and public opinion turned against support for slavery.

The Thirteenth Amendment abolished constitutional slavery and may rightly be regarded as the most important civil rights act in American history. The Emancipation Proclamation was a military order that would cease by its own terms with the end of the war. Lincoln and the Radical Republicans wanted to make sure that slavery ended. Lincoln ran for re-election in 1864 on the promise to push the Amendment through to ratification. The Amendment failed to pass the House when first presented, but finally in January 1865, with a lame duck Congress, it passed. Some, including abolitionist William Lloyd Garrison, saw their work as completed, while others like Frederick Douglass recognized the work had just begun. Douglass knew, "Slavery is not abolished until the black man has the ballot."[4]

Lincoln believed the South had no legal right to secede. Many in Congress believed that the South had committed political suicide by seceding and that the southern states had to apply for readmission to the Union. Almost everyone in Congress believed that the South could not simply pick up where it left off in 1861. Lincoln chose Johnson, a governor of a border state, as his vice-president; he was now dead and Johnson was President. He had professed undying hatred for the slave South and its patrician leadership. He had spoken like a friend of Blacks but when Lincoln died and he became President, he favored pardons for Southerners and encouraged the re-establishment of white governments, composed of the class whose lifestyle he once professed to hate. He expressed contempt for the freedmen and predicted they would be unable to govern themselves. The Radical Republicans in Congress and Johnson were soon at war, and it ended badly for Johnson.

The Radical Republicans repudiated the white governments organized under Johnson's stewardship and embarked on Congressional Reconstruction. The states were required to make abolition part of their new constitutions.[5] Nevertheless former Confederate states all tried to re-establish white governments that recognized no rights for the freedmen.

8. Civil Rights

The right to vote is the basic right of a citizen in a democracy. Without that right the government does not reflect the will of the people. Except for the Fourteenth, Fifteenth and Nineteenth Amendments, the Constitution is sadly and strangely silent on the issue of voting rights. Madison opined at the Convention that "suffrage is certainly one of the fundamental articles of republican government and ought not to be left to be regulated by the legislature" but wanted to restrict it to freeholders (property owners). This met with opposition from not only Benjamin Franklin but others, so it was left to the states.[6]

The Radical Republicans were mobilized by Johnson's racism, his ill-considered treatment of white Southerners encouraging the re-establishment of a white South, his condoning white terror intended to oppress Blacks, and his interference with the military trying to protect freedmen. The Radical Republicans decided that Reconstruction must guarantee Black voting rights and other basic civil rights. There must be equality before the law guaranteed by the national government. Wrestling control from Johnson, they required the states that had been part of the Confederacy to provide for Black voting rights in their constitutions and to adopt the Fourteenth Amendment as prerequisites to readmission to the Union. Southern whites sought by law and intimidation to reestablish a social system like slavery that kept the white foot on the Black man's neck. The Jubilee did not come with the end of the war and the abolition of slavery. White Southerners voting as the result of the leniency of President Johnson's Reconstruction efforts sent men back to Congress who had just months before been in open armed rebellion against the federal government. These former Confederate soldiers and politicians were unreconstructed rebels seeking establishment of a white society that controlled all facets of Black lives.

With Johnson's blessing Southern white governments passed Black Codes to regulate Black lives through vagrancy laws, creating a system of economic peonage, legal kidnaping of Black children, and burdening Blacks economically and financially with laws designed to create a Black underclass.[7] The codes forbade Blacks from entering into certain professions unless they paid substantial taxes. They made it illegal for Blacks to own weapons and imposed taxes on their firearms where they could own them. The codes punished Blacks economically when they quit unreasonable labor contracts and authorized law enforcement persons holding Black prisoners to rent them out as laborers. These codes were enforced by a legal system that excluded Blacks from law enforcement, prosecution and the courts.[8]

Excluding Blacks from voting meant excluding them from government. Excluding Blacks from government meant there was no one to represent their interests. Education was a farce controlled by white legislators who proclaimed a policy of separate but equal. Everything was separate but nothing was equal. Separate schools for Blacks were barely funded and part of a policy of separation from white society. In these early white Reconstruction governments, there were no civil rights for Blacks because Black voting was effectively denied by the former masters. Separate treatment that resulted in separate accommodations made Black economics a disaster and insured a lifetime of poverty for generation after generation.

The Civil Rights Acts

The Civil Rights Act of 1866 was meant to enforce the Thirteenth Amendment. It made all persons born in America citizens. Justice Taney's declaration in the *Dred Scott* decision that Blacks were not and could not be U.S. citizens was nullified. The Act granted all citizens "the equal benefit of all laws and proceedings for the security of persons and property." State law or custom discriminating on the basis of race or color was made illegal. The Act applied to everyone, North and South.[9]

All persons who were citizens had the right to make contracts, own property, sue in court and enjoy all the protections of federal law. Importantly, the federal courts were given jurisdiction over criminal violations of the Act and federal district courts and courts of appeal had concurrent jurisdiction to hear civil violations of the Act.

Lyman Trumbull, the Senator from Illinois who authored the bill, declared its purpose was to secure for all men "great and fundamental rights" and "break down all discrimination between Black and white men." "Tennessee" Johnson, President of the United States, vetoed the Act because he believed it prohibited private discrimination and that Congress had no constitutional power to regulate such matters. Within days, both Houses of Congress overrode the veto, a first in American history. The bill was reenacted in 1870, after passage of the Fourteenth Amendment and in 1874 became Section 1981 of the United States Code.[10]

Interpretation of the Act has not been consistent throughout its history. Its authors believed that it prohibited private discrimination and

8. Civil Rights

early interpretations of the Act were consistent with this argument. In the *Matter of Turner*, Salmon P. Chase, Chief Justice of the Supreme Court, acting as a federal circuit judge in Virginia, ruled that a private person offering apprentice programs had to treat Blacks the same as whites and teach them all how to read.[11] Another case brought under the Act held that a Black woman who purchased a first class ticket on a railroad had a right to ride in the first class section. In 1968, in *Jones v. Alfred H. Mayer*,[12] the Supreme Court finally found Congress intended to prohibit private as well as public discrimination. Jones alleged that he was discriminated against in the sale of real estate and the Supreme Court agreed, finding that the Civil Rights Act of 1866 prohibited private and public discrimination. The Act today remains a powerful tool for all races to enforce civil rights.

The Fourteenth Amendment was an American revolution. It established the primacy of national citizenship and mandated that all persons born in the United States were citizens of the Republic and entitled to due process and equal protection of law. It was meant to block southern attempts to interfere with the enforcement of individual liberties enumerated in the Bill of Rights and to protect all citizens from government interference and private violations of the Bill of Rights. It was drafted by the Radical Republicans, passed Congress in 1866, and ratified in 1868.

The Supreme Court has not consistently ruled the Fourteenth Amendment applied the Bill of Rights to all action, private or state, impairing the rights of citizens.[13] By finding that a violation must be by state action, the Court has through its case law rendered the Privileges and Immunities Clause a nullity. The Privileges and Immunities Clause was meant to protect basic rights from infringement by private or public action. The Supreme Court has impaired the protection afforded by the Privileges and Immunities Clause by limiting it to state action. Edwin Chemerinsky argued, "all private violations of liberties occur because the state has chosen to tolerate and not forbid them. Private power certainly can interfere with fundamental values such as freedom of speech or equality every bit as much as government action."[14]

The Fourteenth Amendment has five sections; the first defines citizenship and prohibits laws that abridge the "privileges and immunities of citizens of the United States" and prohibits any state from depriving "any person of life, liberty, or property, without due process of law ... or equal protection of the laws." As Eric Foner has said, this was "a national guarantee of equality before the law."[15]

Section 2 enabled Congress to reduce the population counted in a state for determining representation in the House by the proportion of those male citizens denied the right to vote. This provision was meant to answer southern attempts to deny Black male suffrage. Unfortunately, Congress never had the courage to enforce this penalty after white Southerners took over state governments and began excluding Blacks from voting.

Section 3 was meant to disqualify those southern men who had previously "sworn an oath to the Constitution as an officer of the federal or state governments and then taken arms against the federal government, from service in the Senate or House, as electors for President or Vice President, or any office, civil or military, under the United States, or under any state." Section 3 was in response to the election of rebels all over the South to state offices and to the Congress of the United States. The election of these men occurred under President Johnson's ill-considered policies for Reconstruction. The men in Congress who had shepherded the federal government through four long years of civil war were not going to sit down in Washington with traitors, many of whom had received pardons mere months after leaving the battlefield.

Section 4 made clear that the United States would not pay debts incurred by the rebel states or the Confederacy as a result of the war. But Section 4 once and for all foreclosed any idea of payment to Southerners for emancipated slaves. Many Southerners returning home told their fellow rebels and former slave owners that they should demand payment for the liberated slaves before reentering the Union.

Section 5 gave Congress authority and power to enforce the Fourteenth Amendment by "appropriate legislation."

The Radical Republicans believed in the gifts of natural law and wanted equality to be the rule of law.[16] That is the purpose of government. During the passage of the Civil Rights Act of 1866 and the ratification of the Fourteenth Amendment, Congress was at war with the President. The Radical Republicans were not willing to stand by and watch Johnson surrender the gains of the Civil War and the future of Black Americans. The Reconstruction Act of 1867 placed the South under military rule, giving the Army the power to protect persons and property, and required the southern states to ratify the Fourteenth Amendment and write new constitutions establishing Black voting rights. These state constitutions had to be ratified by a majority of registered voters. Another bill gave military commanders the right to register voters and hold elections. The Habeas Corpus Act allowed Black citizens to avoid local southern courts

8. Civil Rights

and proceed with actions to enforce their rights in federal courts. Another bill outlawed peonage.[17]

The Fifteenth Amendment did not grant an absolute right to vote but prohibited the use of "race, color or previous condition of servitude" in determining voter qualifications. The Reconstruction Congress wanted the voting rights of Black Southerners protected. Those voting rights were granted by Congress in the Reconstruction Act of 1867 and by the former states that rebelled as a price of readmission to the Union. The amendment was ratified by 1870, but white Southerners immediately began devising other schemes and qualifications that were meant to disenfranchise Blacks. They were imminently successful.

The Civil Rights Act of 1875 was a valiant effort to fight public and private segregation. Charles Sumner, the lifelong advocate for abolition and equal rights, urged passage of a new civil rights act in 1874. This was the same Senator Sumner who was nearly beaten to death on the floor of the Senate because of his abolitionist views by Representative Preston Brooks of South Carolina. Senator Sumner was dying and was at odds with the Grant administration over U.S. policy in the Caribbean. But he persisted in his steadfast views as to the principle of equality. Thus, the Civil Rights Act was passed and signed by Grant in March 1875, after Sumner's death. The bill outlawed racial discrimination. It was revolutionary in its treatment of Black Americans. Not until 1957, eighty-two years later, would there be another civil rights bill.[18]

In 1883 the U.S. Supreme Court considered several civil rights cases together. President Hayes, elected in the disputed 1876 election without a majority of popular votes and only after the math in a disputed Electoral College didn't add up, had begun dismantling Congressional Reconstruction. Pig iron, steel, railroads, commerce and profits had become the driving forces in America. The Civil Rights Cases of 1883[19] presented the question of whether Congress could end private conduct that amounted to discrimination. The Court concluded that Congress did not have the power to regulate private conduct, it could only regulate conduct under the color of state law. It found the Civil Rights Act of 1875 unconstitutional. This decision effectively found segregation to be constitutional, and that principle was not only used to shield private conduct amounting to discrimination, but for 70 years, it also gave the states a pass to discriminate based on race.[20]

There was no new civil rights act until 1957. Dwight Eisenhower was unwilling to intervene in matters involving civil rights. He reluctantly

The Constitution and American Racism

intervened in Little Rock, but believed personally that private racism could not be changed. "I do not believe we can cure all the evils in men's hearts by law." He sent only white soldiers to Little Rock to enforce the federal court's orders. He had opposed a segregated Army during the Second World War. It was Truman, his predecessor, who desegregated the armed forces by executive order in 1949.[21] Eisenhower claimed his worst appointment was Earl Warren: "biggest damned fool mistake I ever made." The Civil Rights Act of 1957 was meant to protect Black voting rights and stirred a vicious debate in Congress as the result of Dixiecrat responses to the idea that the South needed any reforms. The Act was eventually diluted by the Senate and resulted in little real reform. Eisenhower signed another Civil Rights Act in 1960 that permitted federal inspection of voter registration lists.

The 1964 Civil Rights Act prohibited discrimination in public places and employment based on race, color, religion, sex, or national origin. It was the result of a long battle spanning decades. Civil rights workers pressed for its adoption, and it was a near thing. Lyndon Johnson was the only man who could have engineered its passage. Five days after Kennedy's assassination he told the nation, "We have talked long enough in this country about equal rights. We have talked for 100 years or more. It is time now to write the next chapter, and to write it in the books of law." Despite all of his faults, Johnson did the right thing and battled fellow Southerners for a better day for Black Americans. The bill passed the Senate only after a sixty-day filibuster was overcome by cloture.

We have mostly forgotten, or worse never knew, about the hard work done and trying times endured by civil rights workers trying to integrate the South. Young and old, they challenged a decades-old system of segregation, suppression of voting rights and terror. Voting was key to changing the system, and Southerners were not going to allow Blacks to vote without a fight. There were no Black jurors in Haynie, Alabama, in 1965. Jurors in Alabama were chosen from the voter's rolls, which had been purged of all Black voters. Jonathan Myrick Daniels, a valedictorian at Virginia Military Institute, was a 26-year-old white Episcopal seminary student. After Martin Luther King, Jr., called for volunteers to help battle segregation and hate in Selma, Alabama, in March 1965, Daniels went South and cast his lot with the cause of racial equality. Daniels and other young people, Black and white, were arrested while picketing all-white stores in Fort Deposit, Alabama, in August 1965. They were released some days later, on August 20. Daniels, with Catholic priest Father Richard Morrisroe and

8. Civil Rights

two Black women, walked to a nearby store that would serve Blacks, to buy a soft drink. Tom Coleman, an unpaid white special deputy, showed up that day with a shotgun and a pistol. He stood on the sidewalk blocking the entrance to the store, pointing the shotgun at one of the Black women, 17-year-old Ruby Sales. Daniels stepped in front of her and pushed her to the ground. Daniels now stood between a Black woman and a white man with a gun. Coleman pulled the trigger on the shotgun and killed Daniels. When Father Morrisroe grabbed the other Black woman to pull her to safety, Coleman shot him in the back.

Richmond McDavid Flowers, Sr., was attorney general of Alabama in 1965. Flowers opposed Governor George Wallace's segregationist policies. He labeled the Coleman killing another Ku Klux Klan murder. The local grand jury returned a manslaughter charge as a result of the death of Daniels. Flowers publicly said it should have been murder and took over the prosecution. Because the local judge would not delay the trial, the badly wounded Catholic priest was unable to testify. The white jury returned a not guilty verdict, finding that Coleman acted in self-defense when killing Daniels. Flowers was later convicted of official corruption, a charge he said resulted from his opposition to segregationist policies. President Jimmy Carter pardoned him in 1978. Daniels, a martyr to racial equality, was named a saint of the Protestant Episcopal Church.

Tom Coleman lived to be 86. He retired from his county job and said in an interview with CBS News the year after the killings that he had no regrets: "I would shoot them both tomorrow."

Edmund Burke was right that in the public sphere, "Bad men need nothing more to compass their ends, than that good men should look on and do nothing."[22]

The 1965 Voting Rights Act was passed to break down barriers erected by southern states to prevent Blacks from voting. The Act was a victory for Black men and women, civil rights workers and Lyndon Johnson. Men and women died for this Act. The VRA was the centerpiece of the Civil Rights movement because without the right to vote there is no democracy. Poll taxes, literacy tests, absurd registration rules and many other imaginative mechanisms to suppress Black voting that are still common today including violence, were the rule of the day. In support of the Act, Lyndon Johnson told Congress, "Should we defeat every enemy, should we double our wealth and conquer the stars, and still be unequal to this issue, then we will have failed as a people and a nation."[23]

The key provision requiring federal preclearance of southern states'

The Constitution and American Racism

voting regulations was, in *Shelby County v. Holder*,[24] unfortunately struck down by the Supreme Court. Since that decision, elections have been influenced and voters disenfranchised. The Court's view that southern states no longer required regulation of their voting rules because of past discrimination was just plain wrong.[25] Over 80,000 voters were struck from the Georgia rolls prior to the 2018 election, potentially changing the outcome of a statewide election. Requirements for voter ID cards disparately impact minorities, and in some southern states, those states required to seek approval under the Voters Rights Act, the clock is being turned back to a time when voter suppression was business as usual. The Act was amended in 1970, 1975, 1982 and 2006.

The Civil Rights Act of 1968 (Fair Housing Act) was originally intended to protect civil rights workers, but it was expanded to prohibit discrimination in the sale and rental of real estate throughout the United States (title VIII of the Act). It also barred state and Indian governments from violating the constitutional rights of Native Americans (Indian Civil Rights Act of 1968). Another act sponsored by Johnson, it was approved one week after Martin Luther King Jr.'s assassination. Regardless of its intent to create a unitary housing market without regard to race, racially motivated policies in the real estate market continue to play havoc with Black lives and economic status.

The Civil Rights Restoration Act of 1987 was originally vetoed by President Reagan but Congress overrode his veto. The Act applied civil rights laws to all facets of an organization if it was receiving federal funds.

The Civil Rights Act of 1991 addressed no less than eight decisions of the Supreme Court. The Act provided for compensatory and punitive damages and jury trials in cases involving intentional discrimination. It was intended to provide remedies for harassment and intentional discrimination.

The cupboard is not bare, but the law attempting to rectify discrimination and protect civil rights is not extensive. Madison's definition of a Republic in the Federalist Papers made clear that a republican form of government was one elected by a majority of the citizens, not a faction or minority party. Certainly, the abuse of Jim Crow and segregation were possible because of Black voter suppression. If you can't vote, you can't change your government. If you can't vote you have no representation, no say in the operation of the government. If you can't vote you can't be heard and you have no protections. Black Americans needed the right to vote.

8. Civil Rights

Black Americans needed equal educational and employment opportunity. Black Americans needed to be free from the kind of terror that was meant to destroy their lives politically, economically and socially.

Despite the passage of Civil Rights law addressing discrimination, the courts, especially the U.S. Supreme Court, gave up equality for economic Darwinism. The rule of law in the United States for a few brief years involved the search for equality for all Americans, but more often the rule of law was inequality and injustice for Black Americans.

9

Democracy Is Government "by and for the people"

It is really simple. American slavery was based on race. The Europeans who invaded the Americas first enslaved Native Americans, and when that failed, kidnapped millions of Africans and brought them to their plantations and colonies to be slaves. They weren't indentured servants. They weren't serfs. The Africans were brought to toil and die in the sugar cane fields and on cotton plantations. No, this was not the same as slavery in Africa. No, it is not okay because everybody in the Bible did it. However you twist and obfuscate the facts, no white man was a slave in North America. Slavery was wrong. Lots of people before, after and at the time of the writing of the Constitution knew it was wrong. Jefferson talked about it being wrong but then wrote about the inferiority of his slaves and continued to purchase wine from France with money he made from slave labor. He couldn't even free the Black mother of his children. James Madison wrote about slavery being wrong and lived almost all of his adult life on the labor of hundreds of slaves. Madison admitted slavery was based on racism. According to him the difference between the states was not the size of the population, it was slavery.

The Constitution has failed Americans since its ratification. During the seventy odd years after ratification the Republic struggled constantly over slavery. Slavery could only be ended by a civil war that killed 750,000 Americans. All of the pre-war compromises simply preserved slavery. On this evidence alone, on the graves of those Americans, Black and white who liberated the slaves, the Constitution was a failure. Congressional Reconstruction and the Thirteenth, Fourteenth and Fifteenth Amendments were a second American Revolution, trying to make the Declaration of Independence apply to all men. But almost as soon as the last man at Appomattox surrendered, the racism that made slavery possible was redeemed by

9. Democracy Is Government "by and for the people"

terrorism, voter suppression, and segregation. Racism became a political tool used again and again for years, for generations, to get out the white vote and justify Black voter suppression, Jim Crow, lynchings, bombings, beatings and water cannons in the streets.

The Constitution's failure after the Civil War is measured by the failure of any branch of the federal government to do anything about white terrorism and segregation for almost ninety years after the election of Rutherford B. Hayes, who traded his soul and Black lives for a few votes in the Electoral College. The rule of law before the Civil War was slavery. The rule of law after Hayes' election was racism. Madison wrote that a republican form of government is one where the majority of the governed choose their government. That is his definition of a Republic. The Constitution guarantees a republican form of government. But suppressing votes by any method—whether legislative or by rule, through gerrymandering; by intimidating voters and discouraging political participation by violence, by segregating institutions financed and maintained by the states, via onerous requirements or just dirty tricks—are violations of this Constitutional promise.

Madison's Republic is dead. All the veneration in the world cannot change the fact that the Constitution has been repeatedly used first by pro-slavery forces, then by racist anti-democratic forces from the time of the Constitutional Convention until the present. Since the late nineteenth, through the twentieth and into the early twenty-first century, big money crushed opposition, oppressed labor and punished the poor. The racism that slavery was based on created Jim Crow, banned Asians after they built the railroads, killed American Indians and grabbed their land, went after immigrants in the early twentieth century, forcibly removed Japanese-Americans to concentration camps, denied Blacks the right to education, housing and economic opportunity, and is still a glaring presence in today's politics and in law enforcement and immigration policies.

Despite the constitutional guarantee of a "republican" form of government the government that resulted from the Constitution for most of the nineteenth and twentieth centuries aided and abetted segregation, white terror and all manner of voter suppression in the southern states through court approved segregation, voter suppression, and a filibustering Senate. Gerrymandering became a favorite device of both parties to lock in victory. The Electoral College has given two presidential elections in the last twenty years to men who did not win the popular vote. The U.S. Senate, in the last four years of Obama's presidency, blocked any initiatives made by an administration elected by a huge majority of Americans. The Senate that blocked Obama consisted of a majority of Republicans who were elected by a minority of Americans. Madison warned of the tyranny of majorities, but a minority now dictates policy for all Americans. There are no checks and balances. Donald Trump mocked the disabled, women, and veterans, has no character that most men would admire, and as President has repeatedly lied, insulted and degraded immigrants, people of color and the poor, and rewarded the rich. He is President because of the Electoral College, not democracy.

Lincoln ignored the Constitution in order to save the Union and was able to abolish slavery only because the southern states had seceded. The legacy of slavery is racism. Long after the guns were silent the South continued to fight the idea of Black equality and used terrorism as an instrument to deny them civil liberties and the right to vote. Men, women and children were slaughtered by the thousands in lynchings all over the South. Reconstruction ended after the disputed election of Hayes in 1876, and another compromise with the South ended any effort to incorporate Blacks into the body politic as citizens and voters. After Hayes' election the federal government abandoned Black Americans in the South, subjecting them to lynching and segregation. Despite the Constitution's guarantee of a republican form of government the Black vote in every former Confederate state was suppressed, and white power resulted in Jim Crow and segregation at all levels of society. Separate was never equal. There were no republican governments in the former Confederacy. The Rule of Law was and is racism.

The anti-democratic spirit that possessed the drafters continues to consume what is left of the Constitution. In the twenty-first century the checks and balances promised by Madison are dead. In 2020 Republicans through gerrymandering, racism, the Electoral College, voter suppression and money control both the Senate and the Presidency. The Supreme Court has been dominated for the last fifty years by conservatives obsessed with cultural issues and an agenda that is anti-labor and pro-business. Because of this combination, the Supreme Court is an ideological rubber stamp for a conservative Congress and President. Congress, since the Vietnam War, has given up its war powers to the President and U.S. troops are everywhere. Barack Obama was elected by a majority of Americans but stonewalled by a Republican Congress elected by a minority of Americans. With the election of Trump, the Republican Congress has embraced an unqualified, undignified, and anti-democratic President elected by a minority of Americans.

9. Democracy Is Government "by and for the people"

The Electoral College functions as an anti-democratic check on majority rule and without abolition by amendment will only exacerbate the problem of minority rule. Donald Trump is a minority President. Over three million more Americans voted for his opponent. Trump is a disaster for the United States. His supporters claim they have been lied to and abused by the "deep state" yet they embrace a man who is a liar, a racist and adulterer without compassion for anyone. Trump's election represents the end of Madison's Republic. There is no pretense that character matters in the Republican Party. The Trump administration is openly corrupt and abysmally incompetent. The next resident of the White House should count the china.

The gap between rich and poor, white and Black has within years of Trump's election been exacerbated by rulings at the Supreme Court and the Republican tax bill. That gap will grow. The current political parties are surely the factions Madison feared when he warned that a large gap between rich and poor would destroy the Republic. These trends can be reversed only by amending the Constitution to make it a truly democratic document that provides a framework for government in the twenty-first century and guarantees the general welfare of all Americans.

Venerating the Constitution is a singularly destructive tradition. The Constitution failed to prevent the Civil War. The Constitution failed to provide a way to abolish slavery without the deaths of 750,000 Americans. The Constitution was a failure because the government it created did nothing to stop the terror in the South that was aimed at Black Americans, and it failed when the government that was supposed to ensure a Republican form of government did nothing to stop voter suppression for nearly ninety years. It failed when its Supreme Court approved of gerrymandering and laws that opposed equality and favored the rich. The Constitution failed when a minority of Americans elected Donald Trump and George W. Bush.

Democracy

Scholars of the U.S. Constitution and the Federalist Papers have spilled much ink analyzing Madison's view of republican government. The reality is Madison's vision of representative government resulted in a document that protected slavery by way of anti-democratic provisions that were designed to throttle freedom and choice. Democracy is based on the idea of majoritarian rule. Every citizen in a democracy should be able to vote to determine the nature of the government and their representatives and every vote should be counted and every vote should count equally. The right to vote is basic to a democracy. It is the only way for citizens to hold their government accountable. A system that suppresses your vote by gerrymandering or says your vote doesn't count even when it is in the majority is not a democracy. All citizens ought to be able to participate in the direct election of representatives for their government, and their vote should count.

People can only make a democracy work if they assume the duties of a citizen. Citizens must be educated and informed and must participate in their government by voting. Citizens must be able to make choices based on factual information, not propaganda and outright lies. The truth matters and government by lies is dedicated to tyranny. Distorting the truth and outright lying are the tools of despots and tyrants.

Everyone in a democracy should have a certain set of basic liberties guaranteed to them that the government cannot unilaterally withdraw or suppress. Democracy must function with the idea that all of its citizens are equal and entitled to all benefits and protections of the law. State-sanctioned discrimination based on national origin, race, color, religion, sex or sexual preference has no place in a democracy. Racial and religious biases that elevate dogma over choice work against democracy and weaken the notion of equality and a government for all citizens.

Religious Freedom

Government should operate free of religious influence. The great myth of American history is that our government and its founding documents were inspired by God. There are over 100 religious faiths recognized by the U.S. Department of Defense and an estimated 313 religious organizations in the United States. Why so many? They all believe something different. Which if any is the true, divinely inspired doctrine? There should be freedom of religious conscience and practice, but there should be no oppression by or of any particular religious doctrine, or imposition of any doctrine upon those who choose not to believe.

Thomas Jefferson and James Madison were deists. Jefferson invoked God in the Declaration of Independence but also spoke of nature and nature's law. He identified with no particular religious group. He wrote his

9. Democracy Is Government "by and for the people"

nephew: "Question with boldness even the existence of a god; because, if there be one, he must more approve the homage of reason, than that of blindfolded fear." Jefferson placed his faith in reason. He and Madison worked hard to convince Virginia to pass the Statute for Religious Freedom. In Jefferson's *Notes on the State of Virginia* he wrote, "The legitimate powers of government extend to such acts only as are injurious to others. But it does me no injury for my neighbor to say there are twenty gods, or no god. It neither picks my pocket nor breaks my leg.... Reason and free enquiry are the only effectual agents against error."

Nowhere in the Constitution is God mentioned. Madison wrote that

> there remains in others a strong bias towards the old error, that without some sort of alliance or coalition between Gov' & Religion neither can be duly supported: Such indeed is the tendency to such a coalition, and such its corrupting influence on both the parties, that the danger cannot be too carefully guarded against.... Every new & successful example therefore of a perfect separation between ecclesiastical and civil matters, is of importance. And I have no doubt that every new example will succeed, as every past one has done, in shewing that religion & Gov will both exist in greater purity, the less they are mixed together" [James Madison, letter to Edward Livingston, July 10, 1822, *The Writings of James Madison*, Gaillard Hunt, ed.].

Madison acted as he believed and as President during the War of 1812 refused to declare a day of prayer and fasting (people could pray "if so disposed"). The author of the First Amendment believed the office of military chaplain was unconstitutional. He vetoed three bills providing money for church buildings and supplies, and he refused to incorporate a church in the District of Columbia because it would be bad legal precedent.

The Pew Research Center tried to get its hands around religious America and found the best way to represent religion is to imagine it a town of 100 people. Of these 100 people, 25 would be evangelical Protestant; 23 would be unaffiliated; 21 would be Catholic; 15 would be mainline Protestant; 6 would be historically Black Protestant; 2 Mormons; 2 "other" Christian; 2 Jewish; 2 other faiths; 1 Buddhist; 1 Muslim; and 1 Hindu. (The total exceeds 100 due to statistical rounding, refusals to respond not being counted, and those who answered that they "don't know.") So, which is the one true faith, and which should oppress the remaining with their moral or spiritual dogma? Separation of church and state is necessary for a democratic government to operate successfully. Madison warned that factions would destroy his Republic, and clearly from the numerous iterations of religious belief it is imperative that today we operate with a perfect separation of church and state. When religious doctrine dictates law, there will be oppression.

Donald Trump appealed directly to Evangelical and Pentecostal Christians for support. In a true devil's bargain his supporters voted for a man who has been a serial adulterer, is a pathological liar, disrespects women, lacks compassion, does not care for the poor, governs through anger and fear, loves money and demonizes people of color. He has embraced totalitarian regimes that have consistently oppressed Christians of whatever ilk. Where does he regularly attend church? Although these traits violate moral doctrine by any religious standard, American Christians have turned a blind eye to these flaws in order to further their causes. These segments of American Christianity that have supported Trump have proven Madison right: faction will destroy this Republic unless there is an absolute separation of church and state.

Influence of Money on Politics

Money is devouring the electoral process. Alone among today's democracies the United States is addicted to profligate spending on its elections. The Supreme Court has ruled that political donations are speech and cannot be limited. It is appalling that the Supreme Court has found corporations are persons and as such are entitled to First Amendment protections when they deluge their political servants with cash. It is a purely political decision made to protect minority government. There is nothing altruistic about these contributions. Those donations do not seek better government, they seek less government when it interferes with corporate agendas and the desires of the wealthy. Their donations influence politicians to vote the "right way." They check the influence of ordinary private citizens and majority rule in a democracy and create an autocracy, run for the benefit of the wealthy.

In *Federalist* No. 10 James Madison defined faction as "a number of citizens, whether amounting to a majority or a minority of the whole, who are united and actuated by some common impulse of passion, or of interest, adverse to the rights of other citizens, or the permanent aggregate interests of the community." The political action committees and the corporate donors and the religious fanatics who seek control of the country have a vision of America that rewards wealth, narrows the scope of citizenship, suppresses the vote, seeks to save white America,

9. Democracy Is Government "by and for the people"

and has adopted an anti-abortion, anti-feminist, anti-immigrant, anti-worker, anti-education, anti-science and anti–LGBQT agenda. They represent a minority of Americans working against the "permanent and aggregate interests of the community."

According to Madison, "the most common and durable source of factions has been the various and unequal distribution of property." Policies advanced by the Republican Party have increased the gap between the wealthy and the rest of us. One percent of Americans own 40 percent of all the property in the United States, and according to the Brookings Institute, 20 percent of the population holds 70 percent of the country's wealth. During recessions, money flows to corporations and not to ordinary Americans. The 2018 Republican tax plan was the largest transfer of wealth in the modern history of the country. The deficit it will create will last for years. Trickle-down economics is a lie, repeated now by Reagan, Bush and Trump. Gary Wills argued in *Explaining America*, "What Madison prevents [his republic] is not faction, but action. What he protects is not the common good but delay." Today, Madison's Constitution has allowed Republicans to "clog, delay, slow down, hamper and obstruct the majority."

Lobbying does not help the average American citizen. Lobbying benefits corporations and wealthy individuals who don't care about the average American. The money thrown at Congress is reshaping America. Lower taxes and less regulation increase corporate profits and further enrich already wealthy Americans. The legacy for the average American voter is a crumbling infrastructure, substandard education, dangerous products, unsafe water and food, more pollution, greater deficits, higher health care costs, lower wages and a diminishing voice in their own government. The super-rich and corporate interests are taking control of the government in a way that could not have been foreseen by anyone in 1787.

We have a professional political class that has engineered the power of the incumbency through money and gerrymandering to remain in office despite almost any political bias or immoral behavior. In 2020 during America's coronavirus outbreak it was discovered three Senators mysteriously sold stock after a secret briefing weeks before the government admitted the gravity of the situation and the economy, including the stock market, tanked. In 2016, a record $6.4 billion was spent on federal political campaigns. Lobbyists spent $3.15 billion to influence the lucky few who were elected. Martin Gilens, a professor at Princeton University, has said that in the last 40 years American economic policies "strongly reflect the preference of the most affluent, but bear virtually no relationship to the preferences of poor or middle-income Americans."

Defenders of the system argue there is no relationship between these huge sums and government, but why have the contributions increased if money doesn't buy votes? The huge amounts of money necessary for election and that flows through donors and lobbyists can only have a corrupting influence. The huge amount of money necessary to run for office severely limits potential candidates. Those candidates who do not have views acceptable to the monied interests will not receive campaign contributions from them. Once elected it means the candidates immediately begin fundraising for the next campaign, sucking up big donors who expect a return on their money. Money is a corrupting influence that distorts politics. Those with the money seek to marginalize voting and encourage people not to turn out to vote their consciences. This is voter suppression. This system must be changed, starting with repeal of *Citizens United*.

The Electoral College

In the last twenty years we have had two Presidents who were not elected by a majority of Americans. One was Donald Trump, elected by a minority of Americans in 2016. The margin of three million more voters for Clinton was the widest margin in any presidential election where the popular vote was for the candidate who did not win the electoral vote.

An American Bar Association study of the Electoral College in 1967 described it as "archaic, undemocratic, complex, ambiguous, indirect and dangerous." A *New York Times* editorial in December 2016 pointed out "by overwhelming majorities, Americans would prefer to elect the president by direct popular vote." The Electoral College was one of those compromises meant to placate the slave states. Delegates at the Constitutional Convention, James Wilson, James Madison, Gouverneur Morris, Daniel Carroll, and John Dickenson, proposed direct election of the President. These delegates considered the people to be the "purest" and "fittest" electors to choose the President. The slave states recognized that their comparatively small voting populations and large slave populations would dilute their influence in presidential elections. Having won the argument over how representatives to Congress should be calculated—the three-fifths clause—they argued for the same system to calculate electoral votes.

Because of the Electoral College:

9. Democracy Is Government "by and for the people"

1. The popular vote winner can lose;
2. The number of electoral votes assigned to a state does not reflect population changes that occur between censuses;
3. The number of electoral votes a state is assigned is fixed and remains unchanged whether one voter or millions cast a ballot;
4. Some states are trying to change the winner take all aspect of the Electoral College, which currently awards all the state's Electoral College votes to the winner of the popular votes. The National Popular Vote Interstate Compact provides that electors would have to vote for the winner of the national popular vote. Eleven states and the District of Columbia have already passed legislation to adopt the compact; and
5. The Electoral College votes are determined by each state's representation in Congress, but the scale is tipped in favor of smaller states—a Wyoming voter's vote counts 3.6 times more than a Californian's.

The Electoral College is undemocratic. The President should be elected by the people not through an undemocratic system designed to make slave state votes count more. There is no cogent, defensible reason not to eliminate the Electoral College.

The Senate

The Senate of the United States should be abolished. Giving equal votes to the small states is undemocratic. As George Mason predicted, if the same faction controlled both the presidency and the Senate the two institutions would be uncontrolled—no checks and balances. George Will wrote, "Delaware, the least populous state in 1789, understandably was the first to ratify the Constitution with its equal representation of states in the Senate; Virginia, the most populous, had 11 times more voters. Today Wyoming's two Senators' votes can cancel those of California's two Senators, who represent 69 times more people. If that offends you, so does America's constitutional federalism."

The Senate's existence is inconsistent with the democratic principle of one person, one vote. The various rules of the Senate, especially the filibuster, mean that a coalition of states representing a minority of the population can block legislation. In September 2014, fifty-four U.S. Senators tried to pass an amendment overturning *Citizens United*. Those fifty-four Senators represented 55 percent of the population of the United States. Forty-two Senators, representing 37 percent of the population, blocked it. The Senate represents the tyranny of the minority. The population of the twenty-two smallest states is roughly the same as the population of California. But those tiny states have forty-four senators and California only two.

Gerrymandering

Elbridge Gerry was a Massachusetts delegate to the Constitutional Convention. In 1812 he was a Federalist governor of Massachusetts who drew election districts resembling a salamander so that his Federalist party could retain control of the state senatorial districts. Today, parties redraw voting districts to make sure their party stays in power, although most existing gerrymandered districts are drawn by Republicans. Representatives elected from those districts have no incentive to compromise because they have a voter base that makes them unbeatable. The effect of this also diminishes voter confidence in the system, is a powerful incentive for the voters of the opposition party not to vote, and encourages extremists on both sides because the major threat to an incumbent official comes from a primary challenger, who is even more extreme, not from the other party in the general election.

Computer programs have been developed that can fairly draw district lines. But there is a powerful disincentive to adopt these because the existing system benefits the incumbent politician and it would result in a fair election. Gerrymandering is a tool to prevent predominantly Black districts from successfully exercising any power at the ballot box. The line between despotism and democracy is a fair election. As President Obama has said, "In America, politicians shouldn't pick their voters; voters are supposed to pick their politicians." Gerrymandering could be eliminated by using a proportional system for voting, where votes would be assigned to party candidate lists. A voter would mark a ballot for a party and then seats would be allocated based upon the percentage of voters for that party. Gerrymandering is anti-democratic and should be forbidden by the Constitution as inimical to a republican form of government.

9. Democracy Is Government "by and for the people"

The Supreme Court

Article III of the Constitution provides for a federal judiciary. Sparse in its language, it names only one court, the Supreme Court. It provides that Congress can create other Article III courts as it deems necessary from time to time. The Article also stipulates the jurisdiction of the Supreme Court. In one of its first pieces of legislation, the new Congress in 1789 passed the Judiciary Act, providing for a federal trial court in each state and federal courts of appeal. It also set the number of judges for the Supreme Court. Since then judiciary acts have been used to set the pay and the number of justices serving on the Supreme Court, and to create new federal district courts and courts of appeal. The delegates to the Constitutional Convention were convinced that judges should have lifetime appointments in order to be free from political pressures. Federal judges at all levels hold their appointments for life. They hold their office for good behavior, and their salaries cannot be reduced while they are serving. They can only be impeached, but this has happened only a handful of times.

Appointments to the federal bench, especially the Supreme Court, have far-reaching consequences for the citizens of the United States. Trial judges have the power as the first line of federal judges to establish and interpret federal substantive and procedural law in civil and criminal actions. Federal appellate courts have the power to shape federal law through their interpretation of the law as the result of cases appealed to them from the trial courts. The Supreme Court has the final say as to interpretation of federal, and state law in some circumstances, and ultimately sets legal trends for decades, separate and apart from the reality of the operative culture of the day.

Federal trial judges focus on the facts before them and the law to be applied to civil legal actions and criminal matters in the context of a robust motion practice and jury trial system. The federal trial courts have adopted rules of procedure and evidence to make those uniform in use and application throughout the system. The appointment of all the federal judges begins with the President and ends with the Senate. In years past, Congressional members from the various states have recommended candidates to fill vacancies in the federal courts. This process is tainted with faction because it is unlikely that a Republican will nominate a Democrat and vice versa.

How the Constitution is interpreted by the U.S. courts has a significant effect on the operation of the courts and the government. It affects the health and welfare of the people. John Marshall claimed to have used the *Federalist Papers* in his cases. There were no official records of the Constitutional convention and it met in secret. Madison's notes were eventually published but are sketchy. Using the *Federalist Papers* is using propaganda because the papers were written by Hamilton, Madison and Jay to convince state ratification conventions that the Constitution should be ratified.

Many lawyers and politicians argue that to understand the meaning of the Constitution the drafters' intentions would need to be known—the understanding of the document by those who argued for its ratification, and what the people who ratified the Constitution believed it meant. Basic arguments have emerged for interpretation of the Constitution. Originalism is the effort to interpret the Constitution in the way the framers meant for it to be understood. It may rely on the meaning of the text, the intention of the framers and the understanding of the original readers. Non-originalists on the other hand argue that the framers never intended for their understanding of the Constitution to bind those who sought to interpret it. The text is ambiguous, waiting for someone to give it meaning, and most important, the Constitution is living law. It must be interpreted for the times and times change. Finally, overlaying these two methods of constitutional divination is the impression that all decisions are political.

George Mason feared a dangerous coalition of the Senate and the Presidency when controlled by the same faction, or in modern terminology, party. He believed the combination would thwart Madison's system of checks and balances. This has happened many times in the Republic's history. The President and the Senate will appoint their party's men and women to the bench. All of them, despite the President's and the Senate's protests to the contrary, are puppets of the appointing party.

Trump has attacked the federal courts repeatedly. As a businessman he resorted to litigation over 3,000 times, including bankruptcy to avoid his debts, and as President expects the courts to do his bidding. The nomination of appellate court judge Brett Kavanaugh to the Supreme Court follows closely on the heels of the appointment of Justice Gorsuch. A Republican Senate blocked judicial nominations by Barack Obama in his last four years in office. This is another obvious reason why the Senate needs to be reformed or eliminated. The Republicans blocking Obama's appointments represented a minority of Americans. When the Republican Senate majority leader told Obama he would not act on Obama's last Supreme Court nominee, he was not doing the people's bidding, he was

9. Democracy Is Government "by and for the people"

doing the Republicans' bidding. President Obama had been elected by a majority of Americans and the Senate Republicans by a minority.

Trump campaigned hard on appointing right-wing judges to the bench, men or women with a certain ideological and cultural bent, in hopes of reversing law on the issues of abortion, gay marriage, reducing the power and influence of unions and setting a law and order regime that calls for lower taxes on wealth, reduced social benefits, less regulation of financial institutions, oil and drug companies and more strict laws and less order. He used the Supreme Court to influence voters and motivate his base. Republican Senate Majority Leader McConnell had argued that Obama, a President elected by a majority of Americans, had no mandate from the people to put another judge on the Supreme Court. So, he waited for a Republican President, and a Republican Senate, both elected by a minority of Americans, to put an ideologue on the Court for the right. The Trump Court will not reflect a national majoritarian consensus on Constitutional issues like abortion or civil rights but a partisan minority view rendering judgment based on religion and Pentecostal lifestyles and corporate demands rather than the law. The appointment process needs to be taken out the hands of the President and the Senate.

The difference in the political and constitutional views of justices is important because their decisions endure long after appointment. Judges have claimed to analyze the Constitution by using the doctrine of "Original Intent." What this means is that they claim they are trying to figure out what the drafters meant. Other judges view the Constitution as being a living document that can be interpreted to take into consideration modernity and the changing needs of the country and society. The latter also believe that the framers indicated they did not want their specific intentions to control interpretation. Madison told the House of Representatives in 1796 that:

> Whatever veneration might be entertained for the body of men who formed our Constitution, the sense of that body could never be regarded as the oracular guide to expounding the Constitution, as the instrument came from them it was nothing more than the draft of a plan, nothing but a dead letter, until life and validity were breathed into it by the voice of the people, speaking through the several state Conventions. If we were to look, therefore, for the meaning of the instrument beyond the face of the instrument, we must look for it not in the General Convention, but in the State Conventions, which accepted and ratified the Constitution.

"A living Constitution is one that evolves, changes over time, and adapts to new circumstances, without being formally amended." Slavery was abolished by the Civil War and the Thirteenth Amendment. Why should we continue to employ constitutional devices like the Electoral College and the Senate, whose origins are in slavery? These institutions do not reflect democratic virtues or values. Like definitions of democracy, methods used by justices to interpret the Constitution can be lost in academic mumbo jumbo and unending law review articles. The issue is that the intent of the framers was based on a society that communicated by letter over vast distances, was not committed to universal suffrage, was committed to race-based slavery, viewed the world through a provincial lens, that was not egalitarian, that was not in favor of women's legal rights, that was committed to the extermination or removal and concentration of all Native Americans in order to steal the benefits of their homeland, that had a slave population of four million, and had oceans that were huge defensive moats in time of war.

Today we demand instant communication, have a population of 327 million, and we at least give lip service to universal suffrage. We abolished slavery, and the moats are useless, and on and on.

What to Do

1. A system of reparations should be established for African Americans designed to break the poverty that dominates the African American community.
2. Abolish the Electoral College by constitutional amendment.
3. Amend the Constitution to end private financing of elections and provide for public financing of elections and shortening the time for elections for all political offices.
4. Amend the Constitution to end gerrymandering.
5. Amend the Constitution to provide for strict separation of church and state.
6. Amend the Constitution to dissolve the Senate and make the terms of the members of the House of Representatives four years with term limits of two terms.
7. Amend the Constitution to require all candidates for public office to make their tax and personal financial records public, and requiring them to divest themselves of all financial interests that would benefit from their election to public office within 30 days of their election, or an automatic forfeiture

9. Democracy Is Government "by and for the people"

of their public office, and a special election to fill the vacated position.
8. Amend the Constitution to include the Equal Rights Amendment.
9. Amend the Constitution to guarantee voters' rights. The amendment should guarantee all American citizens the right to vote and prohibit any legislative measure that results in impairing the right to vote in any way to include gerrymandering and mass purging of voter registration lists when they target voters by race, age, or national origin. Make voting in federal elections for the President a national holiday giving Americans the day off to vote, and require federal intervention in elections where there is evidence of foreign interference.

Conclusion

The Constitution was from its ratification a "bargain with the devil." It recognized and protected slavery. The many compromises made by Madison were meant to protect slavery. Lincoln had to ignore the Constitution to save the Union. Abolition of slavery by the Thirteenth Amendment, and passage of the Fourteenth and Fifteenth Amendments, were possible only because the South seceded. While the "Radical Republicans" tried to protect Black civil liberties and voting rights, they worked against prejudice and violence. That prejudice and violence won and has been the state of democracy in the United States for generations. There was no "republican" government in the South. The Supreme Court and a handful of federal courts in the South briefly tried to eliminate Jim Crow and segregation. Congress passed legislation, but it has been diluted by the Supreme Court. Racism is the legacy of slavery, and it corrupts and influences voting yet today.

We have been thoroughly indoctrinated by the idea that we live in a representative democracy, established by wise men inspired by God. We did not, and we do not. Power is moving increasingly into the hands of the few. Oligarchy, plutocracy or theocracy—maybe a bit of all of them—is where we are, and we stand on the threshold of dictatorship. Voter suppression was used by Southerners, and has now been picked up by the Republican Party. When Trump declared that he would not accept the

The Constitution and American Racism

outcome of the presidential election in 2016 and again in 2020, he declared our republic dead. His administration has worked to dismantle our democratic institutions and the idea of the rule of law as the centerpiece of our system of justice. Self-dealing and nepotism with a dash of gangsterism is the rule of the day. Trump will leave America in wreckage. Unless there is constitutional reform, he is but the beginning of the end.

Despite the veneration of the Constitution, it has been a failure. The government created by it has failed repeatedly over 240 years to act democratically and seek justice for all Americans. The Constitution recognized slavery and racism as the rule of law in the United States. Slavery was only abolished by the deaths 750,000 Americans. When Reconstruction ended the "white redeemers" replaced democratic governments with segregation and terror. The rule of law was Jim Crow and lynching. Despite the Civil Rights revolution in the fifties and sixties, the new white redeemers and the Republicans in the twentieth and twenty-first centuries have been able to turn the clock back in America with support from racists and bigots, Christians on the right and the money of the wealthy. None of this squares with Madison's definition of a Republic: "we may define a republic to be, or at least may bestow that name on a government which derives all its powers directly or indirectly from the great body of the people.... It is *essential* to such a government that it be derived from the great body of the society, not from an inconsiderable proportion or favored class of it; otherwise a handful of tyrannical nobles, exercising their oppressions by a delegation of their powers might aspire to the rank of republicans and claim for their government the honorable title of republic."

Chapter Notes

Chapter 1

1. Dan Himmelfarb, "The Constitutional Relevance of the Second Sentence of the Declaration of Independence," *The Yale Law Journal* 100, no. 1 (Oct. 1990): 169–87.
2. William W. Freeling, "The Founding Fathers and Slavery," *The American Historical Review* 77, no. 1 (Feb. 1972): 81–93; and William M. Wiecek, *The Sources of Anti-Slavery Constitutionalism in America, 1760–1848* (Ithaca: Cornell University Press, 1977), 71–73.
3. Wiecek, *The Sources of Anti-Slavery Constitutionalism in America*, 41–60 and 71–73, and Paul Finkelman, *Slavery and The Founders: Race and Liberty in the Age of Jefferson* (Amonk, NY: M.E. Sharpe, 2014), 199–201.
4. David McCullough, *John Adams* (New York: Simon and Schuster, 2001), 131–136.
5. Andrew Burstein and Nancy Isenberg, *Madison and Jefferson* (New York: Random House, 2013), 15.
6. Paul Finkelman, "The Centrality of the Peculiar Institution in American Legal Development" –Symposium on the Law of Slavery: Introduction, 68 *Chi-Kent L. Rev.* 1009 (1992): 1009–33.
7. Wiecek, *The Sources of Anti-Slavery Constitutionalism*, 66.
8. Betty Wood, *The Origins of American Slavery: Freedom and Bondage in the English Colonies* (New York: Hill and Wang, 1997), 7.
9. Paul Finkelman, "The Centrality of the Peculiar Institution…," 1028; Rebecca Anne Goetz, "Rethinking the "Unthinking Decision": Old Questions and New Problems in the History of Slavery and Race in the Colonial South," *Journal of Southern History* 75, no. 3 (August 2009): 607; and William W. Fisher III, "Ideology and Imagery in the Law of Slavery-Symposium on the Law of Slavery: Theories of Democracy and the Law of Slavery," 68 *Chi.-Kent L. Rev.* no. 3 (1992): 1051–1083.
10. Edward Baptist, *The Half Has Never Been Told: Slavery and the Making of American Capitalism* (New York: Basic Books, 2016), 9.
11. *Dred Scott v. Sanford*, 60 U.S. (19 How.) 393 (1857).
12. J. David Hacker, "A Census-Based Count of Civil War Dead," *Civil War History* 57, no. 4 (Dec. 2011): 307–48; Williamson Murray and Wayne Wei-Siang Hsieh, *A Savage War: A Military History of the Civil War* (Princeton: Princeton University Press, 2016), 8; James McPherson, *Why the Civil War Still Matters: The War That Forged the Nation* (Oxford: Oxford University Press, 2016) 2; and Jonathan M. Steplyk, *Fighting Means Killing: Civil War Soldiers and the Nature of Combat* (Lawrence: University Press of Kansas, 2018) 231.
13. David Waldstreicher, "The Beardian Legacy, the Madisonian Moment, and the Politics of Slavery," *American Political Thought* 2, no. 2 (Fall 2013), 274–82.
14. Jack N. Rakove, "Philadelphia Story," *The Wilson Quarterly (1976–)* 11, no. 2 (Spring 1987): 105–21.
15. Alan J. Lichtman, *The Embattled Vote in America From the Founding to the Present* (Cambridge: Harvard University Press, 2018), 2–35.

Notes—Chapter 1

16. Christopher Collier and James Lincoln Collier, *Decision at Philadelphia: The Constitutional Convention of 1787* (New York: Ballantine Books, 2007), 100–105 and John R. Vile, "The Critical Role of Committees at the U.S. Constitutional Convention of 1787," *The Journal of Legal History* 48, no. 2 (Apr. 2006): 147–76.
17. Burstein and Isenberg at 15 and Rakove, "Philadelphia Story," 105–121.
18. Rakove, "Philadelphia Story," 105.
19. Collier, *Decision in Philadelphia The Constitutional Convention* of 1787, 104.
20. Robin L. Einhorn, "Patrick Henry's Case Against the Constitution: The Structural Problem with Slavery," *Journal of the Early Republic* 22, no. 4 (2002): 549–73.
21. Andrew Delbanco, *The War Before the War: Fugitive Slaves and the Struggle for America's Soul from the Revolution to the Civil War* (New York: Penguin Press, 2018), 66.
22. Rakove, "Philadelphia Story," 105.
23. Gouverneur Morris as quoted by James Madison in his notes, see Edward J. Larson and Michael P. Winship. *The Constitutional Convention: A Narrative History from the Notes of James Madison* (New York: Modern Library, 2005), 78.
24. *Ibid.*, 112.
25. Richard Brookhiser, "The Forgotten Founding Father," *City Journal*, Spring 2002.
26. Larson and Winship, *The Constitutional Convention*, 97.
27. *Ibid.*
28. Collier, *Decision in Philadelphia*, 103–104.
29. Jack Rakove, *Revolutionaries* (New York: Mariner Books, 2011), 347.
30. *Ibid.*, 347–48.
31. *Ibid.*, 359–60.
32. *Ibid.*, 358–66.
33. Collier, 30.
34. Merrill Jensen, "The American Revolution and American Agriculture," *Agricultural History* 43, no. 1 (Jan. 1969): 107–24; and Gavin Wright, "Slavery and American Agricultural History," *Agricultural History* 77, no. 4 (2003), 527–52.
35. Noel Rae, *The Great Stain: Witnessing American Slavery* (New York: Overlook Press, 2018), 123; and Sowande M. Mustakeem, *Slavery at Sea: Terror, Sex, and Sickness in the Middle Passage* (Urbana: University of Illinois Press, 2016), 59.
36. Paul Finkelman, *Slavery and the Founders*, 47–57.
37. Rakove, "Philadelphia Story," 106–108.
38. Vile, "The Critical Role of Committees at the Constitutional Convention," 147–176.
39. Rakove, "Philadelphia Story," 108 and Collier, *Decision in Philadelphia*, 111.
40. Rakove, "Philadelphia Story," 109–113, and Collier, 111 and 183–90.
41. *Federalist* No. 69.
42. Frank Harmon Garver, "Some Misconceptions Relative to the Constitutional Convention." *The Historian*, 1, no. 1 (Winter, 1938): 24–32.
43. Larson and Winship, *The Constitutional Convention*, 13–18.
44. *Ibid.*, 39.
45. *Ibid.*, 69.
46. *Ibid.*, 69–70.
47. Finkelman, *Slavery and the Founders*, 12–14, and Larson and Winship, 84–85.
48. Larson and Winship, 87.
49. *Ibid.*, 90–91.
50. *Ibid.*, 47–58.
51. Paul Finkelman, "The Proslavery Origins of the Electoral College," *Cardoza Law Review* 3, no. 4 (2003): 1145–1157.
52. Larson and Winship, 97.
53. *Ibid.*, 139–140.
54. Waldstreicher, "The Beardian Legacy," 278.
55. Paul Finkelman, "The Root of the Problem: How the Proslavery Constitution Shaped American Race Relations," *Barry Law Review* 4, no. 1 (2003): 1–19.
56. John Rakove, *The Annotated U.S. Constitution and Declaration of Independence* (Cambridge. Belknap Press, 2009), 110.
57. Finkelman, "The Root of the Problem," 1–19.
58. Larson and Winship, 90.
59. *Ibid.*, 41.
60. *Ibid.*, 130.
61. Peter Wallenstein, "Flawed Keepers of the Flame: The Interpreters of George Mason," *The Virginia Magazine of History and Biography* 102, no. 2 (Apr. 1994): 229–260.

Notes—Chapter 2

62. Keith L. Dougherty and Jac C. Heckelman, "A Spatial Analysis of Delegate Voting on Slavery at the Constitutional Convention," *The Journal of Economic History* 73, no. 2 (2013): 407–44.
63. *National Geographic*, March 6, 2018.
64. Finkelman, "The Root of the Problem," 7.
65. Rakove, *Annotated U.S. Constitution*, 164.
66. Andrew Delbanco, *The War Before the War*, 5.
67. Rakove, *The Annotated U.S. Constitution*, 210.
68. Williamson and Hsieh, *A Savage War*, 45.
69. Edward Bonekemper, *The Myth of the Lost Cause*, p. 39.
70. John P. Kaminski, *The Debate Over the Constitution*, 141.
71. Collier, *Decision in Philadelphia*, 91–94 and 96–101.
72. Akhil Reed Amar, "The Troubling Reason the Electoral College Exists," *TIME*, November 8, 2016.
73. Paul Finkelman, "Proslavery Origins of the Electoral College": 1145–1157.
74. William Cohen, "Thomas Jefferson and the Problem of Slavery," 8–9.
75. Ibid.
76. David McCullough, *John Adams*, 633.
77. *Federalist* No. 39.
78. *Negro History Bulletin*, 9, no. 8 (May 1946): 192; Jacob Heller, "Death by a Thousand Cuts: The Guarantee Clause Regulation of State Constitutions," *Stanford Law Review* 62, no. 6, Symposium State Constitutions (June 2010): 1711–1761.
79. Herbert Aptheker, "American Negro Slave Revolts," *Science and Society* 1, no. 4 (1937): 512–38.
80. Don Glickstein, *After Yorktown: The Final Struggle for American Independence* (Yardley: Westholme Publishing, 2015), 351–61.

Chapter 2

1. Alan Taylor, *American Colonies: The Settling of North America* (New York: Penguin Books, 2001), 38.
2. *Ibid.*, 36–37.
3. *Ibid.*, 42.
4. *Ibid.*, 39–41.
5. *Ibid.*, 39–41.
6. Jared Diamond, *Guns, Germs, and Steel: The Fates of Human Societies* (New York: W.W. Norton & Co., 1997), 78.
7. Taylor, *American Colonies*, 43.
8. Owen Stanwood, "Captives and Slaves: Indian Labor, Cultural Conversion, and the Plantation Revolution in Virginia," *The Virginia Magazine of History and Biography* 114, no. 4 (2006): 434–463; Peter H. Wood, "The Birthplace of Race-Based Slavery," excerpted from Peter H. Wood, *Strange New Land: Africans in Colonial America* (Oxford: Oxford University Press).
9. Michael Guasco, "'To Doe Some Good Upon Their Countrymen': The Paradox of Indian Slavery in Early Anglo-America," *Journal of Social History* 41, no. 2 (Winter 2007): 389–411.
10. *Ibid.*, 389–411.
11. V.C.D. Mtubani, "African Slaves and English Law," *PULA Botswana Journal of African Studies* 3, no. 2 (November 1983).
12. James Farr, "Locke, Natural Law, and New World Slavery" *Political Theory* 36, no.4 (August 2008): 495–522; Holly Brewer, "Slavery, Sovereignty, and 'Inheritable Blood': Reconsidering John Locke and the Origins of American Slavery," *American Historical Review* 122, no. 4 (October 2017): 1038–1078.
13. Guasco, "To Doe Some Good," 399.
14. Linford D. Fisher, "'Why shall we have peace to be made slaves': Indian Surrenders During and After King Philip's War," *Ethnohistory* 64, no. 1 (January 2017): 91–114.
15. Kristofer Ray, "'The Indians of every denomination were free, and independent of us': Anglo-Virginian Explorations Indigenous Slavery, Freedom, and Society, 1772–1830," *American Nineteenth Century History* 17, no. 2 (2016): 139–159.
16. Mathew Mulcahy, *Hubs of Empire: The Southeastern Lowcountry and British Caribbean* (Baltimore: Johns Hopkins University Press, 2014), 94; Alan Gallway, *The Indian Slave Trade: The Rise of the English Empire in the American South, 1610–1717* (New Haven: Yale University Press, 2002).

Notes—Chapter 2

17. Paul Finkelman, *Slavery and the Founders: Race and Liberty in the Age of Jefferson* (Amonk, NY: M.E. Sharpe, 2014), 35.
18. *Robin v. Hardaway*, 1 Jeff. 109 (Va. Gen. Ct. 1772).
19. Gregory Ablavsky, "Making Indians 'White': The Judicial Abolition of Native Slavery in Revolutionary Virginia and Its Racial Legacy," *University of Pennsylvania Law Review* 159 (May 2011): 1457–1531.
20. Paul Finkelman, "The Centrality of the Peculiar Institution in American Legal Development," *Chi. Kent L. Rev.* 68, no. 3 (1992): 1009–1033.
21. Taylor, *American Colonies*, 42–44.
22. Philip Curtin, *The Rise and Fall of the Planation Complex: Essays in Atlantic History* (New York: Cambridge University Press, 1990), 51–52.
23. Gregory E. O'Malley, "Diversity in the Slave Trade to the Colonial Carolinas," in *Creating and Contesting Carolina: Proprietary Era Histories*, edited by Michelle LeMaster and Bradford J. Wood (Charleston: University of South Carolina Press, 2013), 234.
24. David Eltis, *The Rise of African Slavery in the Americas* (New York: Cambridge University Press, 2000), 63.
25. Bernard Bailyn, *The Barbarous Years: The Conflict of Civilizations, 1600–1675* (New York: Alfred A. Knopf, 2012), 41.
26. John J. McCusker and Russel Menard, *The Economy of British America, 1607–1789* (Chapel Hill: University of North Carolina Press, 1985), 61.
27. Kenneth Morgan, *Slavery and Servitude in Colonial North America: A Short History* (New York: New York University Press, 2001), 36.
28. John C. Coombs, "The Phases of Conversion: A New Chronology for the Rise of Slavery in Early Virginia," *William and Mary Quarterly* 68, no. 3 (July 2011): 32.
29. Kenneth Morgan, *Slavery and Servitude*, 37; David Eltis, *The Rise of African Slavery*, 43.
30. Lorena Walsh, *Motives of Honor, Pleasure and Profit: Plantation Management in the Colonial Chesapeake, 1607–1763* (Chapel Hill: University of North Carolina Press), 210.
31. Paul Finkelman, quoting Thomas R.R. Cobb in "Thomas R.R. Cobb and the Law of Negro Slavery," 78.
32. Noah Feldman, quoting Madison in *James Madison's Lessons in Racism, New York Times Sunday Review*, Oct. 28, 2017.
33. Avidit Acharya, Matthew Blackwell and Maya Sen, "The Political Legacy of American Slavery," *The Journal of Politics* 78, no. 3: 621–641.
34. Jane Webster, "The Zong in the Context of the Eighteenth-Century Slave Trade," *The Journal of Legal History* 28, no. 3 (December 2007) 285–298.
35. Taylor, *American Colonies*, 324–329; Paul E. Lovejoy, "The Volume of the Atlantic Slave Trade: A Synthesis," *The Journal of African History*, 23, no. 4 (1982): 473–501; Mustakeem, *Slavery at Sea*, 53–92.
36. John Newton, *Thoughts Upon African Slave Trade* (St. Paul's Church Yard: J. Johnson, 1788), 33.
37. John Newton, *Thoughts Upon African Slave Trade*, 33; Anita Rupprecht, "A Limited Sort of Property: History, Memory and the Slave Ship *Zong*," *Slavery and Abolition* 29, no. 2 (June 2008): 265–77; Srividhya Swaminathan, "Reporting Atrocities: A Comparison of the Zong and the Trial of Captain John Kimber," *Slavery and Abolition* 31, no. 4 (December 2010): 483–499; Jane Webster, "The Zong in the Context of the Eighteenth-Century Slave Trade," *The Journal of Legal History* 28, no. 3 (December 2007): 285–298.
38. James Oldham, "Insurance Litigation Involving the Zong and Other British Slave Ships, 1780–1807," *Journal of Legal History* 28, no. 3 (December 2007): 299–318.
39. Edward E. Baptist, *The Half Has Never Been Told: Slavery and the Making of American Capitalism* (New York: Basic Books, 2016), 1–37.
40. Frederick Law Olmsted, *The Cotton Kingdom: The Classic Firsthand Account of the South in the Years Preceding the Civil War* as quoted in Edward Bonekemper, 14.
41. Kenneth M. Stampp, *The Peculiar Institution*, 18.
42. Oldham, "Insurance Litigation Involving the *Zong*," 300–303.
43. Jonathan A. Bush, "Free to Enslave:

Notes—Chapter 2

The Foundations of Colonial American Slave Law," *Yale Journal of Law & the Humanities* 5, no. 2 (1993): 26 and 30.

44. William W. Fisher, III, "Ideology and Imagery in the Law of Slavery–Symposium on the Law of Slavery: Theories of Democracy and the Law of Slavery," *Chi.-Kent. L. Rev.* no. 3 (1992): 1051–1083.

45. *State v. Harden*, 29 S.C.L (2 Speers) 152 (1832).

46. Fisher, "Ideology and Imagery," 1051–1052; Jonathan A. Bush, "Free to Enslave..." 432–434.

47. Fisher, "Ideology and Imagery," 1053.

48. "An Act Concerning Servants and Slaves," 1705 General Assembly of Virginia 1705.

49. Fisher, "Ideology and Imagery," 1051–1083.

50. Paul Finkelman, "Thomas R. R. Cobb and the Law of Negro Slavery," *Roger Williams University Law Review* 5, no. 1, Art. 4 (1999): 77–78.

51. Bruce W. Frier and Thomas A.J. McGinn, *A Casebook on Roman Family Law* (New York: Oxford University Press, 2004) p. 15.

52. Fergus Miller, *The Crowd in Rome* (Ann Arbor: University of Michigan Press, 2002), 109.

53. Paul Finkelman, "Thomas R.R. Cobb," 78.

54. Fisher, "Ideology and Imagery," 1065.

55. Ibram X. Kendi, *Stamped from the Beginning: The Definitive History of Racist Ideas in America* (New York: Nation Books, 2016): 15–19.

56. William W. Fisher III, "Ideology and Imagery in the Law of Slavery....," 1064–1073 and 1066–1068.

57. Ibid., pp 22–46.

58. Finkelman, "Thomas R.R. Cobb and the Law of Negro Slavery," 83.

59. Wiecek, *The Sources of Anti-Slavery Constitutionalism*, 70.

60. Sidney Kaplan, ed., *The Selling of Joseph: A Memorial*, by Samuel Sewell (Amherst: University of Massachusetts Press, 1969).

61. W. Blackstone, *Commentaries on the Laws of England*, 4 vols. (Oxford: Clarendon, 1765–69), 1: 123.

62. William M. Wiecek, "*Somerset*: Lord Mansfield and the Legitimacy of Slavery in the Anglo-American World," *The University of Chicago Law Review* 42, no.1 (Autumn 1974): 86–88.

63. William R. Cotter, "The Somerset Case and the Abolition of Slavery in England," *History* 79, no. 55 (February 1994): 34–39, and William Wiecek, "*Somerset*: Lord Mansfield and the Legitimacy of Slavery in the Anglo-American World," *The University of Chicago Law Review* 42, no.1 (Autumn 1974): 86–146.

64. Robert Spector, "The Quock Walker Cases (1781–83) and Slavery—Its Abolition and Negro Citizenship in Early Massachusetts," *Journal of Negro History* 53, no. 1 (January 1968): 12–32.

65. Alfred W. Blumenrosen and Ruth G. Blumenrosen, *Slave Nation: How Slavery United the Colonies & Sparked the American Revolution* (Napierville: Sourcebooks, 2005).

66. Ibid.

67. William M. Wiecek, *The Sources of Anti-Slavery Constitutionalism in America, 1760–1848* (Cornell: Cornell University Press, 1977), 40–61.

68. William Peden, ed., *Notes on the State of Virginia*, by Thomas Jefferson (Chapel Hill, 1954), 162.

69. Henry Wiencek, "The Dark Side of Thomas Jefferson," *Smithsonian Magazine*, October 2012.

70. James S. Pula, "The American Will of Thaddeus Kosciuszko," *Polish American Studies* 34, no.1 (Spring 1977), 16–25.

71. Annette Gordon-Reed, "Thomas Jefferson, Tadeusz Kosciuszko, and Slavery," *Atlantic Monthly*, December 2012.

72. Jack N. Rakove, 78.

73. Quoted in David McCullough, *John Adams*, 68.

74. Charles Boyster, *A Revolutionary People at War: The Continental Army and American Character, 1775–1783* (Chapel Hill: University of North Carolina Press, 1996), 12.

75. Bruce Chadwick, The First American Army (Napierville: Sourcebooks, Inc., 2005), 279–285; John Ferling, *Almost a Miracle: The American Victory in the War of Independence* (New York, Oxford University Press, 2007), 341–44, 553; Charles

Notes—Chapter 3

Royster, *A Revolutionary People at War* (Chapel Hill: The University of North Carolina Press, 1979), 241–242.
76. Ferling, *Almost a Miracle*, 341–344.
77. Chadwick, *The First American Army*, 279–80.
78. Paul Finkelman, "Thomas Jefferson and Antislavery: The Myth Goes On," *The Virginia Magazine of History and Biography* 102, no. 2 (April 1994): 193–228.
79. Avidit Acharya, Matthew Blackwell and Maya Sen, "The Political Legacy of American Slavery," *The Journal of Politics* 78, no. 3. Published online May 19, 2016.

Chapter 3

1. David W. Galenson, "The Atlantic Slave Trade and the Barbados Market, 1673–1723," *The Journal of Economic History* 42, no. 3 (Sep. 1982), 491–492.
2. Galenson, "The Atlantic Slave Trade," 433–435.
3. Galenson, "The Atlantic Slave Trade," 433–434, 441 and 449; Jonathan A. Bush, "Free to Enslave: The Foundations of Colonial American Slave Law," *Yale Journal of Law and Humanities* 5, no. 2 (1993): 433.
4. Bush, "Free to Enslave," 433; Edward B. Rugemer, "The Development of Mastery and Race in the Comprehensive Slave Codes of the Greater Caribbean during the Seventeenth Century," *William and Mary Quarterly* 70, no. 3 (July 2013): 429–458.
5. Fisher, "Ideology and Imagery," 1051–1054; Bush, "Free to Enslave," 417–70.
6. Finkelman, "Thomas R.R. Cobb," 76–79.
7. Betty Woods, *The Origins of American Slavery: Freedom and Bondage in the English Colonies* (New York: Hill and Wang, 1997), ch. 2.
8. Bush, "Free to Enslave," 423–425.
9. Bush, 424.
10. Edward B. Rugemer, "The Development of Mastery and Race," 429–458; Fisher, "Ideology and Imagery," 1051–1063.
11. Bush, 443.

12. William Robert Fogel, *Without Consent or Contract: The Rise and Fall of American Slavery* (New York: W.W. Norton, 1989), 394–399.
13. Suzanne Miers and Igor Kopytoff, *Slavery in Africa: Historical and Anthropological Perspectives* (Madison: University of Wisconsin Press, 1977), 3–17; Dorothy Schneider and Carl Schneider, *Slavery* (New York: Checkmark Books, 2007), 1.
14. Bush, 432–434.
15. William W. Fisher, III, "Ideology and Imagery in the Law of Slavery," 1054–1055.
16. Henry Wiencek, "The Dark Side of Thomas Jefferson," *Smithsonian* (October 2012).
17. 25 U.S. (12 Wheat.) 460 (1827).
18. 24 F. Cas. 1042 (C.C.D. Mass. 1835) (No. 14,454); Barbara Holden Smith, "Lords of Lash, Loom and Law: Justice Story, Slavery and *Prigg v. Pennsylvania*," 78, no. 6 (September 1993): 1086–1151.
19. Account of William Wells Brown (1844), reprinted in *A Documentary History of the Negro People in the United States* 246 (Herbert Aptheker ed., 1951).
20. *Prigg v. Pennsylvania*, 41 U.S. (16 Pet.) 539 (1848).
21. Joel Richard Paul, *Without Precedent: Chief Justice John Marshall and His Times* (New York: Riverhead Books, 2018), 45–53.
22. Wiecek, *Anti-Slavery Constitution*, 106–13.
23. Ulysses S. Grant, *Personal Memoirs of Ulysses S. Grant* (New York: Modern Library, 1999), 23–24.
24. Harold Schwartz, "Fugitive Slave Days in Boston, *New England Quarterly* 27, no. 2 (June 1954): 191–212.
25. Samuel Shapiro, "The Rendition of Anthony Burns," *The Journal of Negro History* 44, no. 1 (Jan. 1959): 34–51.
26. 1855 Chap. 489 "An Act to Protect the Rights and Liberties of the People of the Commonwealth of Massachusetts."
27. Jill Lepore, *These Truths: A History of the United States* (New York: W.W. Norton, 2019), 262–267.
28. M. Sinha, "The Caning of Charles Sumner; Slavery, Race, and Ideology in the Age of the Civil War," *Journal of the*

Notes—Chapter 4

Early Republic 23, no. 2 (Summer 2003), 233–262.

Chapter 4

1. Merriam Webster's Collegiate Dictionary, Eleventh Edition.
2. Ambrose Bierce, *The Unabridged Devil's Dictionary* (Athens: University of Georgia Press, 2000), 110.
3. Bonekemper, *The Myth of the Lost Cause* (Washington, D.C.: Regnery Press, 2015).
4. Maurice Landrieu, "How I Learned About the "Cult of the Lost Cause," *Smithsonian*, March 12, 2018.
5. Bonekemper, *The Myth of the Lost Cause*, 1–8.
6. Shelby Foote, *The Civil War: A Narrative. Vol. 1: Fort Sumter to Perryville* (New York: Random House, 1958), 58.
7. Earl J. Hess, *Civil War Infantry Tactics* (Baton Rouge: Louisiana State University Press, 2015), 35–80.
8. Larry J. Daniel, *Shiloh: The Battle That Changed the Civil War* (New York: Simon and Schuster, 1997), 106–115.
9. Williamson Murray and Wayne Wei-Siang Hsieh, *A Savage War* (Princeton: Princeton University Press, 2016), 147–161.
10. *A Savage War*, 111–113.
11. Michael Korda, *The Life and Legend of Robert E. Lee* (New York: Harper Collins, 2014), 324–325.
12. Earl J. Hess, *The Rifle Musket in Civil War Combat: Reality and Myth* (Lawrence: Kansas University Press, 2008). 197–215.
13. J. David Hacker, "A Census Based Account of Civil War Dead," *Civil War History*, 57, no. 4 (December 2011): 307–348; James McPherson, *The War That Forged a Nation* (Oxford: Oxford University Press, 2015), 46–64; Murray and Hsieh, *A Savage War*, 8.
14. James M, McPherson, *War on the Waters: The Union and Confederate Navies, 1861–1865* (Chapel Hill: University of North Carolina Press, 2012), 70–96.
15. Phillip Shaw Paludan, "Dictator Lincoln: Surveying Lincoln and the Constitution," *OAH Magazine of History* 21, No. 1 (Jan. 2007): 8–13.
16. Elizabeth D. Young, "Lincoln and the Constitution," *Saber and Scroll* 1, no. 3 (2015): 31–48.
17. Noah Andre Trudeau, *Like Men of War: Black Troops in the Civil War 1862–1865* (Edison, NJ: Castle Books, 2002), 9–11.
18. James H. Robertson, Jr., *Soldiers Blue and Gray* (New York: Warner Books, 1988), 31–36.
19. McPherson, *The War That Forged a Nation*, 119.
20. Manisha Sinha, "Architects of Their Own Liberation: African Americans, Emancipation, and the Civil War," *OAH Magazine of History* 27, no. 2 (April 2013): 5–10.
21. Doris Kearns Goodwin, *Team of Rivals* (New York: Simon and Schuster, 2005), 61–68.
22. Stephen W. Sears, *Landscape Turned Red: The Battle of Antietam* (New York: Houghton Mifflin, 1983), 32–33; Stephen W. Sears, *Lincoln's Lieutenants: The High Command of the Army of the Potomac* (New York: Houghton Mifflin, 2017) 108.
23. Sears, *Landscape Turned Red*, 112–113.
24. Murray, and Hsieh, *A Savage War*, 225.
25. *Ibid.*, 229.
26. *Ibid.*, *A Savage War*.
27. Sears, *Landscape Turned Red*, 151–297.
28. Foote, *The Civil War*, Vol. I, 694.
29. Sears, *Landscape Turned Red*, 260–267.
30. Murray and Hsieh, *A Savage War*, 240.
31. McPherson, *The War That Forged a Nation*, 132.
32. James M. McPherson, *For Cause and Comrades: Why Men Fought in the Civil War* (New York: Oxford University Press, 1975), 125.
33. McPherson, *For Cause and Comrades*, 126.
34. Dudley Taylor Cornish, *The Sable Arm* (Lawrence: University Press of Kansas, 1987), 288–291.
35. McPherson, *Cause and Comrades*, 129.
36. Deborah Willis, "The Black Civil

183

Notes—Chapter 5

War Soldier: Conflict and Citizenship," *Journal of American Studies* 51, no. 2 (2017): 285–323.
37. Cornish, *The Sable Arm*, 91.
38. William A. Dobak, *Freedom by the Sword* (Washington, D.C.: Center of Military History, United States Army, 2011), 11–23.
39. Dobak, *The Sable Arm*, 92–93.
40. Trudeau, *Like Men of War*, 60.
41. *Ibid.*, 61.
42. *Ibid.*, 61.
43. *Ibid.*, 156–181.
44. Gordon C. Rhea, *The Battle of the Wilderness* (Baton Rouge: Louisiana State University Press, 1994), 42.
45. *Ibid.*, 435–440.
46. Ron Chernow, *Grant* (New York: Penguin Press, 2017), 384–385.
47. Murray and Hsieh, *A Savage War*, 399.
48. Catherine M. Lewis and J. Richard Lewis, eds., *Jim Crow America* (Fayetteville: University of Arkansas Press, 2009): 81.
49. Eric Foner, *Reconstruction* (New York: HarperCollins, 1988), 35.
50. *Ibid.*, 228–234.
51. *Ibid.*, 548–605, and Armistead L. Robinson, "The Politics of Reconstruction," *The Wilson Quarterly*: 2, no. 2 (Spring 1978): 121–123.
52. Foner, *Reconstruction*, 190.
53. *Ibid.*, 35–38.
54. *Ibid.*, 61–62, and *Statutes at Large, Thirty Seventh Congress, Second Session*.
55. Ira C. Colby, "The Freedmen's Bureau: From Social Welfare to Segregation," *Phylon*, 46, no. 3 (3rd Qtr., 1985): 219–230.
56. Kolchin, Peter. "Scalawags, Carpetbaggers, and Reconstruction: A Quantitative Look at Southern Congressional Politics, 1868–1872," *The Journal of Southern History* 45 no. 1 (1979): 63–76; and Ted Tunnell, "Creating 'The Propaganda of History': Southern Editors and the Origins of 'Carpetbagger and Scalawag'". *The Journal of Southern History* 72, no. 4 (2006): 789–822.
57. Foner, *Reconstruction*, 177.
58. *Ibid.*, 183.
59. Armistead L. Robinson, "The Politics of Reconstruction," *The Wilson Quarterly*: 2, no. 2 (Spring 1978): 106–123.
60. Foner, *Reconstruction*, 190, and David Hardin, *After the War: The Lives and Images of Major Civil War Figures After the Shooting Stopped* (Chicago: Ivan R. Dee, 2010), 178–186.
61. James W. Clarke, *The Lineaments of Wrath: Race, Violent Crime, and American Culture* (New York: Routledge Press, 2018), 67.
62. Foner, *Reconstruction*, 199–209.
63. Crouch, Barry A. "A Spirit of Lawlessness: White Violence; Texas Blacks, 1865–1868." *Journal of Social History* 18, no. 2 (1984): 217–32.
64. Foner, *Reconstruction*, 180.
65. U.S. Constitution. Amend. XIII.
66. Foner, *Reconstruction*, 243–251.
67. U.S. Constitution. Amend. XIV.
68. U.S. Const. Amend. XIV.
69. Michael Martinez, *Coming for to Carry Me Home: Race in America from Antebellum to Jim Crow* (New York: Rowman & Littlefield, 2012), 215.

Chapter 5

1. Paul, *Without Precedent*, 350–351.
2. Carol Anderson, *A History of Disfranchisement: How Voter Suppression Is Destroying Our Democracy* (New York: Bloomsbury Publishing, 2018), 2.
3. Douglas R. Edgerton, *The Wars of Reconstruction: The Brief Violent History of America's Most Progressive Era* (New York: Bloomsbury Press, 2014,) 15.
4. Armstead L. Robinson, "The Politics of Reconstruction," *The Wilson Quarterly* (1976) 2, no. 2 (Spring 1978), 106–123.
5. Eric Foner, *Reconstruction: America's Unfinished Revolution: 1863–1877* (New York: Harper Collins, 1988), 604.
6. Mary Frances Berry, *Black Resistance, White Law: A History of Constitutional Racism in America* (New York: Penguin Books, 1994), xii.
7. Anderson, *A History of Disfranchisement*, 3–11.
8. Robert B. McKay, "Racial Discrimination in the Electoral Process." *The Annals of the American Academy of Political and Social Science* 407 (May, 1973): 102–18.
9. Brian Z. Tamanaha, "The History

Notes—Chapter 5

and Elements of the Rule of Law," *Singapore Journal of Legal Studies* 2012, 232–247.
10. Edgerton, *The Wars of Reconstruction*, 119.
11. Paul, *Without Precedent*, 222–225.
12. Judiciary Act of 1801.
13. Schwartz, *A History of the Supreme Court*, 18–20.
14. 2 U.S. (Dall.) 419 (U.S. 1793).
15. 5 U.S. (1 Cranch) 137 (1803).
16. Paul, *Without Precedence*, 241–261; and 1 Cranch at 177–178.
17. Jonathan M. Bryant, *Dark Places of the Earth: The Voyage of the Slave Ship Antelope* (New York: W.W. Norton & Co., 2015), 234.
18. 6 U.S. (2 Cranch) 336 (1804).
19. 7 U.S. (3 Cranch) 324 (1806).
20. 10 U.S. (6 Cranch) 3 (1810).
21. 11 U.S. (7 Cranch) 290 (1813).
22. 11 U.S. (7 Cranch) 496 (1813).
23. 23 U.S. (10 Wheat) 66 (1825).
24. Bryant, *Dark Places of the Earth*.
25. *Ibid.*, 264–273.
26. Paul, *Without Precedent*, 439–440.
27. Don E. Fehrenbacher, "Roger B. Taney and the Sectional Crisis," *The Journal of Southern History* 43, no. 4 (1977): 555–66.
28. 60 U.S. (19 How.) 393 (1857).
29. Alexander Tsesis, "Interpreting the Thirteenth Amendment," *U. Penn. J. of Constitutional Law* 11, no. 5 (March 2009): 1337–1362.
30. Act of April 9, 1866, Ch. 31, 14 Stat. 27 (reenacted by Enforcement Act of 1870, ch. 114, §16 Stat. 140, 144 (1870) (codified as amended at 42 U.S.C. §§1981–1982 [1987]).
31. Cong. Globe, 39th Cong., 1st Sess. (1866), 474–76, 673–87, 1291–93, 1755–61, 1782–85, 1804, 1809.
32. 24 Fed. Cas. 337 (1867).
33. 32 U.S. (7 Pet.) 243 (1833).
34. U.S. Constitution, amend. XIV, sec.1.
35. Eric Foner, *The Second Founding: How the Civil War and Reconstruction Remade the Constitution* (New York: W.W. Norton & Company, 2019), 75.
36. Schwartz, *A History of the Supreme Court*, 158–161.
37. Egerton, *The Wars of Reconstruction*, 236–242, 285–287, 290–293, 295–299.
38. Foner, *Reconstruction*, 425.
39. Report of the Committee on Reconstruction, Part IV, p.75.
40. The Freedmen's Bureau Online: Records of the Bureau of Refugees, Freedmen, and Abandoned Lands freedmensbureau.com., and Philip Dray, *At the Hands of Persons Unknown: The Lynching of Black America* (New York: Modern Library, 2002), 37.
41. Dray, *At the Hands of Persons Unknown*, 48.
42. Dray, 48.
43. *Ibid.*
44. Foner, *Reconstruction*, 437, 550.
45. Thomas F. Gossett, *Race: The History of an Idea in America* (New York: Oxford University Press, 1997), 258.
46. Dray, *At the Hands of Persons Unknown*, 49.
47. Chris Chapman and A.J. Withers, *Violent History of Benevolence: Interlocking Oppression in the Moral Economies of Social Working* (Toronto: University of Toronto Press, 2019) 95.
48. Dray, *At the Hands of Persons Unknown*, 36–37.
49. Foner, *Reconstruction*, 454–459, 530–31.
50. *Ibid.*, 457–458.
51. Egerton, *The Wars of Reconstruction*, 316.
52. Chernow, *Grant*, 795.
53. 109 U.S. 3 (1883).
54. Foner, *Reconstruction*, 582.
55. Richard Wormser, *The Rise and Fall of Jim Crow* (New York: St. Martin's Press, 2003), 30.
56. David Margolick, *Strange Fruit: The Biography of a Song* (New York: Harper Collins, 2002).
57. Dray, *At the Hands of Persons Unknown*, x.
58. *Ibid.*, 7.
59. James Allen, Hilton Als, Congressman John Lewis and Leon F. Litwack, *Without Sanctuary: Lynching Photography in America* (Santa Fe: Twin Palms Publishers, 2000).
60. Harvey Young, "The Black Body as Souvenir in American Lynching" *Theater Journal* 57, no. 4 (2005) 639–657.
61. Amy Louise Wood, and Susan V. Donaldson, "Lynching's Legacy in Ameri-

Notes—Chapter 6

can Culture." *The Mississippi Quarterly* 61, no. 1/2 (2008): 5–25..

62. Michael J. Pfeifer, "At the Hands of Parties Unknown? The State of the Field of Lynching Scholarship," *Journal of American History* 101, no. 3 (December 2014): 832–846.; Equal Justice Initiative, "Lynching in America: Confronting the Legacy of Racial Terror," 3d ed. (2017); Wood and Donaldson, "Lynching's Legacy," 5–25.

63. Equal Justice Initiative, "Lynching in America: Confronting the Legacy of Racial Terror" (3d ed.), 16 and 62–66.

64. Paula J. Giddings, *Ida: A Sword Among Lions* (New York: HarperCollins, 2008), 248–251.

65. Giddings, *Ida: A Sword Among Lions*, 274–275.

66. Dray, 3–6.

67. William F. Pinar, "To Live or Die in Dixie," *Counterpoints* 163 (2001): 117–56.

68. Amy B. Wang, "Lawmaker apologizes after saying 'Leaders should be lynched' for saying Confederate statutes should be removed," *Washington Post*, May 22, 2017.

69. Dray, 152–159.

70. Jeffrey T. Sammons and John H. Morrow, Jr., *Harlem's Rattlers and the Great War: The Undaunted 369th Regiment and the African American Quest for Equality* (Lawrence: University Press of Kansas, 2014).

71. Equal Justice Initiative, "Lynching in America: Targeting Black Americans" (2016), 30.

72. Equal Justice Initiative, "Lynching in America: Targeting Black Americans" (2016), 30–31.

73. Dray, 369–70.

74. Goodwin Liu, "The First Justice Harlan," *Cal. L. Rev.* 96, no. 5 (Oct. 2008), 1383–1393.

75. Nadra Kareem Nittle, "Biography of Homer Plessy, Civil Rights Activist." Thought Co., Jul. 3, 2019, thoughtco.com/homer-plessy-4588299.

76. 163 U.S. 45 (1896); Molly Townes O'Brien, "Justice John Marshall Harlan as Prophet: The Plessy Dissenter's Color-Blind Constitution," *Wm. & Mary Bill of Rts. J.* 753 (1998): 756–761; Goodwin Liu, "The First Justice Harlan," 96 Cal. L. Rev. 1383 (2008): 1386–1391.

77. Dray, 307–315.
78. 287 U.S. 45 (1932).
79. 294 U.S. 587 (1935),
80. Dray, 313–317.
81. 313 U.S. 80 (1941).
82. Dray, 440–442.
83. 325 U.S. 91 (1945).
84. Dray, 441.
85. 334 U.S. 1 (1948).
86. 334 U.S. 24 (1948).
87. 332 U.S. 631 (1948).
88. 339 U.S. 629 (1950).
89. Winston Groom, *1942: The Year That Tried Men's Souls* (New York: Atlantic Monthly Press, 2005), 158–160.
90. Orville C. Shirey, *Americans: The Story of the 442d Combat Team* (Washington, D.C.: Infantry Journal Press, 1946).
91. 347 U.S. 483 (1954).

Chapter 6

1. John Rakove, *Original Meanings: Politics and Ideas in the Making of the Constitution* (New York: Random House, 1997): 289 and 330.

2. Wiecek, *The Sources of Anti-Slavery Constitutionalism*, 106.

3. *Ibid.*, 94.

4. *Annals*, 1 Cong. 2 sess. 1189 (11 Feb. 1970), 1198–1204 (12 Feb. 1790), 1466–1471 (22 March 1790); Wiecek, 94.

5. Wiecek, 98–100.
6. *Ibid.*, 87–88.
7. *Ibid.*, 103–104.
8. *Ibid.*, 97.
9. *Ibid.*, 107.
10. *Ibid.*, 122.
11. *Ibid.*, 279.
12. 60 U.S. (19 How.) 393 (1857).

13. Stephen Cresswell. "Enforcing the Enforcement Acts: The Department of Justice in Northern Mississippi, 1870–1890," *The Journal of Southern History* 53, no. 3 (1987): 421–40.

14. Lois P. Masur, "Why It Took a Century to Pass an Anti-Lynching Law," *Washington Post*, Dec. 28, 2018.

15. Ida A. Brudnick and Jennifer Manning, "African American Members of the United States Congress: 1870–1918," Congressional Research Service, 2018.

Notes—Chapter 7

16. William Barney, ed., *A Companion to Nineteenth Century America* (Malden: Blackwell Publishers, 2001), 53.
17. Vincent P. De Santis, "President Hayes's Southern Policy," *The Journal of Southern History* 21, no. 4 (1955): 476–94.
18. Raphael O'Hara Boyd, "Service in the Midst of the Storm: James Edward O'Hara and Reconstruction in North Carolina." *The Journal of Negro History* 86, no. 3 (2001): 319–35.
19. David A. Bateman, Ira Katznelson, and John S. Lapinski, *Southern Nation: Congress and White Supremacy After Reconstruction* (Princeton: Princeton University Press, 2018), 129.
20. Richard E. Welch, "The Federal Elections Bill of 1890: Postscripts and Prelude." *The Journal of American History* 52, no. 3 (1965): 511–26.
21. J.R. LeMaster and James Daniel Wilson, eds. *The Mark Twain Encyclopedia* (New York: Garland Publishing Company, 1993), 334.
22. Rakove, *The Annotated U.S. Constitution*, 275.
23. David A. Nichols, *A Matter of Justice: Eisenhower and the Beginning of the Civil Rights Revolution* (New York: Simon and Schuster, 2007), 92.
24. James F. Simon, *Eisenhower vs. Warren: The Battle for Civil Rights and Civil Liberties* (New York: Liveright Publishing Co., 2018), 243–247.
25. Simon, 276–289.
26. John Hart. "Kennedy, Congress and Civil Rights," *Journal of American Studies* 13, no. 2 (1979): 165–78.
27. Catherine Fisk and Erwin Chemerinsky, "The Filibuster," *Stanford Law Review* 49, no. 2 (1997): 181–254.
28. *Ibid.*
29. Daron Acemoglu and James A. Robinson, *Why Nations Fail: The Origins of Power, Prosperity and Poverty* (New York: Crown, 2012), 418.
30. Tony Badger, "Southerners Who Refused to Sign the Southern Manifesto," *The Historical Journal* 42, no. 2 (1999): 517–34.
31. Eric Schickler, Kathryn Pearson, and Brian D. Feinstein, "Congressional Parties and Civil Rights Politics from 1933 to 1972," *The Journal of Politics* 72, no. 3 (2010): 672–89.

Chapter 7

1. Larson and Winthrop, *The Constitutional Convention*, 97.
2. *Ibid.*, 20.
3. *Ibid.*, 50.
4. *Ibid.*, 26.
5. *Ibid.*, 139–40.
6. *Federalist*, No.10.
7. Finkelman, *Slavery and the Founders*, 217–218.
8. Baptist, *The Half Has Never Been Told*, 9.
9. Ron Chernow, *Washington: A Life* (New York: Penguin Books, 2011), 490.
10. Kenneth Morgan, ed., *Slavery in America: A Reader and a Guide* (Athens: University of Georgia Press, 2005), 150.
11. Finkelman, *Slavery and the Founders*,183–184.
12. *Ibid.*, 121.
13. *Ibid.*, 203–05.
14. *Ibid.*, 254.
15. *Ibid.*, 264–268.
16. *Ibid.*, 265.
17. Gordon S. Wood, *Friends Divided: John Adams and Thomas Jefferson* (New York: Penguin Press, 2017), 124–127.
18. Baptist, *The Half Has Never Been Told*, 224–29.
19. *Ibid.*
20. 60 U.S. (19 How.) 393 (1857).
21. McPherson, *The War That Forged a Nation*, 15–25.
22. Carl Sandburg, *Abraham Lincoln: The War Years Vol. IV* (New York: Harcourt, Brace & Co., 1939), 402.
23. *Ibid.*, 297.
24. Foner, *Reconstruction*, 143.
25. 109 U.S. 3 (1883).
26. Frank P. Vazzano, "Rutherford B. Hayes and the Politics of Discord," *The Historian* 68, no. 3 (2006): 519–40 and 546.
27. Vincent P. De Santis, "President Hayes's Southern Policy," *The Journal of Southern History* 21, no. 4 (1955): 476–94.
28. Frank N. Schubert, "Buffalo Soldiers at San Juan Hill," *Army History*, no. 45 (1998): 36–38.
29. William E. Leuchtenburg, *The*

American President: From Teddy Roosevelt to Bill Clinton (New York: Oxford University Press, 2015), 36.

30. Dray, 159–162.

31. Kenneth O'Reilly, "The Jim Crow Policies of Woodrow Wilson," *The Journal of Blacks in Higher Education*, no. 17 (1997): 117–21.

32. Patricia O'Toole, *The Moralist: Woodrow Wilson and the World He Made* (New York: Simon & Schuster, 2018) 78–79.

33. O'Toole, *The Moralist: Woodrow Wilson*, 133–135, and Dick Lehr, "President Woodrow Wilson and His Racist Legacy." *Atlantic Monthly*, Nov. 27, 2017, accessed July 3, 2018, https://www.theatlantic.com/politics/archive/2015/11/wilson-legacy-racism/417549/.

34. O'Toole, 324–325.

35. George F. Garcia, "Herbert Hoover and the Issue of Race." *The Annals of Iowa* (1979), 507–515.

36. Doris Kearns Goodwin, *No Ordinary Time: Franklin and Eleanor Roosevelt: The Home Front in World War II* (New York: Simon & Schuster, 1994), 162–165.

37. "Getting to Know the Racial Views of Our Past Presidents: What about FDR?" *The Journal of Blacks in Higher Education*, no. 38 (2002): 44–46.

38. Leuchtenburg, *The American President*, 181–182.

39. Garth E. Pauley, "Harry Truman and the NAACP: A Case Study in Presidential Persuasion on Civil Rights," *Rhetoric and Public Affairs* 2, no. 2 (1999): 211–41.

40. Ibid.

41. James F. Simon, *Eisenhower vs. Warren* (New York: Liveright Publishing, 2018), 384–385.

42. *Ibid.*, 180–181.

43. *Ibid.*, 310–311.

44. Leuchtenburg, *The American President*, 361.

45. Simon, *Eisenhower v. Warren*, 296–310.

46. *Ibid.*, 276–289.

47. Leuchtenburg, *The American President*, 401–402.

48. *Ibid.*, 400–406.

49. *Ibid.*, 430–449.

Chapter 8

1. Thomas D. Morris, *Free Men All: The Personal Liberty Laws of the North, 1781–1861* (Baltimore: Johns Hopkins University Press, 1974).

2. *Prigg v. Pennsylvania*, 41 U.S. (16 Pet.) 539 (1842).

3. Paul Finkelman, "John Bingham and the Background to the Fourteenth Amendment," *Akron Law Review* 36, no. 4, Art. 3 (2003): 671–693.

4. Foner, *Reconstruction*, 67.

5. Ibid., 35, 183 and 276.

6. Larson, *The Constitutional Convention*, 109–110.

7. Paul Finkelman, "The Historical Context of the Fourteenth Amendment," *Temple Political and Civil Rights Law Review* 2 (2004), 389–409.

8. Eric Foner, *Reconstruction*, 199–207.

9. Daniel A. Farber and John E. Muench, "The Ideological Origins of the Fourteenth Amendment," *Constitutional Commentary* 161 (1984), 235–279.

10. Hugh H. Hackney, "Racial Discrimination and the Civil Rights Act of 1866," *SMU Law Review* 23 SW L.J. (1969), 373–383; John Hope Franklin, "Civil Rights Act of 1866 Revisited," *Hastings L.J.* 4 no. 41 (1989), 135–48; Foner, *Reconstruction: America's Unfinished Revolution*, 243–251.

11. *In re: Turner*, 24 F. Cas. 337 (C.C. D. Md. 1867) (No. 14,247).

12. *Jones v. Alfred H. Mayer Co.*, 392 U.S. 469 (1968).

13. Erwin Chemerinsky, "The Supreme Court and the Fourteenth Amendment: The Unfulfilled Promise," *Loyola of Los Angeles Law Review* 25 (1992): 1143–1157.

14. Ibid.

15. Foner, *Reconstruction*, 57.

16. Daniel A. Farber and John E. Muench, "The Ideological Origins of the Fourteenth Amendment," *Constitutional Commentary*, 161.

17. Foner, *Reconstruction*, 276–280.

18. Ron Chernow, *Grant*, 795.

19. Civil Rights Cases of 1873, 109 U.S. 3 (1883).

20. Schwartz, *A History of the Supreme Court*, 165–168.

21. David McCullough, *Truman* (New York: Simon and Schuster, 1992), 650–651.

Notes—Chapter 8

22. William J. (ed.), *American Martyr: The Jon Daniels Story* (Harrisburg, PA: Morehouse Publishing, 1992). Originally published as *The Jon Daniels Story: With His Letters and Papers* (New York: Seabury Press, 1967), and Charles Eagles, *Outside Agitator: Jon Daniels and the Civil Rights Movement in Alabama* (Tuscaloosa: University of Alabama Press, 2000). Published under same title by the University of North Carolina Press (Chapel Hill, 1993).

23. Laurence Tribe and Joshua Matz, *Uncertain Justice: The Roberts Court and the Constitution* (New York: Henry Holt and Company, 2104), 32–38.

24. *Shelby County v. Holder* 570 U.S. 529 (2013).

25. Vann R. Newkirk II, "How *Shelby County v. Holder* Broke America," *Atlantic* July 10, 2018.

Bibliography

Books

Acharya, Avidit, Matthew Blackwell and Maya Sen. *Deep Roots: How Slavery Still Shapes Southern Politics*. Princeton: Princeton University Press, 2018.

Allen, James, Hilton Als, Congressman James Lewis, and Leon F. Litwack. *Without Sanctuary: Lynching Photography in America*. Santa Fe: Twin Palms Publishers, 2000.

Allison, Robert J., and Bernard Bailyn, eds. *The Essential Debate on the Constitution: Federalist and Antifederalist Speeches and Writing*. New York: The Library of America, 2018.

Amar, Akhil Reed. *America's Constitution: A Biography*. New York: Random House, 2005.

———. *The Constitution Today: Timeless Lessons for the Issues of Our Era*. New York: Hachette Book Group, 2016.

Anderson, Carol. *One Person, No Vote*. New York: Bloomsbury Publishing, 2018.

Bailyn, Barnard. *The Barbarous Years: The Conflict of Civilizations, 1600–1675*. New York: Alfred A. Knopf, 2012.

Baptist, Edward. *The Half Has Never Been Told: Slavery and the Making of American Capitalism*. New York: Basic Books, 2016.

Barber, Sotirios A. *Constitutional Failure*. Lawrence: University Press of Kansas: 2014.

Beard, Charles. *An Economic Interpretation of the Constitution of the United States*. New York: Macmillan and Co., 1921.

Berlin, Ira. *Many Thousands Gone: The First Two Centuries of Slavery in North America*. Cambridge: Belknap Press, 1998.

Berry, Mary Francis. *Black Resistance, White Law: A History of Constitutional Racism in America*. New York: Penguin Books, 1994.

Bierce, Ambrose. *Unabridged Devil's Dictionary*. Athens: University of Georgia Press, 2000.

Blackmon, Douglas A. *Slavery by Another Name: The Re-Enslavement of Black Americans from the Civil War to World War II*. New York: Anchor Books, 2009.

Blumenrosen, Alfred A., and Rose G. Blumenrosen. *Slave Nation: How Slavery United the Colonies & Sparked the American Revolution*. Naperville, IL: Sourcebooks, Inc., 2005.

Bonekemper, Edward H. *The Myth of the Lost Cause*. Washington, D.C.: Regnery History, 2015.

Brookhiser, Richard. *Gentleman Revolutionary: Gouverneur Morris, the Rake Who Wrote the Constitution*. New York: The Free Press, 2003.

Bryant, Jonathan M. *Dark Places of the Earth: The Voyage of the Slave Ship Antelope*. New York: W.W. Norton, 2015.

Burgess, John W. *Reconstruction and the Constitution: 1866–1876*. New York: Charles Scribner's Sons, 1903.

Burstein, Andrew, and Nancy Isenberg. *Madison and Jefferson*. New York: Random House, 2010.

Chadwick, Bruce. *The First American Army*. Napierville, IL: Sourcebooks, 2005.

Bibliography

Clarke, James C. *The Lineaments of Wrath: Race Violent Crime and American Culture*. New York: Routledge, 2018.

Cohen, Adam. *Supreme Inequality: The Supreme Court's Fifty-Year Battle for a More Unjust America*. New York: Penguin, 2020.

Collier, Christopher, and James Collier. *Decision in Philadelphia*. New York: Ballantine, 2007.

Cooper, Phillip J. *By Order of the President: The Use and Misuse of Executive Direct Action*. Lawrence: University Press of Kansas, 2002.

Cornish, Dudley Taylor. *The Sable Arm: Black Troops in the Union Army, 1861–1865*. Lawrence: University Press of Kansas, 1987.

Cost, Jay. *The Price of Greatness: Alexander Hamilton, James Madison and the Creation of American Oligarchy*. New York: Basic Books, 2018.

Curtin, Philip. *Rise and Fall of the Plantation Complex: Essays in Atlantic History*. New York: Cambridge University Press, 1990.

Dahl, Robert. *How Democratic Is the American Constitution?* New Haven: Yale University, 2001.

Daniel, Larry J. *Shiloh: The Battle that Changed the Civil War*. New York: Simon & Schuster, 1997.

Degler, Carl N., and Harry P. Owens. *Perspectives and Irony in American Slavery*. Jackson: University Press of Mississippi, 1976.

Delblanco, Andrew. *The War Before the War: Fugitive Slaves and the Struggle for America's Soul, from the Revolution to the Civil War*. New York: Penguin Press, 2018.

Diamond, Jared. *Guns, Germs, and Steel: The Fates of Human Societies*. New York: W.W. Norton & Co., 1997.

Dobak, William A. *Freedom by the Sword: The U.S. Colored Troops, 1862–1867*. Washington, D.C.: Center of Military History of the United States Army, 2011.

Dray, Philip. *At the Hands of Persons Unknown: The Lynching of Black America*. New York: Random House, 2002.

_____. *Capitol Men: The Epic Story of Reconstruction Through the Lives of the First Black Congressmen*. Boston: Houghton Mifflin Company, 2008.

Dunbar, Erica Armstrong. *Never Caught: The Washingtons' Relentless Pursuit of Their Runaway Slave Ona Judge*. New York: Atria Books, 2017.

Egerton, Douglas R. *The Wars of Reconstruction: The Brief, Violent History of America's Most Progressive Era*. New York: Bloomsbury Press, 2014.

Ellis, Joseph R. *American Dialogue: The Founders and Us*. New York: Alfred A. Knopf, 2018.

Eltis, David. *The Rise of African Slavery in the Americas*. Cambridge: Cambridge University Press, 2000.

Fellman, Michael. *Citizen Sherman: A Life of William Tecumseh Sherman*. New York: Random House, 1995.

Ferling, John. *Almost a Miracle: The American Victory in the War of Independence*. New York: Oxford University Press, 2007.

Finkelman, Paul. *Slavery and the Founders: Race and Liberty in the Age of Jefferson*. Armonk, NY: M. E. Sharpe, 2014.

_____. *Supreme Injustice: Slavery in the Nation's Highest Court*. Cambridge: Harvard University Press, 2018.

Finkelman, Paul, and Donald R. Kennon. *Congress and the People's Contest: The Conduct of the Civil War*. Athens: Ohio University Press, 2018.

Finkelman, Paul, and Melvin Urofsky. *Landmark Decisions of the United States Supreme Court*. Washington, D.C.: CQ Press, 2003.

Finley, M.L., and Brent D. Shaw. *Ancient Slavery and Modern Ideology*. Princeton: Markus Weiner Publishers, 1998.

Fogel, William Robert. *Without Consent or Contract: The Rise and Fall of American Slavery*. New York: W.W. Norton, 1989.

Bibliography

Foner, Eric. *Reconstruction: America's Unfinished Revolution, 1863–1877.* New York: HarperCollins, 1988.

———. *The Second Founding: How the Civil War and Reconstruction Remade the Constitution.* New York: W.W. Norton & Co., 2019.

Foote, Shelby. *The Civil War: A Narrative.* Vol. I: Fort Sumter to Perryville. New York: Random House, 1958.

Frassanito, William A. *Antietam: Photographic Legacy of America's Bloodiest Day.* New York: Charles Scribner's Sons, 1978.

Frier, Bruce W., and Thomas A.J. McGinn. *A Casebook on Roman Family Law.* New York: Oxford University Press, 2004.

Gallway, Alan. *The Indian Slave Trade: The Rise of the English Empire in the American South, 1610–1717.* New Haven: Yale University Press, 2002.

Gerbner, Katherine. *Christian Slavery: Conversion and Race in the Protestant Atlantic World.* Philadelphia: University of Philadelphia Press, 2018.

Giddings, Paula J. *Ida: A Sword Among Lions.* New York: HarperCollins, 2008.

Glickstein, Don. *After Yorktown: The Final Struggle for American Independence.* New York: Yardley Westholme Publishing, 2015.

Goodwin, Doris Kearns. *No Ordinary Time: Franklin Roosevelt and Eleanor Roosevelt: The Home Front in World War II.* New York: Simon & Schuster, 1994.

———. *Team of Rivals: The Political Genius of Abraham Lincoln.* New York: Simon & Schuster, 2005.

Grant, Ulysses S. *Personal Memoirs.* New York: Modern Library, 1999.

Hardin, David. *After the War: The Lives and Images of Major Civil War Figures After the Shooting Stopped.* Chicago: Ivan R. Dee, 2010.

Hashaw, Tim. *The Birth of Black America: The First African Americans and the Pursuit of Freedom at Jamestown.* New York: Carrol & Graf Publishers, 2007.

Hess, Earl J. *Civil War Infantry Tactics: Training, Combat, and Small Unit Effectiveness.* Baton Rouge: Louisiana State University Press, 2015.

———. *The Rifle Musket in Civil War Combat: Reality and Myth.* Lawrence: University Press of Kansas, 2008.

Inskeep, Steve. *Jacksonland: President Andrew Jackson, Cherokee Chief John Ross and a Great American Land Grab.* New York: Penguin Books, 2015.

Jefferson, Thomas. *Notes on the State of Virginia.* William Peden, ed. Chapel Hill: University of North Carolina Press, 1954.

Kaminsky, John P., and Richard Leffler, eds. *Federalists and Antifederalists: The Debate Over the Ratification of the Constitution.* New York: Rowman and Littlefield, 1998.

Kelso, William M. *Jamestown: The Buried Truth.* Charlottesville: University of Virginia Press, 2006.

Kendi, Ibram X. *Stamped from the Beginning: The Definitive History of Racist Ideas in America.* New York: Nation Books, 2016.

Kolchin, Peter. *American Slavery.* New York: Hill and Wang, 1993.

Korda, Michael. *The Life and Legend of Robert E. Lee.* New York: HarperCollins, 2014.

Larson, Edward J., and Michael P. Winship. *The Constitutional Convention: A Narrative History from the Notes of James Madison.* New York: Modern, 2005.

Lepore, Jill. *These Truths: A History of the United States.* New York: W.W. Norton, 2018.

Leuchtenburg, William E. *The American President from Teddy Roosevelt to Bill Clinton.* New York: Oxford University Press, 2015.

Levinson, Cynthia, and Sanford Levinson. *Fault Lines in the Constitution.* Atlanta: Peachtree Publishers, 2017.

Levinson, Sanford. *Our Undemocratic Constitution: Where the Constitution Goes Wrong (and How We the People Can Correct It).* New York: Oxford University Press, 2006.

Lewis, Catherine M., and J. Richard Lewis, eds. *Jim Crow America.* Fayetteville: University of Arkansas Press, 2009.

Bibliography

Lichtman, Allan J. *The Embattled Vote in America: From the Founding to the Present.* Cambridge: Harvard university Press, 2018.

Madison, James H. *A Lynching in the Heartland: Race and Memory in America.* New York: St. Martin's Press, 2001.

Maltz, Earl M. *Slavery and the Supreme Court, 1825–1861.* Lawrence: University Press Kansas, 2009.

McCullough, David. *John Adams.* New York: Simon & Schuster, 2001.

———. *Truman.* New York: Simon & Schuster, 1992.

McCusker, John J., and Russel Menard. *The Economy of British America, 1607–1789.* Chapel Hill: University of North Carolina Press, 1985.

McPherson, James M. *For Cause and Comrades: Why Men Fought in the Civil War.* New York: Oxford University Press, 1997.

———. *War on the Waters: The Union & Confederate Navies, 1861–1865.* Chapel Hill: University of North Carolina Press, 2012.

———. *The War That Forged a Nation.* New York: Oxford University Press, 2015.

Merritt, Kerri Leigh. *Masterless Men: Poor Whites and Slavery in the Antebellum South.* Cambridge: University Printing House, 2017.

Miers, Suzanne, and Igor Kopytoff. *Slavery in Africa: Historical and Anthropological Perspectives.* Madison: University of Wisconsin Press, 1977.

Miller, Fergus. *The Crowd in Rome in the Late Republic.* Ann Arbor: University of Michigan Press, 2002.

Morgan, Edmund S. *American Slavery, American Freedom: The Ordeal of Colonial Virginia.* New York: W.W. Norton, 1975.

Morgan, Kenneth. *Slavery and Servitude in Colonial North America: A Short History.* New York: New York University Press, 2001.

———. *Slavery and the British Empire.* Oxford: Oxford University Press, 2007.

Morris, Thomas D. *Free Men All: The Personal Liberty Laws of the North, 1781–1861.* Baltimore: Johns Hopkins University Press, 1974.

———. *Southern Slavery and the Law, 1619–1860.* Chapel Hill: University of North Carolina Press, 1996.

Mounk, Jascha. *The People vs. Democracy.* Cambridge: Harvard University Press, 2018.

Mulcahay, Mathew. *Hubs of Empire: The Southeastern Lowcountry and British Caribbean.* Baltimore: Johns Hopkins University Press, 2014.

Murray, Williamson, and Wei-Siang Hsieh. *A Savage War: A Military History of the Civil War.* Princeton: Princeton University Press, 2016.

Mustakeem, Sowande M. *Slavery at Sea: Terror, Sex, and Sickness in the Middle Passage.* Urbana: University of Illinois Press, 2016.

Nelson, Dana D., and Donald E. Pease. *National Manhood: Capitalist Citizenship and the Imagined Fraternity of White Men.* Durham: Duke University Press, 1998.

Oakes, James. *Freedom National: The Destruction of Slavery in the United States, 1861–1865.* New York: W.W. Norton, 2013.

O'Malley, Gregory. "Diversity in the Slave Trade to the Colonial Carolinas." In *Creating and Contesting Carolina: Proprietary Era Histories,* ed. by Michell LeMaster and Bradford J. Wood. Charleston: University of South Carolina Press, 2013.

Orth, John V. *Due Process of Law: A Brief History.* Lawrence: University Press of Kansas, 2003.

O'Toole, Patricia. *The Moralist: Woodrow Wilson and the World He Made.* New York: Simon & Schuster, 2018.

Phillips, William D. *Slavery from Roman Times to the Early Transatlantic Trade.* Minneapolis: University of Minnesota Press, 1985.

Rae, Noel. *The Great Stain: Witnessing American Slavery.* New York: Overlook Press, 2018.

Rakove, Jack N., ed. *The Annotated U.S. Constitution and Declaration of Independence.* Cambridge: Harvard University Press, 2009.

Bibliography

Rakove, Jack N. *Original Meanings: Politics and Ideas in the Making of the Constitution*. New York: First Vintage Books Ed., 1996.

———. *Revolutionaries: A New History of the Invention of America*. New York: Houghton Mifflin, 2010.

Raphael, Ray. *Constitutional Myths*. New York: New Press, 2013.

Rediker, Marcus. *The Slave Ship: A Human History*. New York: Viking, 2007.

Resendez, Andres. *The Other Slavery*. New York: Houghton Mifflin, 2016.

Rhea, Gordon C. *The Battle of the Wilderness: May 5–6, 1864*. Baton Rouge: Louisiana State University Press, 1994.

Riley, Rochelle ed. *The Burden: African Americans and the Enduring Impact of Slavery*. Detroit: Wayne State University Press, 2018.

Robertson, James, Jr. *Soldiers Blue and Gray*. New York: Warner Books, 1988.

Rosen, Gary. *American Compact: James Madison and the Problem of Founding*. Lawrence: University Press of Kansas, 1999.

Rothstein, Richard. *The Color of Law*. New York: W.W. Norton & Co., 2017.

Royster, Charles. *A Revolutionary People at War: The Continental Army and American Character, 1775–1783*. Chapel Hill: University of North Carolina Press, 1996.

Sammons, Jeffrey, and John H. Morrow. *Harlem's Rattlers and the Great War: The Undaunted 369th Regiment and the African American Quest for Equality*. Lawrence: University Press of Kansas, 2014.

Sandburg, Carl. *Abraham Lincoln: The War Years* (Vol. 4). New York: Harcourt, Brace & Company, 1939.

Schneider, Dorothy, and Carl Schneider. *Slavery*. New York: Checkmark Books, 2007.

Schwartz, Bernard. *A History of the Supreme Court*. New York: Oxford, 1993.

Sears, Stephen W. *Landscape Turned Red: Battle of Antietam*. New York: Ticknor & Fields, 1983.

———. *Lincoln's Lieutenants: The High Command of the Army of the Potomac*. New York: Houghton Mifflin Harcourt, 2017.

Sedgwick, John. *Blood Moon: An American Epic of War and Splendor in the Cherokee Nation*. New York: Simon & Schuster, 2018.

Simon, James F. *Eisenhower vs. Warren: The Battle for Civil Rights and Liberties*. New York: Liveright Publishing, 2018.

Snyder, Timothy. *On Tyranny*. New York: Tim Duggan Books, 2017.

Stampp, Kenneth, M. *The Peculiar Institution*. New York: Vintage Books, 1989.

Stelyk, Jonathan M. *Fighting Means Killing: Civil War Soldiers and the Nature of Combat*. Lawrence: University Press of Kansas, 2018.

Stevens, John Paul. *Six Amendments: How and Why We Should Change the Constitution*. New York: Little, Brown, 2014.

Stoner, James R. *Common-Law Liberty: Rethinking American Constitutionalism*. Lawrence: University Press of Kansas, 2003.

Sunstein, Cass R. *Can It Happen Here?* New York: HarperCollins, 2018.

Taylor, Alan. *American Colonies: The Settling of North America*. New York: Penguin Books, 2001.

Theoharis, Jeanne. *A More Beautiful and Terrible History: The Use and Misuses of Civil Rights History*. Boston: Beacon Press, 2018.

Tribe, Laurence, and Joshua Matz. *Uncertain Justice: The Roberts Court and the Constitution*. New York: Henry Holt & Co., 2014.

Trudeau, Andre Noah. *Like Men of War: Black Troops in the Civil War, 1862–1865*. New York: Little, Brown, 2002.

Tushnet, Mark V. *Slave Law in the American South*: State v. Mann *in History and Literature*. Lawrence: University Press of Kansas, 2003.

Van Cleve, George William. *A Slaveholders' Union: Slavery, Politics, and the Constitution in the Early Republic*. Chicago: University of Chicago Press, 2010.

Bibliography

Waldstreicher, David. *Slavery's Constitution: From Revolution to Ratification.* New York: Hill and Wang, 2009.
Wert, Jeffry D. *The Sword of Lincoln: The Army of the Potomac.* New York: Simon & Schuster, 2005.
Wiecek, William M. *The Sources of Anti-Slavery Constitutionalism in America, 1760–1848.* Cornell: Cornell University Press, 1977.
Wilentz, Sean. *No Property in Man: Slavery and Antislavery at the Nation's Founding.* Cambridge: Harvard University Press, 2018.
Wills, Gary. *Explaining America.* New York, Penguin Books, 2001.
_____. *James Madison.* New York: Henry Holt and Company, 2002.
Wood, Betty. *The Origins of American Slavery.* New York: Hill and Wang, 1997.
Wood, Gordon S. *Friends Divided: John Adams and Thomas Jefferson.* New York: Penguin Press, 2017.
_____. *The Idea of America.* New York, Penguin Press, 2011.
Wood, Peter H. "The Birthplace of Race-Based Slavery," excerpted from Peter H. Wood. *Strange New Land: Africans in Colonial America, 1617–1776.* Oxford: Oxford University Press, 2003.

Journals and Periodicals

Ablavsky, Gregory. "Making Indians 'White': The Judicial Abolition of Native Slavery in Revolutionary Virginia and Its Racial Legacy." *University of Pennsylvania Law Review* 159 (May 2011): 1457–1531.
Acharya, Avidit, Matthew Blackwell, and Maya Sen. "The Political Legacy of American Slavery." *Journal of Politics* 78, no. 3 (2016): 621–41.
Amar, Akhil Reed. "The Troubling Reason the Electoral College Exists." *Time,* November 8, 2016.
Aptheker, Herbert. "American Negro Slave Revolts." *Science and Society* 1, no. 4 (1937): 512–38.
Badger, Tony. "Southerners Who Refused to Sign the Southern Manifesto." *The Historical Journal* 42, no. 2 (1999): 517–34.
Brewer, Holly. "Slavery, Sovereignty, and 'Inheritable Blood': Reconsidering John Locke and the Origins of American Slavery." *The American Historical Review* 122, no. 4 (October 2017): 1038–1078.
Chan, Michael D. "Alexander Hamilton on Slavery." *The Review of Politics* 66, no. 2 (Spring 2004): 207–31.
Chemerinsky, Erwin. "The Supreme Court and the Fourteenth Amendment: The Unfulfilled Promise." *Loyola of Los Angeles Law Review* 25 (1992): 1143–1158.
Colby, Ira C. "The Freedmen's Bureau from Social Welfare to Segregation." *Phylon* 46, no. 3 (3rd Qtr. 1985): 219–230.
Coombs, John C. "The Phases of Conversion: A Chronology for the Rise of Slavery in Early Virginia." *William and Mary Quarterly* 68, no. 3 (July 2011): 332–60.
Cotter, William R. "The Somerset Case and the Abolition of Slavery in England." *History* 79, no. 255 (February 1994): 34–39.
Crouch, Barry. "A Spirit of Lawlessness: White Violence; Texas Blacks, 1865–1868." *Journal of Social History* 18, no. 2 (1984).
Davis, David Brion. "The Significance of Excluding Slavery from the Old Northwest in 1787." *Indiana Magazine of History* 84, no.1 (March 1988) 75–89.
DeSantis, Vincent P. "President Hayes's Southern Policy." *Journal of Southern History* 21, no. 4 (1955): 476–94.
Dewey, Frank. "Thomas Jefferson's Law Practice." *The Virginia Magazine of History and Biography* 85, no. 3 (July 1977): 289–301.
Dougherty, Keith L., and Jac C. Heckelman. "A Spatial Analysis of Delegate Voting on

Bibliography

Slavery at the Constitutional Convention." *Journal of Economic History* 73, no. 2 (2013): 407–44.

Einhorn, Robin. "Slavery." *Enterprise and Society*, 9, No. 3 (Sept. 2008): 491–506.

Farber, Daniel A., and John E. Muench. "The Ideological Origins of the Fourteenth Amendment." *Constitutional Commentary* 161 (1984): 235–279.

Farr, James. "Locke, Natural Law, and New World Slavery." *Political Theory* 36, no. 4 (August 2008): 495–522.

Finkelman, Paul. "The Historical Context of the Fourteenth Amendment." *Temple Political and Civil Rights Law Review* 2 (2014): 389–409.

_____. "John Bingham and the Background to the Fourteenth Amendment." *Akron Law Review* 36, no. 671 (2003): 671–692.

_____. "The Proslavery Origins of the Electoral College." *Cardoza Law Review* 3, no. 4 (June 2002): 1145–1157.

_____. "Slavery, the Constitution, and the Origins of the Civil War." *OAH Magazine of History* 25, no. 2, "Civil War at 150: Origins" (April 2011): 14–18.

_____. "States' Rights, Southern Hypocrisy, and the Crisis of the Union." *Akron Law Review* 45, no. 2, Article 5 (2012): 449–478.

_____. "Thomas Jefferson and Antislavery: The Myth Goes On." *The Virginia Magazine of History and Biography* 102, no. 2 (Apr. 1994): 193–228.

_____. "Thomas R.R. Cobb and the Law of Negro Slavery." *Roger Williams University Law Review* 5, no. 5, Article 4 (1999); 75–115.

Fisher, Linford. "'Why shall we have peace to be made slaves': Indian Surrenders During and After King Phillip's War." *Ethno History* 64, no. 1 (January 2017): 91–114.

Fisher, William W. "Ideology and Imagery in the Law of Slavery—Symposium on the Law of Slavery: Theories of Democracy and the Law of Slavery." *Chicago-Kent Law Review*, 68, no. 3, Article 4 *Comparative Law and Slavery*, 1051–1083.

Fisk, Catherine, and Erwin Chemerinsky. "The Filibuster." *Stanford Law Review* 49, no. 2 (1997): 181–254.

Fleischman, Richard, Thomas Tyson, and David Holroyd. "The U.S. Freedmen's Bureau in Post–Civil War Reconstruction." *The Accounting Historians Journal* 41, no. 2 (December 2104): 75–109.

Franklin, John Hope. "Civil Rights Act of 1866 Revisited." *Hastings Law Journal* 41 (1990): 1135–48.

Freehling, William W. "The Founding Fathers and Slavery." *The American Historical Review* 77, no. 1 (February 1972): 81–93.

Galenson, David W. "The Atlantic Slave Trade and the Barbados Market, 1673–1723." *The Journal of Economic History* 42, no. 3 (September 1982): 491–511.

Garcia, George F. "Herbert Hoover and the Issue of Race." *The Annals of Iowa* (1979): 507–515.

Garver, Frank Harmon. "Some Misconceptions Relative to the Constitutional Convention." *The Historian* 1, No. 1 (Winter 1938): 24–32.

Goetz, Rebecca Anne. "Rethinking the 'Unthinking Decision': Old Questions and New Problems in the History of Slavery and Race in the Colonial South." *Journal of Southern History* 75, no. 3 (August 2009): 599–612.

Guasco, Michael. "'To Doe Some Good Upon Their Countrymen': The Paradox of Indian Slavery in Early Anglo-America." *Journal of Social History* 41, no. 2 (Winter 2007): 389–411.

Hacker, J. Davis. "A Census Based Account of Civil War Dead." *Civil War History* 57, no. 4 (December 2011): 307–48.

Hackney, Hugh H. "Racial Discrimination and the Civil Rights Act of 1866." *SMU Law Review* 23 (1969): 373–383.

Hammond, John Craig. "Slavery, Settlement, and Empire: The Expansion and Growth of Slavery in the Interior of the North American Continent, 1770–1820." *Journal of the Early Republic* 32, no. 2 (Summer 2012): 175–206.

Bibliography

Hart, John. "Congress and Civil Rights." *Journal of American Studies* 13, no. 2 (1970): 165–78.

Heller, Jacob. "Deaths by a Thousand Cuts: The Guarantee Clause Regulation of State Constitutions." *Stanford Law Review* 62, no. 6, Symposium on State Constitutions (June 2010): 1711–1761.

Helo, Art, and Peter Onuf. "Jefferson, Morality, and the Problem of Slavery." *The William and Mary Quarterly* 60, no. 3 (July 2003): 583–614.

Hertzberg, Hendrik. "Framed Up." *The New Yorker.* July 29, 2002.

Himmelfarb, Dan. "The Constitutional Relevance of the Second Sentence of the Declaration of Independence." *The Yale Law Journal* 100, no. 1 (Oct. 1990): 169–187.

Holden-Smith, Barbara. "Lynching, Federalism, and the Intersection of Race and Gender in the Progressive Era." *Yale Journal of Law and Feminism* 8, no. 1 (1996).

Jenkins, Jeffrey A., and Peck Justin. "The Erosion of the First Civil Rights Era: Congress and the Redemption of the White South, 1877–1891." Prepared for presentation at the 2015 Annual Congress & History Conference, Vanderbilt University.

Jensen, Merrill. "The American Revolution and American Agriculture." *Agricultural History,* 43, no. 1 (Jan. 1969): 107–124.

Klarman, Michael J. "Has the Supreme Court Been More a Friend or Foe to African Americans?" *Daedalus* 140, no. 2 (2011): 101–08.

Kolchin, Peter. "Scalawags, Carpetbaggers, and Reconstruction: A Qualitative Look at Southern Congressional Politics, 1868–1872." *The Journal of Southern History* 45, no. 1 (1979) 63–76.

Landrieu, Maurice. "How I Learned About the Cult of the Lost Cause." *Smithsonian,* March 12, 2018.

Lerche, Charles O. "The Guarantee Clause in Constitutional Law." *The Western Political Quarterly,* 2, no. 3 (Sep. 1949): 358–374.

Lovejoy, Paul E. "The Volume of the Atlantic Slave Trade: A Synthesis." *The Journal of African History* 23, no. 4 (1982): 473–501.

Lynd, Stoughton. "The Compromise of 1787." *Political Science Quarterly,* 81, no. 2 (June 1966): 225–250.

Maltz, Earl M. "The Idea of the Proslavery Constitution." *The Journal of the Early American Republic* 17, no. 1 (Spring 1997): 37–59.

Manisha, Sinha. "Architects of Their Own Liberation: African Americans, Emancipation, and the Civil War." *OAH Magazine of History* 27, no. 2 (April 2013): 5–10.

McKay, Robert B. "Racial Discrimination in the Electoral Process." *The Annals of the American Academy of Political and Social Science* 407 (1973): 102–18.

Miller, Randall M., and Jon W. Zophy. "Unwelcome Allies: Billy Yank and the Black Soldier." *Phylon* 39, no. 3 (3rd Qtr., 1978): 234–240.

Mtubani, V.C.D. "African Slaves and English Law." *PULA Botswana Journal of African Studies* 3, no. 2 (November 1983).

Murray, P. "The Historical Development of Race Laws in the United States." *The Journal of Negro Education,* 22 (1) (1953) 4–15. doi:10.2307/2293619

Mustakeem, Sowande. "'I Never Have Such a Sickly Ship Before': Diet, Disease, and Mortality in 18th-Century Atlantic Slaving Voyages." *The Journal of African American History* 93, no. 4 (Fall 2008): 474–496.

Nash, Gary B. "Franklin and Slavery." *Proceedings of the American Philosophical Society* 150, no. 4 (December 2006).

Oldham, James. "Insurance Litigation Involving the *Zong* and Other British Slave Ships. 1780–1807." *Journal of Legal History* 28, no. 3 (December 2007): 299–318.

O'Reilly, Kenneth. "The Jim Crow Policies of Woodrow Wilson." *The Journal of Blacks in Higher Education* no. 17 (Autumn 1997): 117–21.

Paludan, Phillip Shaw. "Dictator Lincoln: Surveying Lincoln and the Constitution." *OAH Magazine of History* 21, no. 1 (January 2007): 8–13.

Bibliography

Pauley, Garth E. "Harry Truman and the NAACP: A Case Study in Presidential Persuasion on Civil Rights." *Rhetoric and Public Affairs* 2, no. 2 (1999): 211–41.
Pfeifer, Michael J. "At the Hands of Persons Unknown? The State of the Field of Lynching Scholarship." *Journal of American History* 101, no. 3 (December 2014): 832–846.
Pinar, William. "To Live or Die in Dixie." *Counterpoints* 163 (2001): 117–56.
Rakove, Jack N. "Philadelphia Story." *The Wilson Quarterly* 11, no. 2 (Spring, 1987), 105–121.
Ray, Christopher. "'The Indians of every denomination were free, and independent of us': Anglo-Virginian Explorations, Indigenous Slavery, Freedom and Society, 1772–1830." *American Nineteenth Century History* 17, no. 2 (2016): 139–59.
Riegel, Stephen T. "The Persistent Career of Jim Crow: Lower Federal Courts and the 'Separate but Equal' Doctrine, 1865–1896." *The American Journal of Legal History* 28, no. 1 (Jan. 1984): 17–40.
Robinson, Armistead L. "The Politics of Reconstruction." *The Wilson Quarterly* 2, no. 2 (2006): 789–822.
Roper, Donald M. "In Quest of Judicial Objectivity: The Marshall Court and the Legitimation of Slavery." *Stanford Law Review* 21, no. 3 (1969): 532–39.
Rugemer, Edward B. "The Development of Mastery and Race in the Comprehensive Slave Codes of the Greater Caribbean During the Seventeenth Century." *William and Mary Quarterly* 70, no. 3 (July 2013): 429–58.
Rupprecht, Anita. "A Limited Sort of Property: History, Memory and the Slave Ship *Zong*." *Slavery and Abolition* 29, no. 2 (June 2008): 265–77.
Schickler, Eric, Katherine Pearson, and Brian Feinstein. "Congressional Parties and Civil Rights Politics from 1933 to 1972." *The Journal of Politics* 72, no. 3 (2010): 672–89.
Schmid, Thomas W. "The Definition of Racism." *Journal of Applied Philosophy*, 13, no. 1 (1996): 31–40.
Schubert, Frank N. "Buffalo Soldiers at San Juan Hill." *Army History* no. 45 (1998): 36–38.
Schwartz, Harold. "Fugitive Slave Days in Boston." *New England Quarterly* 2, no. 2 (June 1954).
Shapiro, Samuel. "The Rendition of Anthony Burns." *The Journal of Negro History* 44, no. 1.
Sinha, M. "The Caning of Charles Sumner: Slavery, Race and Ideology in the Age of the Civil War." *Journal of the Early Republic* 23, no. 2 (summer 2003): 233–262.
Smith, Barbara Holden. "The Lords of Lash, Loom, and Law: Justice Story, Slavery, and *Prigg V. Pennsylvania*." *Cornell Law Review* 78, no. 6 (September 1993): 1086–1151.
———. "Lynching, Federalism, and the Intersection of Race and Gender in the Progressive Era." *Yale Journal of Law and Feminism* 8, no. 31 (1995): 32–78.
Snyder, Christina. "The Long History of American Slavery." *OAH Magazine of History* 27, no. 4: 23–27.
Spector, Robert M. "The Quock Walker Cases (1781–83)—Slavery, Its Abolition and Negro Citizenship in Early Massachusetts." *The Journal of Negro History* 53, no. 1 (January 1968): 12–32.
Stanwood, Owen. "Captives and Slaves: Indian Labor, Cultural Conversion, and the Plantation Revolution in Virginia." *The Virginia Magazine of History and Biography* 114, no. 4 (2006): 434–63.
Swaminathan, Srividhya. "Reporting Atrocities: A Comparison of the *Zong* and the trial of Captain John Kimber." *Slavery and Abolition* 31, no. 4 (December 2010): 483–99.
Tunnel, Ted. "Creating "The Propaganda of History: Southern Editors and the Origins of Carpetbagger and Scalawag." *The Journal of Southern History* 72, no. 4 (2006): 789–822.
Vazzano, Frank P. "Rutherford B. Hayes and the Politics of Discord." *The Historian* 68, no. 3 (2006): 519–40.
Vile, John R. "The Critical Role of Committees at the U.S. Constitutional Convention of 1787." *The American Journal of Legal History* 48, no. 2 (Apr. 2006): 147–176.
Wahl, Jenny B. "The Jurisprudence of American Slave Sales." *The Journal of Economic History* 56, no. 1 (1996): 143–69.

Bibliography

Waldstreicher, David. "The Beardian Legacy, the Madisonian Moment, and the Politics of Slavery." *American Political Thought*, 2, no. 2 (Fall 2013): 274–282.

Wallenstein, Peter. "Flawed Keepers of the Flame: The Interpreters of George Mason." *The Virginia Magazine of History and Biography*, 102, no. 2 (April 1994): 229–260.

Wallis, Jim. "America's Original Sin: The Legacy of White Racism." *Crosscurrents* 57, no. 2 (Summer 2007): 197–202.

Webster, Jane. "The *Zong* in the Context of the Eighteenth-Century Slave Trade." *The Journal of Legal History* 28, no. 3 (December 2007): 285–298.

Wiecek, William M. "Somerset: Lord Mansfield and the Legitimacy of Slavery in the Anglo-American World." *University of Chicago Law Review* 42, no. 1 Article 4 (1974): 86–146.

———. "The Statutory Law of Slavery and Race in the Thirteen Mainland Colonies of British America." *The William and Mary Quarterly* 34, no. 2 (1977): 258–80. doi:10.2307/1925316.

Willis, Deborah. "The Black Civil War Soldier: Conflict and Citizenship." *Journal of American Studies* 51, no. 2 (2017): 285–323.

Wood, Amy Louise, Susan V. Donaldson, and the Equal Justice Initiative. "Lynching in America: Confronting the Legacy of Racial Terror." *The Mississippi Quarterly* 61, no. 1/2 (2008): 5–25.

Wright, Gavin. "Slavery and American Agricultural History." *Agricultural History* 77, no. 4 (2003): 527–552.

Young, Elizabeth D. "Lincoln and the Constitution." *Saber and Scroll* 1, no. 3 (2015): 31–48.

Young, Harvey. "The Black Body as Souvenir in American Lynching." *Theater Journal* 57 (2005) 639–57.

Index

Act Forbidding Importation of Slaves 60
Adams, John 10, 25, 41, 45, 137–138
Adams, John Quincy 137
Adams, Samuel 41
Adams v. Woods 101n18
African slavery 37–38, 51–52
Allen, John 5, 44
Amending the Constitution 16, 20, 27, 163
American Indians 17, 30–33, 40, 47–48, 52, 111, 139, 161; *see also* Native slaves 30–33, 39–40, 48
The Antelope 60
Antietam 76–77, 80, 82, 193, 195
Aristotle 40
Army of Northern Virginia 72, 75, 82, 84
Army of the Potomac 72, 75–76, 79, 80–82, 140
Article I 17–19, 21–22, 42, 123, 129
Article II 23, 77, 99
Article III 171
Article IV 16, 19, 24, 26, 55, 97
Article V 16, 20–21
Article VI 16
Article VII 16
Articles of Confederation 9, 12, 14, 24
Atlantic Slave Trade 18–19, 21, 33, 49, 54–56, 66

Barbados 49
Barber, Sotirios 1 Beauregard, P.G.T. 71
Beecher Bible and Rifle Church 68
Benezet, Anthony 5, 44
Bierce, Ambrose 70
Bill of Rights 16, 22, 104–105, 123, 153
Bingham, John A. 105
Black Codes 90, 105, 151
Black Flag Order 79
Black incarceration rate 47
Black soldiers 74, 78–79, 89, 142
Booth, John Wilkes 85

Boyle, Robert 41
Brig Caroline v. United States 101
British colonialism 51
Brooks, Preston 67, 155
Brown v. Board of Education of Topeka 121, 130
Bull Run 72, 75, 79, 80, 82
Burns, Anthony 64–65
Burnside, Ambrose 80
Butler, Sen. Andrew 67
Butler, Benjamin 141
Butler, Pierce 5, 17

Calhoun, John C. 63
Campbell, John A. 105
Carpetbaggers 88, 93, 126, 198
Carroll, Charles 10
Carter, Jimmy 157
Carter, Robert "Councillor" 5
Chisholm v. Georgia 59, 100
Civil Rights Act of 1866 91–92, 97, 103, 120, 127, 141, 152–154
Civil Rights Act of 1875 109, 128, 141, 155
Civil Rights Act of 1957 129, 156
Civil Rights Act of 1964 131, 146
Civil Rights Acts 7, 99, 104–105, 127, 141, 152
Clay, Henry 63
Cold Harbor 82–83
Coleman, Tom 157
Collingwood, Luke 37
Columbia (Arraganta) 60
Commerce Clause 59
Commonwealth v. Jennison 42
Compromise of 1850 17, 25, 63–64, 66, 149
Confiscation Act 74
Congressional Reconstruction 99, 104, 108, 127, 160
Constitutional Convention 1, 3–5, 9–13, 17–18, 24, 27–28, 33, 35, 54, 58, 100,

201

Index

107, 125, 136, 168, 170–172; *see also* delegates to the Constitutional Convention
Contraband 74, 141
Custer, George Armstrong 106

Daniels, Jonathan Myrick 156
Davis, Jefferson 71, 84, 89
Delbanco, Andrew 4, 19
delegates to the Constitutional Convention 3, 9–11, 27–28, 54, 136, 168, 170–172
Dickinson, John 10
Dixiecrats 130, 132–134, 146–147, 156
Douglas, Stephen A. 66–67
Douglas, Justice William O. 119
Dred Scott v. Sanford 7, 60–61, 102, 126, 139, 149, 152
Dutch 8, 30, 35, 37
Duvall, Justice 60

Eisenhower, Pres. Dwight D. 121, 130, 144, 155–156
Electoral College 2, 4–7, 15, 17, 21, 23–24, 28, 92–95, 99, 123–124, 131, 133, 137, 148, 161–163, 168–169, 174
Eleventh Circuit Court of Appeals 147
Emancipation Proclamation 77–78, 83, 106, 126, 150
Enforcement Acts 99, 108, 111, 129, 141
English legal system 32, 35, 41
Equal Justice Initiative 112
Equal Rights Amendment 21, 175

Farragut, Admiral 84
Federalist Papers 3, 26 58, 78, 98, 100, 158, 163, 172
Fifteenth Amendment 7, 27, 95, 98–99, 104, 117, 126–127, 141, 143, 151, 155, 160, 175
Fifth Circuit Court of Appeals 130, 146–1477
filibuster 28, 94, 105, 110, 123, 130, 132, 148, 156, 161, 169
Finkelman, Paul 1, 13
Flowers, Richmond McDavid, Sr. 157
Foner, Eric 106, 153
Forrest, Nathan Bedford 79, 89, 94
Fort Pillow 79
Fort Sumter 72, 95
Fourteenth Amendment 27, 92, 95, 97–98, 104–105, 111, 117–120, 151–154
Franklin, Benjamin 10, 15, 124, 136, 147
Freedmen 20, 27, 64, 78, 85–99, 103–108, 116, 126, 134, 141, 150–151

Freedmen's Bureau 87–89, 91–92, 106–107, 126, 141
Freedmen's Inquiry Commission 87
French 8, 25, 34, 46, 115
fugitive slaves 19–20, 26, 59, 64–65, 74, 124, 142, 149

Gainish, Robert 40
gerrymandering 1, 4, 28, 148, 161–164, 167, 170, 174–175
Gilded Age 70
Grant, Ulysses S. 63, 72, 79–83, 85, 99, 108, 140–141, 155
Great Barbecue 70, 127
Grotius, Hugo 32
Guarantee Clause 26

Hamilton, Alexander 15, 23, 58, 100, 101, 104, 136, 138, 172
Harlan, John Marshall 109, 114, 116–117
Hayes, Pres. Rutherford B. 94, 108–109, 116, 127–128, 141–142, 155, 161–162
Hemings, Sally 44, 47, 137
Henry, Patrick 10
Holbert, Luther 113–114
Hood, John Bell 84
Hooker, Gen. "Fighting Joe" 80–81
Hoover, Pres. Herbert 143
Hopkins, Samuel 5, 44
Hose, Sam 113
Hughes, Hugh 21
Hurd v. Hodge 119

Indians 17, 30–33, 40, 47–48, 52, 111, 139, 161; *see also* Native slaves
Indigo 6, 12, 22, 34–35, 49, 54
Ironclad Oath 87

Jackson, Andrew 60, 102, 139
Jackson, Stonewall 75
Jamaica 37, 42, 49
Jamestown 34–35
Japanese-Americans 115, 120–121, 161
Jefferson, Thomas 1, 5, 9–10, 12, 23–28, 41–47, 54, 124–125, 130, 137–140, 160, 164–165
Jennison, Nathaniel 42
Jim Crow 1, 7, 28, 62, 103, 109, 118, 129–131, 134, 142, 146–147, 158, 161–162, 175–176
Johnson, Pres. Andrew 88–92, 103–104, 141, 150–151, 154
Johnson, Ed 114–115

Index

Johnson, Pres. Lyndon B. 29, 130, 135, 146, 156–157
Johnston, Joe 72, 84–85, 89, 142
Judiciary Act of 1789 58, 171

Kansas-Nebraska Act 17, 25, 66–67, 126
King Philip's War 32
King, Martin Luther, Jr. 3, 29, 146, 156, 158
Kosciuszko, Thaddeus 44–45
Ku Klux Klan 7, 29, 93–94, 141, 143, 157

Landrieu, Mitch 71
Laurens, Col. John 5
Lee, Robert E. 71–72, 75–77, 80–85, 89, 116
Lewis, Charles 115
Lincoln, Abraham 62, 78, 85, 126, 133, 137, 140–141
Lloyds Insurance 38
Locke, John 38, 41, 54
Lost Cause 71
Louisiana State Seminary 71
lynching 1, 3–4, 7, 21, 28, 62, 71, 99, 106, 109–111, 114–117, 127, 130, 134, 143–144, 148, 161–162, 176

Madison, James 5, 10–11, 13, 23, 35, 44, 98, 123, 138, 160, 164–166, 168
Magna Carta 51
Malvern Hill 83
Marbury v. Madison 59, 101
Marshall, John 59–60, 101–102, 104, 139, 172
Martin, Luther 10
Mason, George 10, 16, 18, 33, 136, 169, 172
Massachusetts Personal Freedom Act 65
Massacre of Black Troops 79
McClellan, George 72, 75–77, 80–83
McDowell, Gen. Irwin 79
Meade, Gen. George Gordon 80–81
Meredith, James 116
Mexican War 62–63, 67, 71–72, 126, 140
Mexico 62–63, 67
Middle Passage 12, 36
Militia Act 74, 78
Miller, C.J. 113
Minkins, Shadrach 64
Missouri Compromise 17, 25, 61–63, 66–67, 102
Mitchell v. United States 118
Mobile Bay 19, 84
monoculture 34–35

Morgan, Margaret 57–58
Morris, Gouverner 10–11, 15–16, 168
Morrisroe, Father 156–157
Murray, William 42

Native Americans *see* American Indians
Native slaves 30–33
New York City Conspiracy 26
Newton Sir Isaac 41
Nixon, Pres. Richard 131, 146–147
Norris v. Alabama 118
Northwest Territories 8, 13, 24
Notes on the State of Virginia 41, 165

Otis, James 5, 41, 44
Overland Campaign 81–82

Paine, Tom 5, 44, 46
Patterson, William 14
Peninsula Campaign 80
Pequot 31–32
Personal Liberty Laws 55, 58, 65, 124, 149–150
Philadelphia 3, 5, 13, 23, 47, 75, 100
Plessy, Homer 116–118, 120–121, 130
The Political Legacy of American Slavery 48
Polk, Pres. James 62, 139–140
Pope, Gen. John 80 Portuguese 30, 34
Powell v. Alabama 118
Powhatan Confederation 32
Presidential Reconstruction 86, 88, 93, 104
Prigg v. Pennsylvania 57–58, 149

Queen v. Hepburn 59, 101

Radical Republicans 75, 86–87, 90–93, 128–129, 134, 141, 150–151, 153–154, 175
Randolph, Edmund 10, 136
Randolph, Gov. John 5, 14
Reagan, Pres. Ronald 131, 147, 158, 167
Reconstruction 3, 7, 86–94, 97, 99, 105–106, 108, 110, 129, 134, 141–142, 150–155, 162, 176; Congressional Reconstruction 99, 104, 108, 127, 160; Military Reconstruction 86; Presidential Reconstruction 86, 88, 93, 104
Redeemers 86, 95, 97, 105, 176
reparations 174
republican form of government 3–7, 14, 26, 28, 44, 54, 73, 91, 96–98, 105, 137, 148, 151, 158, 161–163, 170, 175–176

Index

Republican Party 17, 28, 48, 67, 73, 75, 83, 88, 94, 104–105, 108, 111, 128, 134, 142–143, 146–148, 162–163, 167, 170–173, 176
revisionist history 70–96
Revolutionary War 44, 46, 59, 100
Rhode Island 9, 41, 46
Rice 12, 22, 34–35, 38, 54
Robin v. Hardaway 33
Roosevelt, Pres. Franklin D. 118, 121, 134, 144
Roosevelt, Pres. Theodore 142
Royal Africa Company 36, 38, 49
Rule of Law 3–4, 7, 27, 36, 47, 52, 55, 97–98, 102, 106, 109, 111, 116–117, 122, 134–135, 148–149, 154, 159, 161, 162, 176
runaway slaves 20, 27, 36, 44, 54–55, 64–66, 139, 149
Rush, Benjamin 5, 44

Sales, Ruby 157
scalawags 88, 97, 126
Scott v. Negro Ben 101 *Scott v. Negro London* 101
Scottsboro Boys 117–118
Screws v. U.S. 119
segregation 1, 3–4, 7, 26–29, 36, 62, 86, 95–96, 98, 105, 109, 115, 117–122, 127, 129–135, 142–148, 155–158, 161–162, 175–176
Sewell, Judge Samuel 42
Sharp, Granville 42
Shay's rebellion 8
Shelby County v. Holder 158
Sheridan, Gen. Philip 93, 106
Sherman, William Tecumseh 71, 79–81, 84–85, 95
Shiloh 72, 80
Sipuel, Ada Lois 120
slave codes 35, 38–39, 48–54, 149
slave rebellions 21, 26
slave trade 20–23, 33–37, 41, 47, 49, 54–57, 60, 66, 101–102, 124–125, 138
Smith, Henry 112
Somerset, James 42–43
Somerset v. Stewart 42–43
South Carolina 6, 10, 12, 17, 26, 32–33, 38, 49, 52, 54–55, 67–68, 78, 94, 106, 108, 112, 116, 125, 155, 141, 138, 134, 132, 130
Southern Strategy 131, 147
Spanish 8, 25, 30–32, 34, 60, 63
Squanto 31

Stanton, Secretary of War Edwin 74
State's Rights 70–96
Stewart, Charles 42
Stono Rebellion 26
Strange Fruit 11
Sumner, Charles 67–18, 90–91, 155
Supreme Court 7, 26–29, 36, 56–62, 66, 99–105, 108–110, 114–121, 124, 126, 130, 133, 137, 139, 141, 144, 146–147, 149, 153, 155, 158–159, 162–163, 166, 171–173, 175
Sweatt, Herman 120

Taney, Roger B. 7, 60–62, 102, 126, 139, 149, 152
taxes 8, 17, 19, 22, 90, 95, 129, 151, 157, 167, 173
Texas 62–63, 79, 81, 90, 93, 106, 112, 120, 126, 130, 140, 142, 146
Thirteenth Amendment 7, 21, 27, 35, 83, 91, 95, 98–99, 103–106, 109, 116–117
Three-Fifths Clause 7, 15–19, 23–24, 68, 92, 95, 98, 124, 131, 168
Thurmond, Strom 123, 130, 132, 134, 144
Tilden, Samuel J. 94
tobacco 6, 12, 22, 30, 34–35, 38–39, 49, 54, 56, 60
Treaty of Paris 1783 8
Trucking Statutes 53
Truman, Pres. Harry 121, 144, 156
Twain, Mark 111, 129

Unabridged Devil's Dictionary 70
Underground Railroad 20, 64
Union Army 71–72, 78, 106–107, 116, 140, 142
United States v. Battiste 57
United States v. Gooding 56

Virginia Plan 14
Virginia Slave Code 39
Voting Rights Act of 1965 146

Wade-Davis Bill 86
Walker, Quock 42
Wallace, George 131, 147, 157
War Powers Clause 73, 77, 99
Warren, Earl 121, 130, 144–146, 156
Washington, George 9–10, 13, 46–47, 54, 124, 137–138, 147
Webster, the Rev. Samuel 5, 44
West Indies 6, 32, 35, 49, 51
White League 71, 106
Wiecek, David 1

Index

The Wilderness 31, 81–82
Wilmot, David 140
Wilmot Proviso 140
Wilson, James 14–15, 23, 168
Wilson, Pres. Woodrow 129, 136, 142–143

Wilson's Creek 72
Wood, Betty 6, 50
Woodward, Isaac 116

Zong 37, 38, 42

www.ingramcontent.com/pod-product-compliance
Ingram Content Group UK Ltd.
Pitfield, Milton Keynes, MK11 3LW, UK
UKHW042004140426
5217IPUK00015B/979